Early Professional Development in EFL Teaching

NEW PERSPECTIVES ON LANGUAGE AND EDUCATION

Founding Editor: Viv Edwards, *University of Reading, UK*

Series Editors: Phan Le Ha, *University of Hawaii at Manoa, USA* and Joel Windle, *Monash University, Australia.*

Two decades of research and development in language and literacy education have yielded a broad, multidisciplinary focus. Yet education systems face constant economic and technological change, with attendant issues of identity and power, community and culture. This series will feature critical and interpretive, disciplinary and multidisciplinary perspectives on teaching and learning, language and literacy in new times.

All books in this series are externally peer-reviewed.

Full details of all the books in this series and of all our other publications can be found on http://www.multilingual-matters.com, or by writing to Multilingual Matters, BLOCK, The Fairfax, Pithay Court, Bristol, BS1 3BN, UK.

NEW PERSPECTIVES ON LANGUAGE AND EDUCATION: 68

Early Professional Development in EFL Teaching

Perspectives and Experiences from Japan

Chitose Asaoka

MULTILINGUAL MATTERS
Bristol • Jackson

DOI https://doi.org/10.21832/ASAOKA3217
Library of Congress Cataloging in Publication Data
A catalog record for this book is available from the Library of Congress.
Names: Asaoka, Chitose - author.
Title: Early Professional Development in EFL Teaching: Perspectives and
   Experiences from Japan/Chitose Asaoka.
Description: Bristol; Blue Ridge Summit: Multilingual Matters, 2019. | Series: New
   Perspectives on Language and Education: 68 | Includes bibliographical references
   and index.
Identifiers: LCCN 2018052207 (print) | LCCN 2018057283 (ebook) |
   ISBN 9781788923224 (pdf) | ISBN 9781788923231 (epub) | ISBN 9781788923248
   (Kindle) | ISBN 9781788923217 (hbk : alk. paper)
Subjects: LCSH: English language—Study and teaching (Secondary)—Japan. |
   English teachers, Training of—Japan. | English language—Study and teaching
   (Secondary)—Japanese speakers.
Classification: LCC PE1068.J3 (ebook) | LCC PE1068.J3 A75 2018 (print) | DDC
   428.0071/052—dc23
LC record available at https://lccn.loc.gov/2018052207

British Library Cataloguing in Publication Data
A catalogue entry for this book is available from the British Library.

ISBN-13: 978-1-78892-321-7 (hbk)
ISBN-13: 978-1-83668-148-9 (pbk)

Multilingual Matters
UK: BLOCK, The Fairfax, Pithay Court, Bristol, BS1 3BN, UK.
USA: NBN, Blue Ridge Summit, PA, USA.
Authorised Representative: Easy Access System Europe – Mustamäe tee 50, 10621
Tallinn, Estonia gpsr.requests@easproject.com.

Website: www.multilingual-matters.com
Bluesky: https://bsky.app/profile/multi-ling-mat.bsky.social
Twitter: Multi_Ling_Mat
Facebook: https://www.facebook.com/multilingualmatters
Blog: www.channelviewpublications.wordpress.com

Copyright © 2019 Chitose Asaoka.

All rights reserved. No part of this work may be reproduced in any form or by any
means without permission in writing from the publisher.

The policy of Multilingual Matters/Channel View Publications is to use papers
that are natural, renewable and recyclable products, made from wood grown in
sustainable forests. In the manufacturing process of our books, and to further
support our policy, preference is given to printers that have FSC and PEFC Chain
of Custody certification. The FSC and/or PEFC logos will appear on those books
where full certification has been granted to the printer concerned.

Typeset by Deanta Global Publishing Services Limited.
Printed and bound in the UK by the CPI Books Group Ltd.
Printed and bound in the US by Thomson-Shore, Inc.

Contents

	Acknowledgements	vii
1	Introduction	1
	1.1 Background	1
	1.2 The Linguistic Context of Japan	2
	1.3 Overview of the Book	4
2	Educational Reforms in Japan	7
	2.1 MEXT Policies for English Language Education	7
	2.2 Unclear Standards in Teacher Education	10
	2.3 Initial Teacher Education in Japanese Higher Education	12
	2.4 Initial Teacher Training in Secondary Schools in Japan	16
	2.5 Challenges of Initial Teacher Education in Japan	19
3	Professional Development in Initial Teacher Education	21
	3.1 Models of Professional Development in Initial Teacher Education	21
	3.2 Dimensions of Professional Expertise	26
	3.3 Dimensions of Professional Expertise for English Language Teaching	27
	3.4 Challenges of Putting Theory into Practice	30
4	Teaching Culture in Japan	32
	4.1 Holistic Teaching	33
	4.2 Teaching as Craft	34
	4.3 Challenges of Japanese Teaching Culture	41

5	Case Studies	44
	5.1 Theoretical Framework	44
	5.2 Procedure	51
6	Preservice Teachers' Perspectives on Teaching	68
	6.1 Teacher as a Subject Specialist	69
	6.2 Perspectives on Holistic Teaching	84
	6.3 Theory and Practice: Evolving Student Teacher Perspective	95
7	Factors that Affect Initial Teacher Education	101
	7.1 Previous and Current Experiences as a Learner	102
	7.2 Theoretical Learning in ITE Coursework	108
	7.3 Practical Learning in Informal Settings	111
	7.4 Reflections on Case Studies	114
8	Mediational Tools: Narrowing the Gap between Theory and Practice	115
	8.1 Observation and Emulation	116
	8.2 Impact of Peer Learning	127
	8.3 Reflections on Effective Mediational Tools	136
9	A Critical Reflection: Professional Development in Initial Teacher Education in Japan	141
	9.1 Student Teachers' Struggle in Narrowing the Theory/Practice Gap	142
	9.2 Pedagogical Implications	150
	9.3 Directions for Future Research	152
	9.4 Final Conclusion	154
	References	156
	Index	164

Acknowledgements

As a teacher and a teacher educator, I have always been interested in what it means to be a good teacher and how teachers have arrived at where they are now. Many of my former students are excellent English teachers now and, thanks to a one-year sabbatical from Dokkyo University, I was able to launch a PhD study on the expertise development of such teachers at the Institute of Education, University College London, which is the basis of this book. I wish to thank those student teachers and teacher educators who readily gave their time to this study. I am immensely grateful to the seven student teachers in the main study, Aya, Chie, Kento, Mari, Nana, Saori and Yurika (pseudonyms) as well as the two student teachers in the pilot study, for their willingness to learn with me and to develop their teacher expertise at the time of the study. Without their interest and full cooperation, this book would not have been feasible.

I would also like to thank all those who assisted me in the preparation of this work. My sincere appreciation is especially extended to Dr Shirley Lawes, who gave unsparingly of her time and support and guided me during all phases of the study.

And last but not least, I would like to thank my family: my parents, Yoshiji and Michiko Asaoka, and my husband, Katsuhiko, for being understanding and supportive during all the phases of my work. Thank you.

1 Introduction

> Making a lesson plan using content-based instruction was extremely difficult for me. No matter how much I thought, I couldn't make any progress, only time passing by. What you have never experienced as a student is very difficult to master, I guess.
> (Kento, Fourth interview)

1.1 Background

This study emerged out of my own experiences in Japan as a teacher educator in English as a foreign language (EFL); I have worked in an undergraduate-level initial teacher education (ITE) programme in the country for two decades. In this role, I have endeavoured to guide student teachers, who are mostly native Japanese speakers, without any set framework to define what *teacher expertise* they should have mastered upon graduation. Indeed, a vast amount of theoretical knowledge must be transmitted to student teachers at higher education institutions (HEIs), while student teachers themselves seem desperate for practical experiences as opposed to theoretical knowledge. On the other hand, I am remote from student teachers' school-based experiences and can only monitor their development through teaching logs or stories they relate about their teaching practice. The only opportunity open to me as a teacher educator is a single visit to observe the student teachers' demonstration lessons towards the end of their teaching practice. In other words, it is rare to expect collaboration between HEIs and schools in developing student teachers' expertise in this specific context. In addition, as the opening quote from a student teacher, Kento, indicates, student teachers themselves seem to struggle. At HEIs, they learn about up-to-date teaching approaches and methods, such as employing a communicative practice or a student-centred approach or using English as a medium of instruction; whereas at schools, they face the reality of the classroom and are asked to adjust to school contexts, and thus cannot freely put theory into practice. They may also have no previous experiences of learning English as students through such up-to-date approaches; thus, they may find it a challenge to draw on their own learning experiences.

As a researcher and a teacher educator, I felt the necessity to re-examine what elements should constitute *teacher expertise* in a Japanese EFL context and how student teachers can develop this professional expertise effectively during ITE. For student teachers to become good English teachers, what qualities are necessary and what kind of support can ITE provide? I had already articulated these questions at the onset of this research study.

1.2 The Linguistic Context of Japan

The linguistic context of Japan should first be described, so we can understand the larger context of English language teaching in Japan. In Japan, English is effectively taught at school as a foreign language, since the majority of Japanese do not have to use English in their everyday lives. In fact, Japanese society is drastically changing to become a multilingual society, mainly due to the need to compensate for labour shortages (Heinrich, 2012; Kanno, 2008). Following the 1990 revision of the Immigration Control and Refugee Recognition Act, there has been a dramatic increase in the number of foreign nationals in Japan, including the descendants of Japanese emigrants. The latest figure for the number of foreign nationals legally living in Japan is 2,382,822 as of December 2016, which is 1.8% of the total population (Ministry of Justice, 2017). Chinese constitute the largest group (29.2%), followed by Korean nationals (19.0%) and Filipinos (10.2%). Hence, nowadays, English is more commonly used for intranational communication than before within the domestic context due to ethnic and linguistic diversity. However, as already mentioned, the majority still speak and use Japanese as their mother tongue in daily life, in school as well as in the workplace.

In the early 2000s, following the rapid globalisation of the economy, the Ministry of Education, Culture, Sports, Science and Technology (MEXT) faced the urgent need to upgrade the general level of English language education in order to compete with other countries in a global society, since English is essential as an international lingua franca. As one of the actions to cope with the need, in the 2008 school year, English started to be taught to fifth and sixth graders in primary school as a 'foreign language activity' class in which pupils are expected to experiment and have fun with English. Furthermore, in the 2020 school year, English will become a mandatory subject for fifth and sixth graders, and along with this change, the foreign language activity classes will also become mandatory for third and fourth graders (MEXT, 2017).

In Japan, the compulsory education period is six years of elementary school and three years of lower secondary school, called junior high school. The advancement rate in upper secondary schools, called senior high schools (three years), is currently 98% according to MEXT (2017). English is only one of the elective foreign languages to choose from in the national curriculum for junior high school, but MEXT has encouraged schools to teach English in principle; hence, almost all junior high school students and senior high school students learn English (MEXT, 2010d). This implies that students presently learn English for three years in junior high school and for another three years in senior high school – for a total of six years at least in secondary education. In regard to a medium of instruction, although MEXT (2010a, 2017) encourages secondary school teachers to use English, in reality, most teachers still use Japanese as the main classroom language, or use a mixture of English and Japanese at best. Additionally, as most universities have a section on English as part of their entrance examinations, many senior high school students are instrumentally motivated to study English in order to obtain good scores on the tests rather than learning the language as a communicative tool. At the tertiary education level, most undergraduate students, even non-English majors, are required to take English language courses for at least the first two years of their undergraduate study, although they are usually required to take only one or two courses per week unless they are English majors. As the description so far indicates, students in Japan currently learn English for some 6–10 years in school and college, while there has been ongoing criticism that many do not have a high enough proficiency in English; often teachers and teacher education are the target for this criticism.

At the same time, although English is still not widely used for social interaction or for communication in business or government, its importance is more widely recognised than before, particularly in business and the tourism industry as society has globalised. For instance, obtaining a good score on the Test of English for International Communication (TOEIC), which is a widely used proficiency test that evaluates a learner's English language competences in the workplace, is essential in Japan for finding a job or for promotion. Some companies have even made a rule to use English as an official language in their workplaces. Also, due to technological advances, it is not very difficult for learners in Japan to access materials in English: a wide range of both authentic and edited materials are available nowadays beyond the classroom, ranging from films, news, podcasts, online materials and e-learning courses to digital textbooks. This situation has led to what is currently called an 'English boom' in Japan.

This section has briefly described the context in which EFL student teachers, teachers and teacher educators in Japan are situated and the issues that they need to make sense of while working on their professional development in ITE. In the newest national curriculum called Course of Study, MEXT (2017) puts more emphasis on the active role of English language learners as an agent rather than a passive recipient of knowledge about the language, which EFL student teachers also need to be aware of. Due to the upcoming 2020 Olympic Games in Tokyo, the English language as well as English language teaching will also be more economically significant and valuable in Japan.

1.3 Overview of the Book

This is a qualitative study situated in a Japanese context. It is also an illustration of my own professional learning as a teacher educator through a 'reflective conversation with the situation' (Schön, 1983: 295). Employing a case-study approach, I conducted the study with the aim of exploring and interpreting EFL student teachers' development processes in their ITE programme. The student teachers' experiences during their training at HEIs as well as at schools were investigated in order to examine *what factors* (e.g. theoretical knowledge transmission, observation and emulation of an expert teacher, reflection, actual teaching) impacted on their expertise development and *how* student teachers themselves reflected on their own professional development.

Since the main purpose of the study is an in-depth exploration of student teachers' *experiences* and *perceptions* of their own development in ITE, the methods employed to collect and analyse data are based on the principles of qualitative studies (Brown & Dowling, 1998; Cohen *et al.*, 2000; Silverman, 2000) since qualitative research allows more descriptive and interpretive inquiry and focuses more on a detailed picture of the particular. The main overarching research question that I formulated at the initial stage of the research that guided this research study was:

(1) How do pre-service EFL student teachers in Japan perceive their professional expertise development over time?

However, as the data analysis proceeded along with the data collection, more specific key concepts emerged from the data, which led to the articulation of some sub-questions. These remain general in character but gave more specific directions to this research study:

(2) How do student teachers perceive theory and practice in their training? Which factors do they find more influential in shaping their professional expertise development?
(3) How do student teachers' perceptions of theory and practice change over time?
(4) Do student teachers perceive that there is a gap between theory and practice? If so, how do they address the problem?
(5) If student teachers see it as a problem, how do they mitigate the disparity between theory and practice? What are the tools (i.e. emulation, reflection) that they employ and why?

Through reflective journals and in-depth interviews, this study aims, in particular, to investigate how student teachers develop their teacher expertise; how their views on what makes a good English teacher shift and develop; and what factors, such as interaction with or emulation of others, impact on their learning-to-teach processes. As we shall see later, emulation of others, the implicit use of which is often criticised in professional development (Lunenberg *et al.*, 2007) as it may not effectively allow student teachers to link their own pedagogical choices to abstract theory, turns out to be an important element in student teachers' expertise development in this study.

Seven participants who were EFL student teachers in an ITE programme at a Japanese university joined this study in April 2009. Six of them, Kento, Chie, Mari, Yurika, Nana and Saori (pseudonyms), were lower secondary school student teachers, whereas the other participant, Mari (pseudonym), was a prospective upper secondary school English teacher. The participants were followed over one-and-a-half years, both in formal settings (e.g. journals, interviews, observation) and additional *ad hoc* opportunities such as observation of teaching, which took place on a voluntary basis outside the statutory requirements. The data collection for this study is divided into two phases: training in an ITE programme at an HEI, and teaching practice at a secondary school. Multiple tools were employed for collecting the qualitative data which included interviews, journals and observation in order to maximise the validity and reliability of the research study.

Chapter 2: Educational Reforms in Japan, provides a detailed background on educational reforms in Japan, including those in English language education as well as the ITE system. I first offer an historical overview of educational reforms in Japan in English language teaching, as pressured by globalisation. I then discuss reforms and challenges in the ITE system in Japan by referring to both parties: HEIs where student teachers basically gain theoretical knowledge; and secondary schools, where they experience actual teaching. The chapter concludes that those challenges that ITE in Japan faces are twofold: variability in student teachers' experiences and no general agreement of what goals and standards should be achieved in professional development in ITE.

Chapter 3: Professional Development in Initial Teacher Education provides an in-depth discussion of the theoretical concept of teachers' professional expertise. First, it discusses the different ways in which we can understand how student teachers learn to become teachers and the dimensions of knowledge bases that they need to develop and draw upon in making professional judgements. For EFL student teachers, content knowledge and pedagogical content knowledge of Shulman's (1987) seven dimensions of knowledge bases are of particular interest, in addition to their own proficiency in the target language. The chapter concludes by contending that student teachers' professional development is constructed not only at an individual level but through the dialogical interaction of various constructs.

Chapter 4: Teaching Culture in Japan provides a background on the culture of teaching in Japan. Two salient characteristics will be delineated: holistic teaching and perspectives on apprenticeship in Japan. The chapter then discusses that these two aspects can in fact bring about challenges and difficulties for EFL student teachers. Finally, I present a tentative model of the dialogical process of theory and practice in ITE in Japan with the help of mediational activities, which will be further developed and revisited in Chapter 8.

Chapter 5: Case Studies describes the methodological framework of this study. The chapter explains three specific choices I make: a sociocultural perspective, a case-study approach and an emic approach. From a sociocultural perspective, I discuss how human cognition is shaped and mediated by the social activities in which a learner engages. I choose the case-study approach for this study since this approach enables me to focus on a small number of participants and study them closely over an extended period of time. Furthermore, I employ an emic approach with the role of researcher as insider, which allows me to engage in in-depth conversations with the participating student teachers in regard to their professional development.

The following three chapters are portraits of seven student teachers in ITE in Japan: Chie, Aya, Nana, Mari, Kento, Yurika and Saori. Chapter 6: Preservice Teachers' Perspectives on Teaching concerns the discussion of student teachers' shifting perspectives on teaching. The chapter will elaborate on the student teachers' struggle with the dilemma between subject teaching and holistic teaching, in addition to what kinds of knowledge base they value and how their perspectives on teaching change or fail to change. I will also explain the cultural connotations of *kaizen*, *hikidashi* and *waza-o-nusumu* in shaping student teachers' identities. On the other hand, Chapter 7: Factors that Affect Initial Teacher Education and Chapter 8: Mediational Tools: Narrowing the Gap between Theory and Practice will focus on the factors that affect student teachers' professional development. Chapter 7 highlights the following factors that benefit EFL student teachers in shaping their expertise: experiences as a learner, theoretical learning in ITE coursework and practical experiences in informal settings. However, I will argue that each factor in itself does not fully contribute to the development of student teachers' professional expertise. Chapter 8 sheds light on the struggle of student teachers in terms of how they narrow the gap between theory and practice with the use of mediational tools such as observation and emulation and peer interaction. The chapter then revisits my conceptualisation of the professional development of student teachers in ITE in Japan.

Finally, Chapter 9 concludes the study, providing a summary of the main arguments. I also critically reflect on our current practice and speculate about the future practice of ITE in Japan.

The accounts of the participants in this book are mostly narrated in the present tense. However, the time of actual data collection was between April 2009 and August 2010. A little has changed since the years of my data collection and what I describe in this book may not necessarily represent student teachers' experiences as they are today. Whenever relevant, I provide updates throughout the study.

2 Educational Reforms in Japan

To better understand the participating English as a foreign language (EFL) student teachers' perspectives and experiences in initial teacher education (ITE) in Japan and how they make sense of their experiences, it is crucial to understand both the larger context in which English language teaching is situated and the particular context in which we find ITE. As Chapter 1 described the bigger context, the overall linguistic context of Japan, this chapter will delve into the particular context of ITE in Japan.

2.1 MEXT Policies for English Language Education

Since the national curriculum provides an outline of core knowledge to promote the development of pupils' and students' knowledge and skills, and teachers are influenced by the curriculum to some extent, we should first examine the government's policies on English language education in Japan in more detail.

A new education system began in Japan after World War II. The Course of Study, which is the national curriculum in Japan, was first published by the Ministry of Education, Culture, Sports, Science and Technology (MEXT) in 1947. Since then, it has been revised several times to meet the needs of the changing times. More recently, in the early 2000s, aiming at internationalisation, MEXT initiated drastic reform in English language education. The first change was observed when MEXT (2003b) formulated a five-year action plan that urged society to improve their general level of English language education in order to compete with other countries in an increasingly global society. This was the first time that MEXT clearly stated its aim to improve the national standard of English language education.

According to the action plan, all teachers and students were asked to act in the improvement of English language education for the future of Japan. The plan not only suggested general improvement in English language classes and the evaluation systems for selecting school and university applicants, but also provided specific targets and goals for learners to achieve before 2008:

- English language abilities for junior high school graduates should be at the third level of the Society for Testing English Proficiency (STEP)[1] on average.
- English language abilities for senior high school graduates should be at the second level or the pre-second level of the STEP on average.
- Each university should establish attainment targets from the viewpoint of fostering personnel who can use English in their work.

In order to upgrade the overall English language teaching system, it was also necessary to upgrade the quality of Japan's English teachers. Thus, in this action plan, four goals regarding English teachers were established to be achieved before 2008. As the plan aimed at fostering a community open to external participants, hiring more assistant language teachers[2] (ALTs) or using people with high English proficiency in the community was proposed as an easy solution. In addition, improving the teaching abilities of prospective English teachers was also a target to be achieved in the action plan. The plan recommended that secondary school English teachers attain a certain proficiency in their level of English:

- Almost all English teachers will acquire English skills (STEP pre-first level, Test of English as a Foreign Language [TOEFL][3] 550, Test of English for International Communication [TOEIC] 730 or over) and the teaching ability to conduct classes to cultivate communication abilities through the repetition of activities making use of English.
- Centring on leading teachers at the local community level, the improvement of English abilities in the community will be enhanced.
- A native speaker of English will participate in English classes at junior and senior high schools more than once a week.
- People living in the local community proficient in English will be positively utilised.

It was noteworthy that upgrading the quality of English teachers was explicitly stated in the action plan; however, this proposal needed further consideration. First of all, one of the foregoing recommendations, the achievement of a high proficiency in English, is not necessarily equivalent to the high-quality professional expertise of teachers.

Additionally, the MEXT's proposal did not elaborate specifically on what kind of teaching abilities teachers should acquire. This was partly because there was a lack of common understanding of what skills, knowledge and attributes should constitute professional expertise for good EFL teachers in Japan. According to a study conducted by JACET SIG on English Education (2005), although the results of a quantitative survey showed that some senior high school teachers expect student teachers to have achieved a certain level of English language proficiency demonstrated by the TOEIC or STEP before they start their teaching practice, the same study also suggested that among practicing junior high school teachers, many placed greater importance on the student teachers' willingness to work with ALTs and their ability to conduct a class in English, rather than their high English language proficiency or subject knowledge. This indicates that there is no general agreement, even among practising teachers in Japan, about what professional expertise is necessary to become an effective English teacher in Japan, let alone among student teachers.

The national curriculum was revised in 2008 for elementary schools and lower secondary schools and in 2009 for upper secondary schools in response to criticism of a decline in scholastic ability that the light curriculum invited. As mentioned in Chapter 1, the revision in English language teaching included the introduction of foreign language activities for fifth and sixth graders in elementary school, an emphasis on the development of communication skills and the introduction of a teaching English through English approach at the upper secondary level. In fact, it was the very first time that MEXT stated in the national curriculum that, in principle, senior high school EFL teachers must use English as a medium of instruction for English language classes.

The national curriculum was again revised in 2017, and will be implemented in 2020 for elementary schools, in 2021 for lower secondary schools and in 2022 for upper secondary schools. The Central Council for Education (2006) in Japan states that in order to live in a global society and communicate effectively with people from different cultures with various values, it is essential to improve English language competence, and active learning is key to promoting student-centred, interactive and deep learning. In response to the council's suggestion, the revision includes a greater shift towards an active learning approach and an emphasis on integrating the four language skills, in addition to introducing English as a mandatory school subject for fifth and sixth graders in elementary school, introducing foreign language activities for third and fourth graders in elementary school, as well as increasing the curriculum content. MEXT also encourages in the new Course of Study that junior high school EFL teachers use English as a medium of instruction in principle.

As this section has discussed, globalisation has impacted greatly on those policies concerning English language teaching in Japan. As the number of people using English as an international lingua franca grows, fostering motivated human resources who can communicate and negotiate effectively in English through English language education in schools and colleges is more urgent than ever, a fact about which prospective EFL teachers need to be well aware. These teachers also need to be trained to teach English effectively and promote their students' English language competences and their agency as learners.

2.2 Unclear Standards in Teacher Education

In addition to the policy changes in English language education, Japan has also seen a series of educational reforms since the 1980s. In the 1980s, Japanese society was struggling through a stagnant economy, which put pressure on children who were fighting to pass entrance examinations and get into prestigious universities, since entering reputable institutions was considered in Japan as a guarantee of a good job and a good life. This pressure, partly due to economic concerns, led to a cramming system of education as well as excessive competition for entrance examinations. Students who studied mainly for instrumental purposes, including English, were often called 'study robots'. This resulted in many at-risk students, those who were left behind in examination competition. It also led to serious education issues, such as bullying, school violence and children unwilling to go to school.

In trying to respond to the changing situations in education, a report titled 'National Commission on Education Reform' was compiled in 2000, prompted by then Prime Minister Ryutaro Hashimoto. After careful consideration of the recommendations in the report, the MEXT (2001) then produced the 'Education Reform Plan for the 21st Century', also known as the 'Rainbow Plan'. The plan clearly delineated specific measures and issues of educational reforms to be undertaken. The following list enumerates seven priority strategies mentioned in the reform plan:

(1) Improve students' basic scholastic proficiency in 'easy-to-understand classes'.
(2) Foster open and warm-hearted Japanese through participation in the community and various programmes.
(3) Improve the learning environment to one that is enjoyable and free of worries.
(4) Promote the creation of schools trusted by parents and communities.
(5) *Train teachers as 'educational professionals'*. (My italics)
(6) Promote the establishment of world-class universities.
(7) Establish a new educational vision for the new century, and improve the foundations of education.

These seven strategies indicate that the reform aimed to foster a community, so schools would be more open to external participants from the wider community, where problems would be solved jointly between these participants and students, and where students, who were so-called 'study robots' studying to meet their instrumental purposes, would learn in a more stress-free setting, enhance their individuality and acquire skills that would be useful in a global economy.

Above all, the major reform that actually took place after these recommendations was the implementation of a new national curriculum in

2002 (MEXT, 2003a), with the introduction of a new 'integrated study' course for both primary and secondary schools, which stresses more individualised, cross-curricular thematic projects, as well as a reduction in instructional content and classroom hours, with the emphasis placed on *yutori* (literally, *having the free time and space for relaxation*) for students so as to foster *ikiru chikara* or 'zest for living' in English (MEXT, 2003a). Yoshida (2001) explains that *yutori kyouiku* can be interpreted as pressure-free education. The younger Japanese who go through pressure-free education would become more skilful, innovative and independent, and were expected to have the strength to live in a global society and reinvigorate the Japanese economy, whereas teachers were expected to be responsible for implementing these reforms and achieving these goals.

Educational reforms under the Rainbow Plan (MEXT, 2001) covered a wide range of educational issues, and improvement in teacher training was certainly one issue to be tackled. The recommendations specifically made for training teachers to become more 'educational professionals' were threefold:

(1) Introduce a commendation system and special increases in the salaries of excellent teachers.
(2) Take appropriate measures for teachers who lack teaching abilities (e.g. not letting them teach until improvements are made).
(3) Improve the teacher qualification system, establish a new teacher training system and increase the opportunities to undertake work experience in the community.

Responding to these measures, particularly the second point, a new law, the Licensing Act of Educational Personnel, was enacted in the Diet on 20 June 2007, and the teaching certificate renewal system was implemented in April 2009. During this time, the government was headed by the Liberal Democratic Party. Under this law, currently practising secondary school teachers are required to renew their qualifications every 10 years by participating in conferences and seminars for 30 hours. Although this change seems to have more of an impact on practising teachers, it also has some impact on pre-service teachers in that they are made aware that teaching is a lifelong profession, and that teachers must continue to work on their professional development throughout their careers.

Asaoka (2008, 2012) criticises the vagueness of the goals for student teachers described in the governmental documents. I pointed out earlier that the expression 'teaching abilities' in the five-year action plan is not clearly defined. Similarly, what the expression 'teaching abilities' specifically means has not been clarified in this plan, either. The goals set by the government do not specify what kind of knowledge base or pedagogical skills need to be cultivated in ITE, and do not show whether abstract theory or practical skills should be stressed.

Additionally, the Democratic Party of Japan, which was the ruling party between September 2009 and December 2012, reviewed and proposed the possibility of introducing a six-year ITE programme, including a two-year graduate school-level training, and completely abolishing the teaching certificate renewal system. Consequently, these new policy changes have created more confusion on the part of teachers in Japan, both in-service and pre-service, with no clear direction provided by the government.

2.3 Initial Teacher Education in Japanese Higher Education

Before World War II, teacher education was conducted exclusively at higher education institutions (HEIs) that specialised in teacher education. This benefited students from poor family backgrounds, since the tuition was free and a teaching position was guaranteed upon graduation. However, the system was criticised on the basis that there was a tendency to create teachers who blindly submitted to authority and who were not critical enough against the nationalism prevalent in Japan during World War II (Jinnai, 2008). In the teacher education system, then, teachers were regarded more as government officials whose main duty was to serve his or her country, not as professionals who were responsible for public education. Thus, after the war and in light of the failures of the past, ITE was changed. It lost its exclusivity and became available through liberal arts education at any general university with a curriculum meeting the prescribed conditions (Sato, 2008). The aim was to train teachers who served the people rather than the nation.

Through the new ITE system, it was expected that teachers would become more intellectually independent, able to help build a solid foundation for democracy and the refashioning of society through education. This new system will be referred to as an 'open' system (*kaiho-sei* in Japanese) throughout this study. This means that ITE is not restricted to colleges and institutes of education, and that HEIs in Japan that offer ITE still enjoy relative autonomy due to the decentralised teacher training system. A contrast would be the system in the UK, which is often criticised as being more subject to central government education policy.

Under the present system, in order to become a school teacher in Japan, students are first required to attend an ITE programme offered at undergraduate level at HEIs and acquire a teaching qualification upon graduation. There is usually no specific requirement for students to join ITE programmes at universities, although this is often criticised because students who are less committed can enter the programme. ITE can be further divided into two levels: one for primary school teachers and one for secondary school teachers. ITE for prospective secondary school teachers is provided in various subject areas. This study focuses specifically on ITE for secondary school teachers whose subject area is

English language teaching. It should also be pointed out that in becoming an English teacher, there is usually no specific requirement of living or studying abroad experiences. In fact, many EFL student teachers in Japan are non-native speakers of English without any experience of studying abroad; thus, many likely lack cultural knowledge and confidence in their use of English.

As previously mentioned in this section, one of the characteristics of ITE in Japan is its 'principle of openness' (Ota, 2000), which is similar to many other regions in East Asia, such as Taiwan or South Korea (Asaoka & Ito, 2006; Chang, 2004; Kim, 2005). Due to this principle, ITE for secondary school teachers is mainly offered at undergraduate level by ITE programmes at more than 800 universities across Japan as of April 2016, even at universities without colleges of education. With a bachelor's degree, a first-class certificate is given, whereas with a master's degree, the advanced certificate is awarded. At a two-year junior college graduate-level, the second-class certificate is issued. Most Japanese teachers hold first-class certificates: in 2016, for example, 82.0% of upper secondary school teachers held these certificates, while 16.2% held advanced certificates and 1.0% held second-class certificates. Regarding lower secondary school teachers, 86.7% held first-class certificates, whereas 8.8% held advanced certificates and 4.4% held second-class certificates (MEXT, 2017). These figures show that most secondary school teachers receive ITE at the undergraduate level in Japan. In contrast, in the UK system for example, the majority of prospective secondary school teachers receive their initial teacher training at the post-graduate-level programme, called Post-Graduate Certificate in Education (PGCE), in order to achieve qualified teacher status (QTS), although a number of other routes are possible to becoming a teacher, such as a more employment-based training route called Schools Direct or a more classroom-based training route called School-Centred Initial Teacher Training (SCITT) (Department for Education, n.d.).

In Japan, in line with its open principles, the content of ITE programmes is at the discretion of each HEI. Ota (2000) argues that academic freedom has been maintained to a certain extent in ITE in Japan. However, this variability may cause inconsistency among student teachers' experiences in professional development, although the minimum requirements of the curriculum, prescribed by the Educational Personnel Certification Law and the Regulation for the Establishment of University Standards, ought to be met for accreditation. For instance, student teachers are required to meet specific qualification criteria in order to be licensed by a local government upon exiting the programme, which is usually four years long, starting at their matriculation. Under the current system in Japan, proposed in 1997 and partially revised and implemented in 1999 and 2000 by the Educational Personnel Training Council (EPTC), student teachers in ITE programmes are required to complete 31 credits regarding general education-related courses at a minimum, such as educational psychology, educational philosophy or moral education. Two credits are usually provided after attending a 14- to 15-week-long content course in Japan, meeting once a week for 90 minutes. These student teachers are also required to earn 20 credits of subject-specific courses as a minimum, including target language skills, literature and linguistics in the case of becoming an English teacher. At the research site, at the time of this study, student teachers had to complete two methodology courses[4] (two credits each) in their subject-specific areas, each lasting one semester. Earning 20 credits is roughly equal to completing five one-semester-long courses. These methodology courses are counted as a part of their general education-related courses in the current curriculum. Table 2.1 shows the number of credits currently required in ITE programmes at the secondary school level in Japan. As for the elective courses, student teachers can take either subject-specific courses or general education courses.

Before the legislation for teacher certification was revised, the minimum requirement for subject-specific courses was 40 credits, much more than that in the current situation in which only 20 credits of subject-specific courses are required. However, the post-revision minimum requirement for general education-related courses has increased in the current ITE system, mainly to address the criticism from society that many teachers do not possess enough general pedagogical knowledge or generic teaching skills to deal with various problems in the classroom, such as bullying or class disruption, also mentioned as issues to be tackled in the Rainbow Plan. The increase in general education credits was also a result of recommendations made by the EPTC, approved by the Ministry of Education in 1996, which says that by 'creating a new kind of teacher' (Ota, 2000: 47), serious social problems such as bullying and school phobia should be resolved.

However, there is a caveat in that the shift towards acquiring generic teaching skills occurred at the expense of a decrease in subject-specific courses. This is one of the more significant components of teachers' professional expertise (San, 1999), particularly for upper secondary school teachers. Shulman (1987) asserts that the central feature of teachers' knowledge base with which they make choices and actions in the classroom must be the blending of knowledge on subject matter *and*

Table 2.1 The number of course credits required in ITE in Japan

Courses	Lower secondary school level	Upper secondary school level
Subject-specific courses	20	20
General education-related courses	31	23
Electives	8	16

pedagogical skills. In many cases, absorbing theoretical knowledge and consolidating one's knowledge base take place at HEIs (Eraut, 1989). With a decreased emphasis on subject-specific courses, however, student teachers in Japan may lose some sources of their knowledge base for teaching, and hence find it more challenging to cultivate their ability to teach the subject. For example, a lack of appropriate pedagogical content knowledge on teaching methods for reading skills, such as schema theory or top-down processing (Carrell & Eisterhold, 1983; Grabe, 1993), may result in an inability to teach reading properly. As the case of two participants of this study, Aya and Nana (pseudonyms), indicates, in teaching reading skills, student teachers may depend on the traditional grammar-translation method without critically analysing the benefits and drawbacks of using this method (see Chapter 6 for a detailed discussion on this issue).

In 2017, MEXT (2017) provided a core curriculum for ITE in English language teaching for the first time in Japan and asked all HEIs offering ITE programmes in teaching EFL to reapply for accreditation to prove their ITE curriculum meets the expectations of MEXT. The core curriculum, which is to be implemented in the school year 2019, includes four content areas (teaching methodologies, linguistics, literature and cross-cultural understanding) for the programmes to cover, with a set of statements that describe standards to achieve in each area, and English language skills that student teachers need to improve before exiting the programmes. For example, student teachers need to earn eight credits on teaching methodologies (four credits only for student teachers who wish to become high school teachers) and achieve the following standards in regard to this content area, just to give a few examples:

- To understand how to teach listening skills and apply it to classroom practice.
- To understand how to teach speaking skills and apply it to classroom practice.
- To understand how to teach reading skills and apply it to classroom practice.
- To understand how to teach writing skills and apply it to classroom practice.
- To understand how to teach multiple language skills in an integrated way and apply it to classroom practice. (MEXT, 2017: 7)

Although the introduction of the core curriculum has been generally favourably received, many issues are still at the discretion of each ITE programme, which can create further confusion among student teachers and teacher educators.

2.4 Initial Teacher Training in Secondary Schools in Japan

Although the introduction of the core curriculum has had a strong impact on the ITE curriculum at HEIs across the nation, most of the changes have been made to the university coursework offered by ITE, and none to school-based training.

One of the challenges currently facing ITE in Japan is the theory–practice dichotomy (Hartley, 1993). While a theoretical knowledge base provided through HEIs is significant in student teachers' development of expertise, the quality and quantity of time that student teachers actually spend in school also has some influence on their professional development. In the case of the UK, after major educational reforms in the late 1980s and 1990s, the length of school-based training has currently been extended to 120 days for prospective secondary teachers in one-year PGCE courses. In addition, usually serial and block practice is carefully implemented during school-based training so that student teachers can regularly go back to HEIs for both academic and emotional support and follow-up (Furlong et al., 2000).

In comparison, in Japan, while experiential training in ITE has been considered more important than in the past in order to teach effectively and deal with new challenges in education, it still does not play a central role in student teachers' development of expertise. In 2001, one week of hands-on experiential training at a facility for the elderly or at a school for children with disabilities was implemented as a requirement during student teachers' third year of training. This hands-on experience is assumed to provide prospective teachers with work experience to enable them to understand and effectively deal with problems that challenge traditional Japanese values, such as juvenile delinquency or students with developmental disabilities. Another change implemented in 2001 was the extension of the length of the teaching practice. During their fourth year, student teachers are required to go to a local secondary school of their choice for a teaching practice. This spanned only two weeks for both upper and lower secondary schools until 2000; however, for the same reasons mentioned above, the length of time was extended to four weeks for lower secondary school teachers in order to gain a better understanding of the work of schools (i.e. administrative work, student counselling, supervision of extracurricular activities) and of various problems such as bullying, non-attendance at school or class disruption, which are more commonly found at lower secondary schools. This slight extension of teaching practice may raise student teachers' awareness of the reality of the workplace; however, it may not directly enhance the quality of their training as a subject teacher.

The length of teaching practice in ITE in Japan is two weeks for upper secondary schools and four weeks for lower secondary schools as a minimum requirement. Thus, on the one hand, colleges and institutes of education may offer a longer period of teaching practice with the cooperation of affiliated schools. For example, one university of education in northern Japan offers a one-week class observation and participation period at school during the first and second year, then a three-week classroom-based training period during the third and fourth year. On the other hand, secondary schools may make their own interpretations of the new law, as Bowe and Ball (1992) argue, and these schools are allowed to take student teachers for only three weeks, not four, owing to their various work circumstances. As a result, the majority of student teachers across Japan, particularly those who are in ITE programmes at universities without strongly established partnerships with schools, seem to experience a teaching practice of only three weeks. In this way, due to the length of school-based training, a lack of consistency in student teachers' expertise development is found not only in the ITE curriculum across HEIs but also in individual student teachers' teaching practice experiences.

Longer-term practical experience could possibly provide student teachers with more opportunities to try out their ideas in specific contexts, communicate with pupils, reflect on their actions and teaching techniques, and gain confidence as a teacher. Considering other contexts in which student teachers gain longer-term school-based experiences, such as six months in Taiwan (Chang, 2004) or at least one month in South Korea (Asaoka & Ito, 2006) or at multiple sites, such as in the UK (Lawes, 2004), the present ITE system in Japan does not seem to offer enough practical experience, and this is clearly a major challenge currently facing school-based training in Japan. San (1999: 17) asserts that this shortcoming is partly due to the fact that 'the university faculty values liberal arts more than teaching skills in teachers' preparation'. Moreover, with no additional financial incentives, schools are unwilling to accept student teachers for a longer term, since 'supervising trainees will increase the workload of teachers' (San, 1999: 18). School teachers' unwillingness to mentor student teachers also arises from the fact that in Japan not all student teachers will actually enter the teaching profession after graduation (Sato, 1992). Hence, the educational policy changes in ITE is an example that fails to understand the school contexts, as Bowe and Ball (1992) assert, and has led to a more challenging problem (Ota, 2000: 53) that ITE in Japan must manage, such as finding suitable schools and supervising teachers for school-based training.

The following description elaborates on a typical process of school-based training in Japan and points out that the lack of partnership between schools and HEIs is another challenge of school-based training. It is usually student teachers who choose which school to go to for their teaching practice. In most cases, they return to a school at which they were previously educated, although this may result in limiting the range of experiences that student teachers can experience. Prior to the teaching practice, student teachers are provided with a series of pre-teaching practice induction sessions at HEIs to ask questions and share concerns. Very often, experienced teachers in the local community or teachers who are graduates of the programmes are invited to share their expertise and experiences.

During the teaching practice, each student teacher is assigned a supervising teacher who can coach subject instruction as well as overall classroom management. According to Ito (2011), regardless of the subjects they teach, lower secondary school teachers in particular in Japan are responsible for a wide range of homeroom activities including daily class meetings, school events like sports days or school festivals where students work together on art or drama projects, serving and eating lunch together and daily classroom cleaning. Thus, the development of class management skills is crucial during teaching practice. This issue will be further discussed in Chapters 4 and 6.

Student teachers are usually required to keep logs in Japanese in which they keep a record of what they do each day (e.g. observing teachers and peers across subjects; preparing for lessons; reflecting on teaching classes; supervising students, homeroom activities and club activities; getting feedback from peers and supervising teachers), and receive written feedback from their supervising teachers at the end of each day. As mentioned at the start of this book, a lecturer from an HEI normally pays a visit during a teaching practice, observes student teachers' final demonstration lesson called *kenkyu jugyou* and has a meeting with a student teacher and a supervising teacher afterwards for feedback. If a student teacher is from a remote town, however, nobody from the HEI may go to observe his or her lesson.

After the teaching practice, a post-teaching practice course is provided by the HEI, in which student teachers share with cohort students their experiences and reflect on their own teaching practices. An assessment of the teaching practice is first provided by supervising teachers and HEI teacher educators finalise the grades based on the supervising teachers' assessment. There is usually no discussion between a supervising teacher and an HEI teacher educator, either on student teachers' professional development or on finalising their grades. This lack of partnership between schools and HEIs, along with fewer established expectations for supervising teachers' roles in school-based training, is one of the major challenges that must be taken into account in a Japanese context when discussing student teachers' professional development during ITE.

Another challenge, in addition to the length of the teaching practice and a lack of partnership systems between schools and HEIs, is the wide range of school experiences of each student teacher. Although the typical process of the teaching practice is as described above, each school has a different context in terms of school characteristics and students' needs, interests and proficiency levels; consequently, student teachers often undergo various experiences during their teaching practice. For instance, student teachers may be asked to teach only the first grade, while schools may ask student teachers to teach a number of different grades, from the first to the third. Furthermore, the number of classes taught over the two to four weeks varies considerably, ranging from 4 or 5, to more than 30 in total. Some may be asked to team teach with ALTs in English, while others may have to teach solely in their mother tongue, Japanese. The great variability in student teachers' experiences in school-based training may result in difficulty when attempting to standardise student teachers' final assessment. How the variability of student teachers' experiences influences the quality of their experiences should be questioned as well.

2.5 Challenges of Initial Teacher Education in Japan

One of the universal challenges that teacher education faces across cultures is the balance between theory and practice, and ITE in Japan is no exception. In this chapter, I first elaborate on recent educational reforms in English language education and the current ITE system in Japan in an attempt to elucidate the major problems that ITE in Japan currently faces under the theory–practice dichotomy. The main challenges in educating prospective secondary school English teachers in Japan are twofold.

First, due to its 'open' principles, a variability in student teachers' experiences in the content of the ITE curriculum across HEIs is a major challenge, although academic freedom in providing ITE is one of the merits that HEIs in Japan still enjoy. The variability of student teachers' experiences can also be found in school-based training. These experiences are not only variable but also isolated and limited to one school context. The variability in the quality of student teachers' experiences implies a lack of consistency across the ITE curriculum.

A lack of consistency leads to another problem in ITE in Japan in terms of teaching as a lifelong career. Currently, there is no general agreement on the goals or standards to achieve in professional development among each stakeholder in teacher training. Many student teachers in Japan are likely to be left confused, and yet, are struggling to develop their professional expertise in their own way, something that is discussed in later chapters in this study. The term *teaching abilities* used in many governmental documents is not clearly defined and often refers equally to teachers' language proficiency levels. Currently, both teachers and student teachers cannot see a clear direction in the content of professional expertise to be developed. Although the impact of the recent introduction of the core curriculum in English language teaching on student teachers' development still needs to be explored, the process of how a student teacher can become more autonomous in critically making professional choices and adapting effectively to new changes should be clarified.

With an understanding of the challenges that currently confront ITE in Japan, this study will seek to investigate how EFL student teachers in ITE in Japan perceive their own expertise development processes and try to mitigate the disparity between theory and practice.

Notes

(1) STEP is an English language proficiency test conducted by a Japanese non-profit organisation, the Society for Testing English Proficiency.
(2) ALTs are native English-speaking teachers hired through the Japan Exchange and Teaching Programme on a contractual base without a teaching certificate of Japan. Currently, English teachers with a teaching certificate are mostly Japanese natives.
(3) TOEFL and TOEIC are created by the Educational Testing Service, a US non-profit test development institution. Here, TOEIC refers to the TOEIC Listening and Reading Test and TOEFL is about the TOEFL Paper-Based (PBT) Test. TOEFL is used as an admission requirement for English-speaking universities, and 550 is based on their PBT.
(4) The curriculum at the research site was revised in the academic year 2017 so as to take four methodology courses as a requirement in order to promote student teachers' subject matter knowledge as well as pedagogical content knowledge.

3 Professional Development in Initial Teacher Education

A goal set for student teachers is to develop teacher expertise and become more professional while in the initial teacher education (ITE) programme. This enables them to teach and control their classes effectively, even on their first day of work at school. Hence, it is crucial to understand both *how* student teachers learn to take control of their own learning in ITE and *what* constructs of teacher expertise are important in the process of teacher development.

In this chapter, I first discuss the different ways we can understand how student teachers learn to become teachers. Next, the dimensions of knowledge bases that student teachers need to develop and later draw on in making professional judgements are discussed. In this study, 'content knowledge' (*what* to teach) (Shulman, 1987) is of particular importance among the constructs of teacher expertise for English as a foreign language (EFL) student teachers, since, unlike in other subjects, the subject matter is not only the content taught, but also the medium through which students learn and teachers teach the subject (Nunan, 1999). 'Pedagogical content knowledge' (PCK; *how* to teach) (Shulman, 1987) is also of interest to this study, since a good teacher needs to be able to select the most effective approach to present a content area, catering for a particular teaching context. I also explore not only the role of theoretical learning but also the role of reflective practices and social interactions. This study takes the stance that student teachers' professional development is constructed not only at an individual and internal level but also claims that how the constructs dialogically interact with each other in the process should be of particular interest.

3.1 Models of Professional Development in Initial Teacher Education

One way of understanding teachers' professional development is to explore how student teachers learn to become teachers. A number of studies into teachers' professional development have provided a model that identifies stages or phases that teachers are likely to go through (e.g. Furlong & Maynard, 1995; Kolb, 1983). In this section, I focus on the four major models of professional development: Furlong and Maynard's five-stage model, Kolb's work on experiential learning, Schön's view of reflective thinking and Johnson's sociocultural perspective in teacher learning, as these models are closely related to the participating student teachers' expertise development in this study.

Learning to teach as a linear process

Furlong and Maynard's (1995) five-stage process of student teachers' professional development is one of the best known models in ITE. In this model, the authors claim that student teachers go through five stages in a linear manner in school-based training: 'early idealism', 'personal survival', 'dealing with difficulties', 'hitting a plateau' and 'moving on'. At the first stage of their training, student teachers tend to hold idealistic views about students and themselves as a teacher, often influenced by their own positive learning experiences as a student. In many cases, they do not remember how exactly they were taught, but liked learning because of their teacher's personality and the relationship they established with their students. This also implies that student teachers at this stage are not yet fully able to analyse classroom practices based on theoretical knowledge bases. The second phase is usually observed when student teachers begin their school-based training. They realise then that they are seen as a teacher by their students, and often try to fit in with the school contexts and other teachers' expectations, although they may find some conflicts between their prior perspectives and the reality of the classroom. The third stage is shifting from personal survival to survival 'as a teacher' (Furlong & Maynard, 1995: 82), when student teachers begin to make sense of what is going on in a classroom, and very often, in order to deal with difficulties, they try to 'mimic' what they believe to be teacherly behaviour. Without understanding how complex teacher thinking behind the stage is, they can at least adopt the outward appearance of being a teacher. This means that student teachers are likely to emulate teaching behaviours without fully appreciating the theoretical knowledge that underpins them, which will confine them to one approach, meaning that they cannot develop solutions to problems they face in the classroom. Towards the end of their school-based teacher training, which is the fourth stage, student teachers often gain some confidence and feel a little more relaxed, although their teaching still remains shallow. Therefore, Furlong and Maynard believe that what is more important in the process is the final stage of 'moving on'; student teachers need to move on to a more professional understanding of classroom practices. This model, however, does not yet fully succeed in explaining everything in the complex process of learning to teach, particularly how student teachers gain a more professional understanding of teaching and become able to proceed onto the next stage.

Learning to teach as a cyclic process

Although the stages suggested by Furlong and Maynard (1995) are described as a series of stages in a linear process, some models of professional development, such as Kolb's (1983) experiential learning cycle, suggest that it is more like a cyclic process with the help of reflection. Based on the idea that knowledge is created through the transformation of experience, Kolb argues that learning starts with concrete experience, and the experience needs to be reflected on, analysed and transformed into a conceptual understanding of a situation. This conceptual understanding is used for planning the next action, which leads back to the start of this learning cycle. What this cycle suggests is that simply experiencing something is not sufficient for learning to take place; experience needs to be reflected on, acted upon and transformed into new experience – improvement in teaching – with the help of a conceptual understanding of teaching.

Schön is another researcher well known for the following two types of reflection on practice in professional development: reflection-in-action and reflection-on-action. Although Schön does not write particularly about teachers, the model of a reflective practitioner has already been practised in many teacher training programmes, both in in-service teacher training (see, e.g. Richards & Lockhart, 1994) and in ITE (Grenfell, 1998; LaBoskey, 1993; McIntyre, 1993; Orland-Barak & Yinon, 2007; Tann, 1993).

Underpinned by Dewey's (1938) theory of experiential learning, Schön (1983) introduces and defines the notion of 'reflecting-in-action' – that professionals engage in reflective conversation with practical situations – setting problems while working on tasks, testing out new solutions and readjusting. Both Dewey and Schön view learning as an adaptive process. Through reflection-in-action, an unobservable element of professional expertise, which Schön (1983: 276) refers to as 'artistry', can be made explicit; as a result, it is easier to adjust or modify one's teaching, if necessary. Hartley (1993) also maintains that the strength of reflective pedagogy is that teacher thinking, which is grounded in everyday situations and has merely been habitual, becomes tacit. Schön further argues that learning to teach is the dialogical process that integrates knowledge, experience, action and reflection, and in this cycle, reflection is viewed as the bridge that helps narrow the gap between cognition and examination of the concepts, principles and experiences through which teachers test ideas, solve problems and adapt to new situations.

Criticisms of notion of reflective teaching in ITE

Many researchers in the field of teacher education have suggested that the reflective practitioner approach is effective in foreign language teacher education in narrowing the gap between theory and practice, in which teachers are provided with opportunities to reflect on their theoretical knowledge and the experiential knowledge gained through teaching practice. However, this reflective approach has not escaped criticism, in particular in ITE.

Some researchers (e.g. Heilbronn, 2008; LaBoskey, 1993; Nagamine, 2008; Suzuki, 2013) point out in their respective studies that the use of the term *reflection* is not always clear or consistent among researchers, practitioners and teacher educators; thus, concepts, topics, skills or tasks used or emphasised in reflective practices in ITE vary. The confusion is not just the term loosely used by researchers and practitioners. As Akbari (2007) criticises, there is, as yet, little evidence to show improvements in teachers' or students' performance due to teachers' reflective practices. The results of many of the abovementioned studies indicate that the participants developed better reflective skills; however, this does not necessarily imply that teachers became better at teaching with a better understanding of the theoretical concepts and disciplines. Additionally, reflection may not always bring about ideal results, whereas there may also be *bad* reflection (Moore, 2000) that may reinforce wrong values or behaviours in student teachers.

The most notable challenge for novice teachers in the teacher-as-a-reflective-practitioner approach is that reflective discourse assumes a certain *a priori* sophistication in the skill of introspection (Atkinson, 2004). The learner is assumed to have a transcendent and rational subjectivity before experiencing reflective tasks, whereas reflection may be challenging for student teachers because they may not have enough of either a knowledge base or 'intuitive knowing' (Schön, 1983: 276) or practical experiences to draw upon. This is a major challenge for many novice teachers, especially in a context where reflective teaching approaches in ITE are just beginning to be developed, such as in Japan. Reflection is still a new skill for student teachers in ITE in Japan, requiring specific instruction and support, such as setting aside specific times for reflection in the coursework (Kojima, 2008). Funaki (2008) also points out that ITE in Japan has not developed a deep enough yearning for autonomous learning; thus, many student teachers in ITE lack an inquiring mind and problem-solving abilities, as can be seen in Yurika's case in Chapter 6 (Section 6.2), which are essential for reflection. As Suzuki (2013: 86) points out, when the term *reflection* is translated into Japanese, it becomes the word *hansei*, which emphasises 'a negative form of reflection'. Both the terms *reflection* and *hansei* involve looking back at one's thoughts and behaviours; however, while *reflection* is expected to result in a new perspective, *hansei* does not necessarily do so. Thus, confused with the concept of *hansei*, student teachers in Japan may individually focus more on negative aspects of their ideas and practices, rather than generating newer insights and perspectives based on reflection.

What Schön (1983) refers to as reflection-*on*-action, reflecting on teaching *afterwards*, is also challenging for student teachers without the vocabulary to articulate their experiences (Kennedy, 1993). Student teachers are usually more concerned with self-image and acquiring routines (Akbari, 2007) rather than critically evaluating their own teaching or teaching contexts. Without a knowledge base to critically analyse teachers' experiences in a particular teaching setting, 'teacher education can lapse easily into an almost narcissistic, self-reflective mode' (Hartley, 1993: 85). In addition to lack of a rational subjectivity, established routines and practical experiences, other constraints, such as emotional pressure and time constraints to get through ITE, may also hinder pre-service teachers' reflection (Kerr, 1994).

The previous section has discussed the importance as well as the challenge of reflective practices for novice teachers' professional development, especially when there remains a disparity between theory and practice. Learning to teach is ideally a dialogical process that integrates knowledge, experience and action through reflection. In this cycle, reflection is viewed as the bridge between theoretical knowledge and practical classroom experiences, with which student teachers test ideas, solve problems, adapt to new situations, gain new understanding and improve their teaching. The reflective model of professional development, however, suggests that student teachers may focus on the individual, not the dynamic nature of interaction among themselves, their peers, colleagues and supervising teachers and students. Learning is fundamentally a social phenomenon, and cognitive development does not always take place individually; thus, the social dimension of learning in ITE needs to be emphasised as well.

The sociocultural perspective

Another model of teachers' professional development is based on the sociocultural perspective (Johnson, 2009), informed by Vygotsky's work on psychology (Roth & Lee, 2007). In this model, student teachers who are learners of teaching often work as a group (community) and engage in a shared activity, which is mediated by various tools (for example, beliefs, theories, concepts and artefacts), and the cognitive assistance is provided by other members of the community. Their professional knowledge is shaped by the social activities of thinking, talking and acting embedded in the communities of practice. Learners in this model support one another and mutually construct assistance in ways that are similar to how experts support the performance of novices. In becoming more professional, student teachers need to make connections between the scientific concepts to which they are exposed to in ITE and their everyday concepts about language, language learning and language teaching with the assistance of appropriate mediational tools. In this model, the process of learning to teach is not individualistic but rather is promoted through peer interaction as student teachers collectively struggle through issues and problems related to their professional experiences.

3.2 Dimensions of Professional Expertise

In this section, I address *what* constitutes teachers' professional expertise. While learning in ITE, student teachers need to develop the professional expertise to draw on in making professional judgements in their own teaching practices. Many researchers in the field of teacher development have used various terms to describe the professional expertise that student teachers should attain by the end of the programme (Borg, 2003, 2005; Elbaz, 1981; Richards, 1996, 1998; Roberts, 1998; Shulman, 1987; Wallace, 1991).

One such term, *teacher expertise*, for example, is defined by Tsui (2003). She argues that the teacher expertise of second language teachers is a process by which teachers consciously theorise their practical knowledge through reflection and transform their formal knowledge into practical knowledge. In other words, teacher expertise is *not* a state of theoretical learning but a constant and reciprocal process between theory and practice, in which a student teacher needs to play a central role in meaning-making.

What Tsui refers to as 'formal knowledge' that student teachers are expected to acquire in ITE is quite complex. According to Shulman (1987), there are seven dimensions of teachers' formal knowledge:

(1) *Content knowledge*: central feature of the teacher knowledge base, substantive and syntactic structure of a subject.
(2) *General pedagogical knowledge*: principles and strategies of classroom management.
(3) *Curriculum knowledge*: knowledge of curriculum, materials and programmes.
(4) *Pedagogical content knowledge*: knowledge that blends content and pedagogy into an understanding of how particular topics, problems, or issues can be presented comprehensibly to learners.
(5) *Knowledge of learners and their characteristics*.
(6) *Knowledge of educational contexts*: knowledge of groups, classrooms, schools, communities, and cultures.
(7) *Knowledge of educational ends, purposes, and value*. (Shulman, 1987: 8)

PCK is of particular value to this study. Shulman (1987: 8) defines it as 'the blending of content and pedagogy into an understanding of how particular topics, problems, or issues are organised, represented, and adapted to the diverse interest and abilities of learners, and presented for instruction'. This implies that a subject specialist with an immense amount of content knowledge is not necessarily a good teacher; rather, a good teacher should be able to determine the best and most effective approach to present a content area, catering for a particular group of learners' needs and interests, based on PCK.

I would like to conclude that while Shulman's seven constructs offer a fruitful framework of teacher expertise for ITE, they are largely cognitive and individual and do not elucidate how the constructs interact with each other in the process of professional development. In Shulman's thinking, they are to be achieved at the individual level through reflection on individual cognition and experiences. Concerning this individualised aspect of professional development, Shulman admitted later that a teacher is 'a member of a professional community who is ready, willing, and able to teach and to learn from his or her teaching experiences' (Shulman & Shulman, 2004: 258). This implies that student teachers should learn from both individual experiences and those of others, if they are to be regarded as learners who try to achieve professional autonomy through actively engaging in social practices, and influencing, or being influenced by, them. This is particularly crucial for EFL student teachers in Japan with a limited amount of engagement in practical experiences, already criticised earlier in this book as one of the problems faced by ITE in Japan.

3.3 Dimensions of Professional Expertise for English Language Teaching

In Japan, the improvement of English language proficiency is a pressing need. As MEXT (2003b) addressed in their five-year action plan on English language education in the country, one action to improve English language education is the improvement of English teachers' teaching ability, which should precede the improvement of learners' language competences. Therefore, in this study it is important to examine how student teachers develop their expertise as *English language* teachers, not just teachers in general terms, and how this theoretical principle learned in ITE can be translated into practice, since this greatly influences pedagogic decisions that EFL teachers make and the strategies they employ in teaching English. Firstly, the dimensions of teacher expertise are discussed, which are particularly relevant to EFL student teachers in Japan.

Similar to Shulman's categories of teachers' formal knowledge, it is widely understood that second/foreign language teachers are also expected to build various categories of knowledge base in ITE. Among the seven constructs of teacher expertise, in addition to PCK, *content knowledge* is also important for EFL student teachers in teaching the English language because, unlike in other subjects, the subject matter is not only the content taught, but also the medium through which students learn the subject (Nunan, 1999).

For instance, student teachers in social sciences take Japanese-medium content courses in social sciences. When they teach during school-based training, they teach the content in Japanese, the first language of the majority of student teachers and students. However, EFL student teachers in Japan ought to understand how the English language is structured, learned and used, while they also have to be able to use it competently themselves. Therefore, becoming an EFL student teacher in Japan is often more challenging than becoming a teacher in a different subject. EFL teachers cannot cease to develop their own knowledge of culture and English language competence even after they join ITE, since they are mostly non-native speakers of the English language and culture. Studying abroad, for example, is not a requirement of the ITE curriculum and student teachers of EFL in Japan do not need any experience of spending time in an English-speaking country. On the one hand, EFL student teachers need to learn content knowledge about, for instance, the English language system and theories on second language acquisition and foreign language teaching; on the other hand, they are to improve their competence in the English language by applying what they learn as content knowledge to their classroom performance.

In addition, student teachers' *curriculum knowledge* as well as *knowledge of educational contexts* are closely related to the student teachers' English language competence. For example, in the case of English language teaching (ELT) in Japan, very recently it was officially announced for the first time in the Course of Study that, in principle, English language teachers needed to use English as the medium of instruction for upper secondary schools as of April 2013 (MEXT, 2010a) and for lower secondary schools as of April 2021 (MEXT, 2017). In this way, constructs of the teacher expertise of EFL student teachers are closely intertwined with one another, and thus their professional development is no doubt a complex and multifaceted process.

Furthermore, it should be pointed out that teachers' cognition and experiences inform their PCK as well as their actual teaching practices. As already discussed, a good teacher is not only a subject specialist but can adjust their teaching methods and approaches to adapt to a particular group of learners' needs and wants in a particular teaching context. This is also true of EFL student teachers in Japan. For example, in ITE courses on PCK they typically learn that there was a shift in approaches to teaching a second/foreign language from the grammar-translation method, which many of the participants in this study experienced as a learner (for example, see the discussion in Aya's case in Section 6.1 in Chapter 6), towards more communicative language teaching (CLT). As a foreign language teacher, they learn that they themselves need to make pedagogical choices between the two methods of teaching English by drawing on their PCK.

Up to the 1960s, language was considered a system of descriptive rules for the coding of meaning (Richards & Rodgers, 2001). In this structural view, language learners were to master these rules and syntactic structures, such as phonological units (e.g. phonemes), grammatical units (e.g. phrases, clauses and sentences) and vocabulary items. The most suitable teaching approach for this, particularly in Japan where teacher authority has been highly valued due to Confucianism and filial piety (Shimahara, 2002), was a grammar-translation method in a teacher-centred mode, which stressed the form of the language and considered meaning less important. However, during the 1970s, researchers and linguists started to see language more as a tool for expressing functional meanings (Richards & Rodgers, 2001), where learners are agents who interact, negotiate and co-construct meanings using language (Nunan, 1999). CLT, an approach that focuses on learners as well as developing their communicative competence (Savignon, 2005), became more accepted and learners were expected to create social relations and build linguistic fluency, not just accuracy. Moreover, in a CLT class, teacher roles and student roles significantly differ from those in earlier methods and approaches. The role of a teacher is that of a facilitator, not an all-knowing expert, whereas students are encouraged to engage in linguistic interaction with other students and collaboratively construct meaning 'under the guidance, but not control, of the teacher' (Brown, 2007b: 47).

The view of language as a system for expressing and negotiating meanings in a social context has had a significant impact on second/foreign language teaching as well as on second/foreign language teacher education. As a result, in many cases across nations, teachers have attempted to respond by making changes in ELT in accordance with the reform initiatives from the Ministry of Education. ELT in Japan is no exception, and student teachers also need to develop PCK, knowledge of educational contexts, as well as knowledge of educational ends accordingly. For example, MEXT in Japan introduced a communicative syllabus at secondary school level in the 1980s in order to 'prepare students to cope with the rapid pace of change toward a more global society' (Wada, 2002: 32). In reality, however, it is often reported that there has been a dilemma between teachers' 'ideas of communication-oriented English and a hidden goal of examination-oriented English' (Sato, 2002: 54). Sato notes that many in-service teachers in his study find it a challenge to place total emphasis on the development of communicative competence in English because of entrance examinations:

> To the surprise of the researcher, although in their first interviews they expressed their individual ideas about communication-oriented English, a majority of them conformed to an established pattern of teaching with heavy emphasis on grammar explanation and translation ... These new

ideas and activities remained marginal and had little impact on instruction in regular English classes. (Sato, 2002: 58)

As this quote suggests, even when teachers acknowledge the need for teaching how to use English communicatively, they stress the centrality of explicit grammar teaching due to contextual factors. Nishimuro and Borg (2013) add other contextual factors, such as learners' low proficiency and motivation, a lack of time as well as collective targets in explaining Japanese EFL teachers' pedagogical choices of explicit grammar teaching over CLT; although, as Nishimuro and Borg admit, their choices and practices are largely experiential and not well informed by formal theory or methodological concepts in ELT. A similar dilemma can be found among EFL student teachers in ITE when considering how they should approach their own teaching practices during the teaching practice. They may base their professional judgement on their language learning experiences of explicit grammar teaching in previous schooling, although they learn in ITE that CLT is currently one of the ideal teaching approaches in ELT in Japan.

Of course, CLT is not unproblematic or the only teaching approach in ELT in Japan. As the resistance encountered from many EFL teachers in Japan above shows, the approach has some problems, which student teachers need to learn as part of PCK. According to Savignon (2005), for instance, the methods for properly assessing learner achievement in CLT are not well defined. Additionally, the previous research findings in second language acquisition indicate that the acquisition of the target language is not largely affected by classroom instruction in CLT. Thus, it should be stressed that pedagogical content knowledge, 'the blending of content and pedagogy' (Shulman, 1987: 8), is particularly significant in the development of teacher expertise for EFL student teachers. It is situated and practical because it is closely related to specific teaching contexts.

3.4 Challenges of Putting Theory into Practice

In this chapter, I outlined *how* student teachers typically develop their teacher expertise by referring to influential models of learning theories. These models are not in themselves sufficient. Learning within one particular model does not provide opportunities for student teachers to encounter different and new views. Their professional development is a dynamic and complex process shaped by the social activities of thinking, talking and acting, but the models of professional development above do not fully allow for such collective struggle.

I also discussed *what* constructs of teacher expertise EFL student teachers in Japan need to learn: theory on the subject as well as approaches to teaching the subject. These knowledge bases are what Shulman (1987) calls content knowledge and PCK, respectively. Additionally, unlike other subject teachers, student teachers of EFL are themselves *learners* of the target language that they are to teach, having learned in various learning environments and approaches and informed by former teachers and former school contexts. They are non-native-speaking teachers who may not yet be suitably proficient in the target language to be able to teach effectively. Thus, they need to continue making efforts to develop their English language competence as well as the contextual knowledge of the target language. This adds another layer of complexity to the already complex process of professional development.

As we shall see later, student teachers' pedagogical choices may fluctuate, since they are in the middle of the development of the multifaceted process of internalising various constructs of teacher expertise. They are also affected by the teaching culture in Japan, which will be discussed in the next chapter.

4 Teaching Culture in Japan

Previous research in teachers' professional development has indicated that a teaching culture profoundly reflects its contexts (Lortie, 1975). Shimahara (2002) also speaks of a teaching culture that can capture both salient and latent features of teaching, although the concept itself is quite elusive. Thus, it is the purpose of this chapter to explore the teaching culture in Japan, particularly at the junior high school level, paying close attention to two areas deeply ingrained in Japanese culture: holistic teaching and teaching as craft. These themes are closely intertwined and make the Japanese teaching culture distinctive. They can also affect not only in-service teachers but also student teachers' perspectives and their professional development.

As mentioned in Chapter 2, despite the economic imperative to raise students' English language abilities in order to remain competitive in a global market, the primary educational goal for students in primary and secondary education in Japan is to foster a 'zest for living' (MEXT, 2003a). To go into a little more depth, in order to live in a rapidly changing society, the Ministry of Education, Culture, Sports, Science and Technology (MEXT) cites that students in Japan are expected to enhance the following three qualities in a balanced way: solid academic abilities (to acquire basic knowledge and skills, to utilise them and think, judge and express, to deal with and solve various problems); well-rounded character (self-discipline, collaboration with others, consideration for others); and health and physical strength. Even though the recently revised Course of Study is to be introduced in the 2020 school year, the main aim of fostering a zest for living, based on these three qualities, will remain the same. Among the three, the second quality in particular belongs to personal and social education, as Robson et al. (1999) argue. It suggests that a strong emphasis is currently placed on the social, personal and affective domains of education, not only the cognitive domain, in Japanese teaching culture. The tension between the emphasis on the personal/social and cognitive aspects of education, along with the need to raise the level of English language abilities due to economic imperatives, results from the two dominant characteristics of Japanese teaching culture: holistic teaching and teaching as craft.

4.1 Holistic Teaching

In response to the aforementioned educational goals, particularly that of fostering a well-rounded character, one of the major characteristics of teaching in Japan is its holistic nature. Based on the concept of whole-person education, or *zenjin kyoiku* in Japanese, personal traits and interpersonal relations are essential aspects of teaching that teachers are expected to embrace (Shimahara, 2002). Thus, teachers in Japan are responsible for fostering students' social development through social interactions. All the efforts to become a holistic teacher are geared towards achieving the objective set by MEXT in 1981, which claims that each individual student's personality should be respected and developed while becoming empowered in order to foster 'a zest for living'. This is more salient especially at the primary education level but it is also pivotal at the lower secondary education level (Shimahara, 2002; Shimahara & Sakai, 1992). Unlike in the case of primary school teachers, middle school teachers specialise in academic subjects, such as English or maths; however, they are also responsible for holistic teaching, and in fact, this is often more dominant in teachers' lives in Japan.

Among the seven categories of the knowledge base for teaching classified by Shulman (1987) in Chapter 3, the knowledge base that enables holistic teaching can be referred to as 'general pedagogical knowledge', referring to the theoretical principles and skills of classroom management. More specifically, as Ito (2011) and Shimahara (2002) argue, holistic teaching in Japan includes far more aspects of students' school life than classroom management. For example, middle school teachers in Japan need to give *educational guidance* such as placing students in high schools, which would involve consultation with students and parents, performance assessment based on school records and tests, selection of high schools, preparation and filing of applications, among other things.

In addition to educational guidance, offering *seito shido*, literally translated as *student guidance* in English, to students also occupies a place in teachers' work in Japan. So-called student guidance in the context of Japan can be defined as educational activities in and beyond the curriculum (Inagaki & Inuzuka, 2000). It concerns every aspect of student life in school, ranging from counselling students on behavioural and emotional problems, which belongs to a domain of specialised counsellors in the United States (Shimahara, 2002), to the supervision of extra-curricular club activities, student government, school cleaning, school lunch and homeroom activities. It also includes planning for relevant activities out of school, such as school picnics and trips, sports festivals, chorus contests and patrolling after school and on weekends.

In this, in addition to subject matter teaching, junior high school teachers in Japan are expected to be involved in *all* aspects of student life and development, which is believed, in turn, to enhance their classroom management skills. As a supervising teacher of a student teacher in Shimahara's (2002: 118) study suggests, 'classroom management is key to teaching effectively. Its purpose is to develop *shudan* [a group] and an environment where children can express their problems openly'. This resonates with the beliefs of many in-service teachers in Japan, as well as the supervising teachers of some participants in this study. Their belief in the importance of holistic teaching can greatly affect student teachers' teaching practices during school-based training.

Although holistic teaching is a significant quality for student teachers in any teaching context to acquire in the process of learning to teach, there are problems as well. For instance, placing more emphasis on holistic teaching may overshadow the process of becoming a good *subject* teacher. In Japan, students at middle school are usually grouped heterogeneously and belong to 'homerooms', and a teacher is assigned to each 'homeroom' class regardless of his or her academic subject. During compulsory education, great importance is attached to group life in Japan, and thus, the primary responsibility of a homeroom teacher is to promote a classroom community, provide student as well as educational guidance and supervise non-academic activities (Shimahara, 2002). This may cause a dilemma between classroom management and subject matter teaching for some student teachers, whose perspectives on teaching are still in the process of forming and evolving. In fact, two of the supervising teachers of the participants of this study placed holistic teaching before cognitive domain teaching, which largely affected how they interacted with the student teachers. This case will be further discussed in Chapter 6.

4.2 Teaching as Craft

In the teaching culture of Japan, another salient characteristic is the view of teaching as craft; teaching is often considered as a craft that can be learned, transmitted, emulated and reformulated.

In teacher education and professional development theories, a new perspective has emerged in response to criticism of the view of a good teacher being a rational-autonomous professional (Elliott, 1993). The newer view based on behaviourist principles assumes that a good teacher is a competent practitioner (Furlong *et al.*, 2000), equipped with observable competences and skills, and teaching is considered as craft knowledge that can be learned and transmitted from one teacher to another. The competency-based view of a good teacher has also been criticised, however, mainly for two reasons: the implicit and mere acquisition of a set of behaviours will not necessarily lead to creative teacher development (Moore, 2000; Pring, 1995), nor will mere behaviour emulation enable novice teachers to cope with new situations and future contexts later in their careers (Furlong *et al.*, 2000). In other words, implicit and mere acquisition of craft may not contribute much to teacher creativity and autonomy.

Despite this criticism of the view of teaching as craft, this view has been traditionally more positively accepted in the teaching culture of Japan. As Shimahara (2002: 24) points out, teachers in Japan are likely to believe that classroom teaching is a craft embedded in classroom practices, which teachers learn and share through experiences. It is a form of teacher expertise that can be accumulated through 'pedagogical wisdom'. Shimahara (2002) further argues that in-service teachers in Japan do not consider craft knowledge in teaching the same as mere habitual practice. Rather, through emulation and reflective practice, not only is craft knowledge learned and transmitted as it is, but it is also developed and reformulated to add *new* meanings to their practice. Their reformulated practice is equivalent to what is called *kaizen* in Japanese by Chie, one of the participants of this study (see Chapter 6: Section 6.1).

In order to understand why the view of teaching as craft has been largely accepted in the teaching culture of Japan, next I would like to delve into the concept of apprenticeship in teacher education.

A newer approach to apprenticeship in teacher education

In discussing cognitive learning theory, Rogoff (1995) states that *apprenticeship* is a kind of human mediation in human learning. A model is provided by an expert to a novice learner so that the learner emulates the tasks that the model performs and eventually learns to perform them autonomously. This can be observed not only between a parent and a child but also in teacher education, and of special note is that emulating a model is considered one possible transformative activity (from external/social to internal/psychological), not mindless copying, in novice teachers' cognitive development.

Growing up is a process of social learning, and children are expected to develop their cognitive abilities through participation and interaction with the people who surround them (Rogoff, 1990). Children are, in one sense, *apprentices* in the process of socialisation. From the day they are born, their apprenticeship starts; they observe peers and adults, imitate their behaviours, interact with them and jointly solve problems. Imitation in child development is considered to be one of the most important tools for 'enhancing human competence and the strength of attachment among human beings' (Yando *et al.*, 1978: 156). Through participation, imitation and interaction, children learn a language, learn cultural norms and acquire cognitive thinking skills. Events and activities that children take part in may be supported and guided by adults; for example, adults may adjust the activities or language they use to suit the developmental level of children. However, adults do not take the entire responsibility for children's learning. As Dewey (1916) explains, in order to play an effective role in the community, a child needs to imitate others' actions and behaviours of his or her own will. Although the infinitive 'to imitate' may imply an unconscious aspect of copying the 'ends' of actions, Dewey asserts that one imitates not only to conform to the patterns of others and to be accepted by the group, but also to voluntarily improve the situations in which actions take place, which is similar to *kaizen* in Chie's case mentioned above. Thus, child cognitive development is a two-way process in which both participants – children and adults – can benefit from participation, albeit differently, since this is a lifelong process, though adults are usually at a higher stage of cognitive development.

In some ways, socialisation in child cognitive development is similar to teacher socialisation. Novice teachers learn to teach and develop professional expertise through participation, observation and interaction with experienced teachers, peers and pupils. They are *apprentices* in the teacher socialisation process, learning behaviours and routines, language and norms appropriate within a professional culture. However, there are some differences between these two socialisation processes that are important to acknowledge. The major difference is that teachers' participation, observation and interaction have to be based on their theoretical knowledge bases, which is not the case with children. As Kagan (1992: 136) argues, what distinguishes professional from non-professional people is 'a stock of esoteric knowledge and skills not available to the layman'. Hence, teachers, as professionals, are expected to depend on their professional expertise to plan, teach and evaluate their teaching through an intellectually dialogical process between theory and practice. Novice teachers, as apprentices, are also expected to acquire theoretical knowledge while trying it out in practice as a foundation of their professional development.

The notion of 'apprenticeship' in teacher education is not favourably accepted, however. Lortie (1975) argues that pupils spend quite a long period of time in the classroom unconsciously observing how their teachers teach and deal with pupils, the process of which he claims as 'apprenticeship of observation', regardless of whether or not pupils want to become teachers themselves, and these experiences have a major influence in shaping student teachers' thinking about teaching and their own teaching performance. Due to this implicit process of apprenticeship as a pupil, many are likely to enter their profession with pre-fixed beliefs about teaching, strongly influenced by their former teachers, without critical examination of their models (Almarza, 1996; Kagan, 1992; Pajares, 1992). Similarly, in many contexts, teacher training has been traditionally considered as 'best accomplished by sitting on the job, watching others and absorbing what they do, and so slowly being inducted into the skills of the craft' (Grenfell, 1998: 7), which promotes the implicit process of apprenticeship, even after becoming a teacher. An apprentice teacher learns to teach through an implicit process of observing expert teachers, without critically examining how they teach. Thus, teachers in a traditional apprenticeship approach are not considered to be fully equipped with either theory to draw back on or critical thinking skills with which they can analyse teaching.

Lortie is not the only author who claims this kind of apprenticeship is intuitive and implicit. It is implicit in that the thinking process of experienced teachers is often tacit and difficult to observe for student teachers. Therefore, student teachers may observe and copy what experienced teachers do in practice, which may lead to the acquisition of craft, but may not necessarily lead student teachers to an explicit understanding of what teachers actually think or how they plan, monitor and evaluate their teaching. Wallace (1991) also asserts that imitative and static craft knowledge of teaching do not allow for theoretical knowledge intervention. Student teachers' beliefs about learning to teach established through this intuitive process of apprenticeship are considerably strong; as a result, these beliefs are unlikely to be modified through initial teacher education (ITE) (Kagan, 1992; Peacock, 2001; Richardson, 1996). As previously mentioned, student teachers' pre-fixed perspectives are difficult to change even through reflective practices. Thus, the traditional notion of apprenticeship cannot provide teachers with abilities with which they can critically examine their particular practices and seek to improve them.

Apprenticeship may carry a different connotation in different times and contexts, however. In some of the more recent streams of teacher education literature, an 'apprenticeship' model has been used more favourably. Roberts (1998), for instance, argues that in the case of a stable society that values seniority and tradition such as Japan, an apprenticeship may be effective at least for ITE. Tomlinson (1995: 48) further asserts that apprenticeship can be powerful if mentors can effectively lead student teachers to 'experimental imitation' by supporting student teachers' observations at every step, from planning to reflection. Similarly, in a sociocultural approach, the process of student teachers' learning to teach as an apprentice is not a unidirectional process from a master/mentor to a student/mentee. Student teachers may still be considered as peripheral participants of the learning community, as Lave and Wenger (1991) would term them, but the concept of apprenticeship can be broadened to focus more on a community of practice in which novice members of the community grow as they engage in social interaction and activities with other members. Furthermore, emulation can be understood as one mediational activity in this approach, as Dunn (2011: 56) argues in his study on second language teacher education. In his study, when asked to explain the theoretical concepts that student teachers learned in a workshop, they used the ideas that they discussed with peers during the workshop by connecting newly learned concepts with their prior experiences, not simply copying ideas and concepts that they acquired, and he called this a 'creative form of imitation'.

This newer approach to apprenticeship will be further discussed in the next section. In the teaching culture of Japan, where seniority and tradition are valued, emulation is culturally endorsed in some forms of professional training (Hare, 1996; Ota, 2000). How apprenticeship in teacher training is conceptualised in Japan, and how teachers try to reduce the disparity between theory and practice with the help of emulation and reflection, will be discussed next.

Maneru: Conceptualisation of apprenticeship in Japan

In the Japanese language, a verb for 'to learn' is *manabu*. According to the dictionary *Kojien* (Shinmura, 2008), the word originally comes from another verb for 'to emulate', *manebu*. This indicates that learning and emulation are historically closely linked, both linguistically and culturally, in Japan. Emulation can be a mere copy of craft knowledge and the skills of experts and peers if effected without an intellectual examination of the theory behind specific actions and behaviours. At the same time, craft can be observed either implicitly or explicitly, and can be improved, if followed by a critical examination of imitated actions, which is a 'creative form of imitation' (Dunn, 2011: 56) and can result in *kaizen*, improvements in teaching. Emulation can be a powerful mediational tool for learning a great deal from expert teachers and peers, especially if the goals and means are clearly recognised by student teachers. Lantolf and Thorne (2006) assert that understanding the goals and the means is central to emulation in cognitive development.

According to Hare (1996), in the training of the traditional arts of *noh* drama in Japan, which is the oldest dance drama originating in the 14th century AD, for example, younger actors are required to observe, emulate and master a set form of physical skills from senior actors in order to proceed to the next level. At the next level, they will learn another set form of skills through emulation until they gradually reach the final level of liberation and freedom. This is recursive and experience-based training, and the gradual approach of observing seniors' performance and mastering their physical behaviours leads to a cognitive understanding of the art, which is not learned through a 'rational, and intellective process' (Hare, 1996: 337) of didactic teaching of *noh* drama. This idea of *noh* training and emulation in the training process indicates that there are some differences in the perception of apprenticeship between Japanese and Western pedagogical ideologies. In *noh* training, through the process of observation and emulation, apprentices are expected to learn without any explicit teaching, although the model is explicitly provided. Lewis (1992: 403) supports this point by stating that in the arts and industry in Japan in particular, mastery of set forms through emulation and repeated practice 'may have a very different relationship to creative endeavor in Japan' than in other contexts, such as in the United States. In this learning process, at the final stage after learning craft knowledge through emulation, trainees are expected to develop autonomy even without explicit teaching of the theory behind specific actions and behaviours.

Hare and Lewis' arguments are based on apprentice training in the arts and industry. The process by which an apprentice learns through observation and repeated emulation, without rational or intellectual examination of the theory behind the art, is culturally and traditionally accepted in Japan. Similarly, but not as extensively researched as of yet, in the teaching culture of Japan, some research studies indicate that apprenticeship is often perceived differently in Japan when you see apprenticeship from a Western pedagogical perspective. More specifically, in-service teachers in Japan are expected to learn from their peers or senior teachers through apprenticeship of observation and emulation (e.g. Shimahara & Sakai, 1992) as well as 'the power of collaboration' (Howe, 2006: 293) among colleagues. Emulation is not simply copying others' behaviours as with children but is a more complex process of analysing teacher thinking and improving teaching skills.

Shimahara and Sakai (1992: 371) explain this point by saying that the process of induction training in Japan is viewed as 'an apprenticeship in which interns learn to teach by observing and interacting with other teachers'. In Japan, novice teachers in the first year of teaching at a public school are required to undergo one year of teacher training, usually offered by each prefecture's board of education. Experienced teachers who are mentors for novice teachers are likely to treat the new teachers as equals and do not offer any explicit advice or guidance. Instead, novice teachers in induction training are expected to 'steal' ideas and skills from experienced teachers by observing, emulating and interacting with them in a more informal context such as sharing ideas in meetings and in the teachers' rooms. To 'steal' is a literal translation of a Japanese verb, *nusumu*, which in this context implies a positive connotation of emulating somebody's, usually experts' ideas or strategies, not necessarily with his or her consent.

Additionally, in emulating others, novice teachers are expected not only to adhere to the routines and patterns of others and to fit into the group, but also to voluntarily improve the situations in which they teach, which is similar to what Dunn (2011: 56) calls a 'creative form of imitation', and what Chie in this study called '*kaizen*'. Similar to Dewey's (1916) assertion earlier in this chapter that a child imitates not only to conform to the patterns of adults, but also to make improvements in the situations in which actions take place, in-service teachers in Japan also go through trial-and-error attempts to improve their practices. As one novice teacher in Shimahara and Sakai's (1992: 375) study claimed, 'I do not imitate everything. I imitate only the things that are relevant to my concerns'. This suggests that these novice teachers try to develop a cognitive process that enables them to make professional judgements and adapt themselves to specific teaching contexts, not just imitate their senior teachers uncritically. As Howe (2006: 293) discusses, they learn greatly from experienced teachers through informal contact as well: 'Rather than working in isolation, Japan's teachers recognize the power of collaboration'. In one sense, they are still novices but are allowed to be autonomous in making choices and negotiating meaning in their expertise development as a peripheral member of the shared culture of the craft of teaching, although their training may be conducted without explicit guidance from experts.

In contrast, in another case study conducted at a private high school in Japan (Sato & Kleinsasser, 2004), some in-service teachers admit that they rely on their own second language learning experiences in developing as a teacher, which they confirm is 'vague' and 'personal', similar to what Lortie (1975) terms *apprenticeship of observation*. Since there are no clear, established goals of teaching to achieve, novice teachers in their case study have no alternative but to imitate their former teachers, as well as their colleagues, and then adapt and tailor their styles to their specific teaching contexts. In line with the results of this case study, other scholars also argue that emulation may lead novice teachers to 'merely imitate' (Alexander, 2002: 26) experts' skills, even when the quality of their practice is not as good, in order to adapt to the patterns of teaching in a particular school and conform to a school culture rather than to improve their own teaching. This conformity to a particular school setting has been examined by Hooghart (2006), for example. Hooghart asserts that ideally, practising teachers in Japan may enjoy relative autonomy in professional development because of its decentralised teacher training system with no explicit goals. On the other hand, Hooghart (2006: 297) also finds that, in in-service teacher training in Japan, models are sometimes explicitly provided as demonstration lessons, which are made public to peers as well as to teachers at other schools, and these models are expected 'to be imitated in exact detail'. Despite a lack of empirical evidence, Hooghart (2006: 297) argues that the public nature of demonstration lessons may compel teachers to 'make their practice conform to the expectations of the staff group that collaborates to develop the lesson'. Thus, explicitly providing a model to imitate may also increase pressure to conform to established forms, which could hinder teacher autonomy. Hooghart's claim indicates that the role of theory to inform teachers' judgements and help them to think objectively needs to be emphasised more in Japanese in-service teacher training.

As discussed so far, the idea that recursive practice and mastery of craft can eventually add a new perspective to teaching should be considered as one significant characteristic of the teaching culture in Japan. In the context of Japan, where learning to teach has been highly linked to emulation culturally, in-service teachers are allowed to be autonomous to some extent in making choices and negotiating meaning in their expertise construction through emulation, even without explicit guidance from experts. In contrast, there has been some criticism of this approach. Teachers may emulate a model without critical analysis, or they may struggle with pressures to uncritically follow the well-established forms of experienced teachers, which may adversely affect their teacher expertise development. This impact of emulation on student teachers' professional development is not yet well researched; whether emulation can be one effective shared mediational activity that greatly contributes to participants of the learning community or not should be investigated further. What is at least clear from previous studies is that, currently, one of the major problems in teacher training in Japan is that teachers are likely to depend on emulation without any proper training, where proper training can in fact result in its more effective use in order to link theory and practice. The issue of emulation in apprenticeship is further explored when analysing the development of student teachers' expertise in this study (see Mari's section in 6.1).

4.3 Challenges of Japanese Teaching Culture

This chapter has discussed the two salient characteristics of teaching culture in Japan. One is the emphasis on holistic teaching, based on the view of whole-person education. Although a holistic approach is a significant aspect in terms of students' growth, it can create tension among some teachers, particularly pre-service student teachers, between subject matter teaching and holistic teaching. The second feature is the value placed on teaching as craft knowledge. Many teachers believe that teaching can be learned, transmitted and reformulated as craft. This idea is reflected in professional development practices for in-service teachers in Japan: experiential learning particularly through observation and through a collaborative approach as a group. However, the impact of experiential learning through observation and group collaboration in ITE needs to be further investigated since student teachers in Japan do not necessarily have enough practical experiences during ITE.

The present study tentatively proposes the foregoing model, which focuses on the dynamic nature of interaction among participants in the community of practice. Figure 4.1 is a schematic representation of the dialogical process of theory and practice in ITE in Japan with the help of mediational activities, such as potentially, observation, emulation and reflection, although *which* socially mediated tasks are more effective will be examined later in this study (see section 6.1).

Figure 4.1 illustrates the beginning stage of teacher expertise development. Firstly, student teachers are influenced by former schooling experiences, whether positively or negatively, and the extent of the

Figure 4.1 A dialogical process of theory and practice in ITE in Japan

influence will be explored in this study. Student teachers also learn abstract concepts, theories and principles at HEIs. Among various kinds of knowledge bases, content knowledge (*what* to teach) is the central feature of the teacher knowledge base. As prospective English as a foreign language (EFL) teachers, they ought to learn theoretical principles on the English language system, its culture, second/foreign language acquisition and second/foreign language teaching. In addition, they are expected to learn pedagogical knowledge (*how* to teach), especially what Shulman (1987) calls pedagogical content knowledge, as was mentioned in Chapter 3 on dimensions of teacher expertise. Then, student teachers try to theorise knowledge bases in order to adapt to new classroom contexts. For instance, in classroom practices, student teachers may ask themselves reflective questions, such as 'Why didn't it go well?' or 'What could I have done differently?' in order to understand and then improve their teaching by referring back to the theoretical knowledge that they acquired at HEIs.

However, in the case of ITE in Japan, because of the theory and practice divide, student teachers often encounter a gap between what they know and what the actual classroom context is like. Since professional development is not an individual process of cognitive development in this model, student teachers are considered as situated in a social context and are peripheral members of their learning community. How student teachers try to bridge the gap between theory and practice and what kinds of mediational activities and social interactions are useful (or not useful) for them will be considered in this study.

The schematic representation in Figure 4.1 is still a tentative one: it will be further developed and revised as the data analysis proceeds. Of course, many other aspects related to teacher development in ITE are not shown in Figure 4.1, such as previous beliefs and experiences or contextual factors. These are excluded from the figure at this point since where to situate these elements is not clear (i.e. either as an individual factor or as a social contextual factor) at the start of this study. What kinds of social activities are in fact employed in ITE are not well examined yet either. Therefore, this study will revisit the model in Chapter 8 by referring to the data and indicate what factors are more influential in connecting theory and practice in the case of EFL student teachers in Japan.

5 Case Studies

5.1 Theoretical Framework

With no set standards of teaching competences such as in the UK, and with no established system of reflective practices such as the European Portfolio for Student Teachers of Languages (EPOSTL) in Europe, the contents of initial teacher education (ITE) programmes in Japan are at the discretion of each higher education institute (HEI) due to the principle of openness and the decentralised teacher training system. Thus, both teacher educators and student teachers often feel disoriented and, even after the students become teachers, this problem seems to carry over to in-service teacher training (Sato & Kleinsasser, 2004). In addition, little research has been conducted regarding ITE in Japan, in particular examining student teachers' perspectives and experiences (Nagamine, 2008). Thus, this qualitative enquiry will contribute to a deeper understanding of the learning community to which I belong and have witnessed as a teacher educator.

A sociocultural perspective

At the centre of the theoretical framework of this book is a sociocultural perspective on elucidating teacher professional development. Sociocultural theory originates in Vygotsky's contention that 'human cognition originates in and emerges out of participation in social activities' (Johnson & Golombek, 2011: 1), rather than only in the minds of individual human beings. Vygotsky (1960/1997: 67) states that 'any higher mental function was external and social before it was internal'; thus, human cognitive development is understood as a highly social process of the mind from a sociocultural theoretical perspective. One of the major challenges that remain in ITE is the theory and practice divide, where theoretical principles and scientific concepts that individual student teachers are exposed to at HEIs are often dissociated from everyday classroom experiences. When there is a discrepancy between content knowledge (*what* to teach) and pedagogical content knowledge (*how* to teach) (Shulman, 1987), without the stance of a sociocultural theoretical perspective, student teachers' struggle to tackle complex realities in the classroom may seem individual and internal to those who have enough subject knowledge, with little procedural knowledge or understanding of particular teaching contexts. Hence, a sociocultural theoretical perspective is helpful to more fully understand the complex process of teacher development. This is because, in this approach, cognition development is understood as not necessarily an internal and individual process, but emerges through socioculturally mediated activities, and social interactions are central to the development of new forms of thinking.

Vygotsky (1978) argues that humans use various tools to mediate their activities and develop their cognition. This process is referred to as 'internalization' (Johnson, 2009: 18), or is understood as a transformation from external to internal and from social to psychological. This means that human cognition is initially and largely shaped by specific social activities in which learners engage, but later on they learn to control and regulate their activities as they learn to reconstruct resources, such as time management, pedagogical content knowledge and knowledge of learners and their characteristics in the case of ITE.

The process of internalisation does not take place independently and instantly. It requires time and depends on the learning environment. Thus, mediation is essential in the internalisation process. Humans use various tools to make sense of their learning and adults teach these tools to children in their joint activities so that children learn to regulate their behaviour. These mediational tools include cultural artefacts and activities, concepts and social relations with others (Johnson, 2009).

According to Johnson and Golombek (2011), cognitive development through mediation is not limited to children. In teacher education as well, mediational tools of scientific concepts, cultural artefacts and activities, and social relations with others are essential for teachers and student teachers to develop their expertise and narrow the gap between theoretical concepts and actual teaching in a classroom. Those mediational tools include, for example, textbooks, which have been culturally developed over time and socially designed with specific purposes. Teachers use textbooks to create certain kinds of instructional activity in a classroom in order to meet specific purposes and contexts. The materials that teachers create to go with the textbooks are also an example of cultural artefacts. These are created with a particular purpose and through considering the particular needs and levels of students. By utilising these tools, teachers engage in various social activities embedded in the communities of practice, such as in classrooms, teacher education programmes and schools, and through acting and interacting there they construct and reconstruct teachers' knowledge and values. The concepts reconstructed through such socially mediated activities become 'the psychological tools that enable teachers to instantiate not only locally appropriate but also theoretically and pedagogically sound instructional practices for the students they teach' (Johnson & Golombek, 2011: 5), transforming from external and social interactions to internal and psychological elements.

In addition to cultural artefacts, social relations with others – another mediational tool – is also paramount to an understanding of teacher expertise in the development of student teachers' expertise, particularly concerning the role of peer interaction in this study. Human mediation enables student teachers to transform scientific concepts that they acquire in ITE to 'locally appropriate but also theoretically and pedagogically sound' classroom practices in particular teaching contexts (Johnson & Golombek, 2011: 5). In this study, the role of peers is of particular importance in mediating learning, as student teachers in Japan are more exposed to peer interaction through ITE coursework at HEIs due to the imbalance between theory and practice. Student teachers in ITE in Japan do not have many opportunities to actually enter classrooms, interact with students and teachers, interpret real contexts and make professional judgements about what and how to teach until they engage in school-based teaching practice in their fourth year into the ITE programme.

Johnson (2009: 25) argues that novice teachers are often mediated by a 'temporary other' including peers; peer interaction is important in teacher education in foreign language teaching since peers are not necessarily more capable experts but rather everybody collectively experiences cognitive struggle in the process of expertise development. This can be further explained by one of the most investigated Vygotskian concepts in the educational literature, the zone of proximal development (ZPD). The ZPD is defined as: 'the distance between the actual developmental level as determined by independent problem solving and the level of potential development as determined through problem solving under adult guidance or in collaboration with more capable peers' (Vygotsky, 1978: 86). It concerns the difference between what an individual learner can perform by themselves and what he or she can achieve by working collaboratively with others or experts. Lantolf (2000: 17) describes the concept as a 'metaphoric space where individual cognition originates in the social collective mind and emerges in and through engagement in social activity'. It is also a space where what a person can do with others' assistance can be observed, which Johnson (2009: 6) calls 'an arena of potentiality'. As a matter of fact, it is important to note that assistance within the ZPD is not only provided by more capable peers or experts, but also by cohort peers; learners can mutually construct assistance in a similar manner to the way experts assist and lead the development of novices.

The following studies on peer interaction from a sociocultural perspective have shown that peers can support one another and mutually construct meaning because 'differences in peers' experience and expertise are not fixed, but fluid, dynamic and contingent on how and what is being accomplished in and through the group's activities' (Johnson, 2009: 100). For example, Nagamine (2008) uses a collaborative journal to identify English as a foreign language (EFL) student teachers' beliefs and their development processes. As a result of the 'social nature of textual interactions' (Nagamine, 2008: 82) of the journal as well as biweekly group discussions with peers, he concludes that the participants succeeded in reconstructing their beliefs both at individual and group levels. Particularly at the group level, the participants developed a similar collective identity to professional teachers; for example, 'establishing a good teacher–student relationship' turned out to be a common essential element of being a professional teacher among the participating student teachers. The results of these studies imply that peer interaction is significantly influential on the professional development of student teachers, and peers serve as co-meaning makers who can construct assistance with each other and provide constructive feedback. From a sociocultural perspective, the quality of human mediation, even when it is mediated by non-expert others, is critical when trying to understand the development of expertise in student teachers in ITE.

Other concepts can be found among social theories that are closely related to sociocultural theory and can contribute equally to our understanding of student teachers' professional development. For example, Lave and Wenger's (1991) 'community of practice' is an application of Vygotsky's ideas about human learning and actions. While Vygotsky focuses on the relationship between the individual and society with regard to development of the mind, Lave and Wenger pay less attention to cognitive processes and focus more on how social practices shape the practices of an individual. The authors are understood in this study to share the common thought that people learn and develop through interaction and complement each other in many ways.

A case-study approach

Since the purpose of the present study is to explore student teachers' layered *experiences* and *perceptions* of their own development in ITE, the methods used to collect and analyse data are based on the principles of qualitative inquiry, which allows a researcher to examine individual characteristics and differences in depth (Friedman, 2012) and prioritise 'the study of perceptions, meaning, and emotions' (Silverman, 2000: 10) of the participants being studied. The qualitative research approach enables me to understand the variety of perspectives of pre-service teachers as well as the sense-making processes of their individual contexts and experiences, while also allowing me to make 'fuzzy' generalisations (Bassey, 1999: 52) among these perspectives. In addition, there have been limited qualitative research studies in teacher education in Japan, particularly in the area of ITE (Collinson & Ono, 2001; LeTendre, 1999; Yoshimoto Asaoka, 2015).

Based on the following three characteristics of qualitative research, namely, examining in a naturalistic setting, generating a detailed description of particular cases and theory-building from the detailed description of particular cases, it was considered that a qualitative research design was the most suitable for this study. First of all, according to Hatch (2002: 6), one of the purposes of qualitative research is to examine 'the lived experiences of real people in real settings'. The primary goal of this study is also to explore how an individual student teacher behaves in the course of their everyday activities including classrooms at the university and at school, and how they make meaning of their experiences and development of expertise in their teacher education programme, which is deeply situated in context. Furthermore, 'to understand the world from the perspectives of those living it' (Hatch, 2002: 7) is another overall objective of qualitative research. Therefore, not just how an individual student teacher *behaves* but how he or she *feels* about his or her ITE experiences is explored in this study. Utilising research tools such as interviews and journals, the perspectives or views of student teachers are also elucidated and the meanings that they construct in order to participate in their learning community are described in detail and interpreted. In addition, qualitative approaches are often associated with inductive (Hatch, 2002) and theory-generating (Merriam, 2001) research. Qualitative studies do not necessarily begin with hypothesis or theories to test; rather, they collect 'as many detailed specifics from the research setting as possible, then set about the process of looking for patterns of relationship among the specifics' (Hatch, 2002: 10). As Corbin and Strauss (2008: 12) also rightly put it, one of the main purposes of conducting qualitative research is 'to discover rather than test variables'. Thus, this study also began with an examination of the individual participants in their natural settings as much as possible, allowing the focus of this study to emerge during data collection and analysis. Subsequently, a whole picture of the current ITE situation in Japan is constructed by examining parts and looking for patterns or relationships among them.

The basic mode of inquiry of the study in this book is a case-study approach due to the nature of the research study: focusing on a small number of participants and studying them closely over an extended period of time. In this study, multiple cases (ITE student teachers) are jointly examined in order to investigate a phenomenon (ITE in Japan).

A 'case' is usually defined as a 'bounded system' (Merriam, 2001: 27). This means that it is an individual, such as a student, or an entity, such as a language programme or a school, that a researcher wishes to investigate. Case studies are exploratory and descriptive, they can offer in-depth insights and a thick description about a phenomenon (Dörnyei, 2007; Duff, 2008, 2012). The primary goal of the case-study approach is not to prove something and establish rules across cases, but rather to deeply and holistically understand particular cases and how they make sense. Due to the possible variability of student teachers' perspectives and experiences, this study employs a case-study approach by examining particular cases and creating a thick and rich description of the cases and the context. I then bring the individual cases together and interpret the importance of these phenomena to 'make broader inferences' (Silverman, 2005: 126) about current ITE practices in Japan.

In this study, for each student teacher's case, data were collected from a variety of sources. Furthermore, key themes and features of individual cases were identified and used for cross-case analysis to describe how each individual makes sense of their professional development and how their professional expertise develops over time.

An emic approach: The researcher as an insider

Any qualitative researcher is required to carefully consider degrees of involvement and detachment (Bryman, 2004). The fact that the research site chosen for this study is the higher education institution where I have taught as a teacher educator may raise the question of the kind of role I should adopt in relation to the setting and the participants in the study. For example, as Patton (2002) argues, a researcher may adopt the role of a complete insider in contrast to an *etic* approach in which a researcher is totally detached from the case being studied and thus is able to be objective in data collection and analysis. Some even argue that a researcher should avoid his or her own contexts. Hatch (2002), for example, insists that it is:

> ... too difficult to balance the sometimes-conflicting roles of researcher and educator when the enactment of both roles is required in the same setting. It is just too difficult for educators to pull back from their insider perspectives and see things with the eyes of a researcher. It is just too difficult for participants in the study to respond to the researcher as researcher not teacher, colleague, or both. (Hatch, 2002: 47)

One of the significant elements of this study, however, is that it employs an *emic* approach with the role of teacher/researcher; in other words, I studied my own workplace and tried to engage in in-depth conversations with my own students regarding their teacher expertise development. A researcher as an outsider may offer an objective view of any observations, whereas a teacher/researcher could offer a 'privileged view of the classroom and learners, relatively free from the reactions learners may have to being observed by an outsider' (Fujii, 2005).

The extent to which the self is exposed in interaction is often influenced by the specific cultures to which one belongs (Cousins, 1989; Triandis, 1989). Therefore, cultural specificity should be recognised and taken into account in the research design. In the Japanese context, for example, the distinction between *uchi*, meaning insiders, and *soto*, meaning outside the group, is explicit and important in understanding the extent to which people disclose themselves to others, as has been repeatedly argued by many anthropologists such as Barnlund (1989) and Condon (1984). Barnlund, for example, argues that Japanese people are very careful about who to let inside their group. Unless a person becomes a part of *uchi*, a member of the community, Japanese are less likely to express their inner feelings and attitudes. They share their ideas and inner feelings only with 'trusted acquaintances' (Barnlund, 1989: 79), not much with strangers or untrusted acquaintances. Therefore, the role of the researcher is significant in this study since the main purpose is to investigate the student teachers' self-exploration process of their development of teacher expertise. At the start of the study, the participating student teachers were already familiar with me as their teacher trainer to some extent, through the induction sessions, in classrooms, as well as casual encounters on campus. Having already some professional relationship with the participants prior to the study, entry to their group was rather smooth, as a member of their community in the ITE programme.

The distinctive role of the teacher/researcher also led to the elicitation of honest and rich descriptions in interviews due to the familiarity and trust between the participants and me. Being a member of the community made the participants feel safe about disclosing their feelings and ideas and engaging in in-depth interaction with me, particularly during the interviews, although less so in writing especially at the start of the study because expressing ideas in writing is usually considered more formal. Many of the participants, however, started to voluntarily consult with me regarding their own teaching even outside of office hours or not for the interviews of this study, or invited me to observe their practice of microteaching on a voluntary basis. This in-depth interaction, in turn, led to a richness of data, both verbal and textual, collected over one-and-a-half years. The empathy I had as their teacher educator also enabled me to take and understand the stance, position, feelings and experiences of the participants, whereas I attempted to be neutral and *non-judgemental* (Silverman, 2000: 256) at the same time towards their thoughts and behaviours as a researcher, not as an evaluator of their performances. In one sense, the book describes the interesting process of my own professional development as a teacher educator, by learning how student teachers feel about their expertise development and how they handle the issues they face during ITE.

Being an insider of their group also made it easier for me to have frequent meetings with the participants and communicate regularly with them, which motivated them to keep working on their expertise development. I attempted to offer feedback to all participants, whenever necessary, such as in a classroom straight after their microteaching or a casual conversation in the hall. As Chie, one of the participants, expressed at the end of the final interview, participation in the study made her more conscious that teacher development was a long-term project. Chie built awareness through the process of engaging in self-reflection, peer interaction and mentoring both at school and at the HEI. Participation in this research study engaged some of the participants in the process of developing their abilities to reflect on their practices and thus contributed to their professional development.

In qualitative research, researchers are considered the main research instrument themselves. Therefore, one major drawback of qualitative research is the 'subjectivity' of researchers (Croker, 2009: 11). As they go into research settings and collect and analyse the data, their own personal background and life experiences that they take with them, such as age, gender, ethnicity, educational background and cultural background, greatly affect how they see, interpret and reconstruct the data. However, the subjectivity of the researchers is a strength of qualitative research at the same time, since they are the participants of their own enquiry who can reveal the meanings and interpretations of their experiences with 'insider perspective' (Dörnyei, 2007: 38). In order to mitigate the problem of subjectivity, though, I attempted to constantly reflect on my impact on the participants and the research settings through keeping field notes, and I employed a process called triangulation. Triangulation is the process of qualitative research through which multiple research methods and sources of data are applied to the analysis (Friedman, 2012) to reveal a fuller picture of a case or a system and increase the validity of research. In this study, for example, the data were obtained from a variety of individuals (for example, interviews with ITE lecturers of the participants), and different data collection methods such as interviews and observation were used.

5.2 Procedure

Research site

The enquiry began with my observation and interaction with graduates of the ITE programme, as well as future teachers of the programme, where I have been teaching as a teacher educator for over 15 years. The ITE programme described in this chapter is conducted by the Department of English Studies at the Faculty of Foreign Languages at a private university in the suburbs of Tokyo, Japan, where I work as a teacher educator. Our students graduate with a BA in English language and literature. Within the curriculum of the department, there are four courses: linguistics and education, literature and culture, communication studies and international relations. Students choose one major from these four content areas.

In Japan, in order to become a secondary school English teacher, students are required to attend an ITE programme called *kyoshoku-katei* offered at the undergraduate level at an HEI, while pursuing a bachelor's degree in their own majors, and acquire a teacher's qualification upon graduation. Although the contents of ITE programmes are at the discretion of each institution due to the decentralised teacher training system, ITE programmes in Japan usually begin upon matriculation, and for the first two years, student teachers are required to take general education-related courses in ITE such as educational philosophy, educational psychology or moral education in addition to courses related to their majors, such as linguistics, literature or international relations in the faculties they belong to. Then, in the third year of the four-year ITE programme, students typically enrol in a course called Methods of Teaching English. At the time of the case study, the participants were required to enrol in two courses, Methods of Teaching English I and II, in sequence, at the research site. According to the course guidelines at the research site, some key objectives of the courses are to explore various teaching EFL principles and theories on second language acquisition, to reflect on their own learning and teaching and to practise teaching. A variety of learning experiences and tasks are usually provided to enable student teachers to attain these objectives, which may include observing experienced teachers' lessons, or microteaching in small or large groups. Student teachers also often collaborate in planning and revising a lesson and giving feedback to each other. In addition, the study examined student teachers' experiences during a school-based teaching practice at local secondary schools. The school-based teaching practice in Japan is typically practised for approximately three weeks when student teachers are in their fourth year. ITE at the HEIs has often been criticised that transmission of theory is more emphasised in the Japanese context. More recently, however, the necessity of longer practical training has been recognised, although not officially implemented yet.

Although this institution does not have a faculty of education, it remains one of the top universities that annually produce aspiring English teachers in the area. However, the number of student teachers in the *kyoshoku-katei* at this institution has been on a downward trend, which is a national tendency because of the nationwide decline in the population of children as well as classroom teaching facing various problems. Teaching is nowadays considered to be a more challenging job, rather than a prestigious and secure job with a good salary. Additionally, we can consider the minimum requirement of English language proficiency that student teachers need to attain, which is a Test of English for International Communication (TOEIC) score of 700, equivalent to 550 of the paper-based Test of English as a Foreign Language (TOEFL) test, by the end of the third year, in order to practise teaching at a secondary school. Therefore, many of the students who enter ITE upon matriculation are likely to leave the programme due to non-fulfilment of the required proficiency level. At the onset of the study, four of the participants, Kento,

Chie, Mari and Yurika, did not meet the English proficiency minimum requirement set by the programme. However, they all attained the minimally acceptable score on the TOEIC test by the end of the academic year 2009. Therefore, they were allowed to do teaching practice in the academic year 2010.

The EFL student teachers

At the time of the study, six case-study student teachers – Kento, Chie, Nana, Yurika, Mari and Saori – were English major, third-year undergraduate students who enrolled in the same ITE programme in Japan. Aya was an English major, fourth-year student when the project began. She left the programme in the previous year to the project to pursue a career in the private sector. However, Aya re-entered the programme in April 2009, meaning that she would have to remain as a non-degree student for two more terms to complete the programme after she graduated from the university in March 2010. Saori was a transfer student from another private college in the Tokyo area, regarding the ITE curriculum at her previous school as unsatisfactory. Nana was another transfer student from a foreign language institute where she studied English and early childhood English education. All the student teachers appeared keen to participate, partly to assist in the research but also because they saw this as an opportunity to improve their own teaching. Except for Mari, they wanted to become junior high school English teachers. Table 5.1 provides a full description of each student teacher.

At the research site, four lecturers including me offered Methods of Teaching English courses I and II to third-year students. Most of the student teachers in these courses were in their third year of the four-year ITE programme and there was usually approximately 30 registrants in each course. I first recruited the participating student teachers based on an open invitation in my Methods of Teaching English course I in the spring term of the academic year 2009. I chose this course for the recruitment of possible participants since this was the first course in the ITE

Table 5.1 Description of the student teachers

Name	Gender	Year as of April 2009	TOEIC score as of April 2009	Lecturer
Kento	M	3rd year	680	Researcher
Aya	F	4th year	810	Researcher
Chie	F	3rd year	650	Lecturer A
Mari	F	3rd year	650	Lecturer C
Yurika	F	3rd year	695	Lecturer B
Nana	F	3rd year	795	Researcher
Saori	F	3rd year	800	Lecturer B

programme in which student teachers learned theoretical principles on foreign language teaching and learning. At the end of the first Methods class in April 2009, I briefly informed the student teachers of this project and asked them to indicate in writing their willingness and availability to participate. I emphasised that participation would not affect their course grades, while I also emphasised that participation would probably enhance their understanding and appreciation of their own development as a teacher. This was a self-selection process and the principal criteria were the students' willingness to become an English teacher and their availability to meet with me. I recruited the participating student teachers based on the following two criteria: (1) students who enrolled in the course of Methods of Teaching English I in the spring term of 2009, and (2) those who were committed to becoming a secondary school English teacher upon graduation. The study began with seven participants in May 2009, one male and six female student teachers. All the participants reported that they were seriously considering a teaching job as their career option and planned to take an employment examination in summer 2010, which all of them eventually did and became teachers upon graduation, except for Saori who decided to enter show business, although she did become a teacher at a special support education school in the United States a few years later.

Since four of the student teachers enrolled in the other lecturers' Methods of Teaching English courses I/II, it was necessary to understand the course goals and course content set by each lecturer. In the programme, a common understanding of the Methods courses was formulated among the lecturers; however, there was little sharing among us prior to this study. Thus, I invited the three lecturers to participate in this study and they all agreed to be interviewed. This in fact contributed not only to further understanding the student teachers' layered experiences and ideas on professional development while they were in ITE, but it also improved my own understanding of the members and practices of this learning community of which I was a member. Table 5.2 summarises the background of each lecturer.

Table 5.2 Description of the three lecturers

	Gender	Age	Nationality	Teaching experiences in ITE (years)
Lecturer A	F	Mid-60s	Japanese	40
Lecturer B	M	Mid-50s	American	20
Lecturer C	F	Mid-30s	Japanese	2

Research process and interventions

The data collection involved the following two stages: from April 2009 until February 2010 and from May 2010 until August 2010. In the

Table 5.3 The timeline of the study

First phase	In-class tasks	Tasks for the study
May 2009		First semi-structured interview, starting journals (approx. January 2010)
July 2009		Second semi-structured interview
Oct 2009		Third semi-structured interview, card-sorting exercise 1
Nov–Dec 2009	Lesson planning microteaching	Observation by the researcher
Jan 2010		Final journal submission
Feb 2010		Fourth semi-structured interview, card-sorting exercise 2, video-viewing and think-aloud protocol
Second phase	**School-based training**	
May 2010	Daily teaching logs	Fifth semi-structured interview
June–July 2010	Demonstration lesson	School visit and observation by the researcher
Aug 2010		Final semi-structured interview, card-sorting exercise 3

spring and autumn terms of the 2009 academic year, all participating student teachers enrolled in the Methods of Teaching English I (in spring) and II (in autumn) courses in the ITE programme at the research site. In the spring term of the 2010 academic year, six student teachers experienced a school-based teaching practice at secondary schools in either May or June depending on the school contexts, except for Mari who did her student teaching in September 2010 due to contextual reasons at her school. Table 5.3 provides a brief summary of the overall data collection activities of the study.

In this study, data are collected using interviews, journals, lesson observation and materials including teaching plans, teaching materials and teaching logs during the teaching practice. Non-participant observations of both the microteaching and actual classroom teaching of the seven student teachers were conducted.

Interviews

One of the main qualitative methods used in this study is semi-structured interviews. As many researchers argue (Brown & Dowling, 1998; Bryman, 2004; Cohen et al., 2000; Hatch, 2002; Silverman, 2000), qualitative interviews enable interviewees to investigate their own thoughts, beliefs and perspectives of the world in which they live for greater depth and to reconstruct events they experience. For example, Silverman (2000: 154) argues that interviews allow researchers access to not only 'external reality (e.g. facts, events)' but also 'internal experience (e.g. feelings, meanings)'. Hatch (2002) even ventures the suggestion that in order to capture participants' perspectives and obtain rich data, interviewing in some form is essential.

On the part of the interviewer, this method leads to deeper understanding and richer descriptions of interviewees' experiences and contexts from their perspectives. Furthermore, this method of qualitative interviews is commonly found in ITE research studies (Almarza, 1996; Borg, 2005; Johnson, 1994; Lim & Chan, 2007).

In this study, I conducted six interviews over a period of one-and-a-half years with each student teacher. I explored the world from their perspective regarding the process of learning to teach in order to construct an understanding of how they make sense of their experiences, and to see what factors in ITE influence their development of expertise.

The interviews were open-ended since I wanted to create a flexible space where the student teachers could talk freely, although the interviews were not unstructured. For each interview, I prepared an interview guide with a set of questions in mind to be covered, although I understood that the questions were open and flexible. The interview guides for each interview were first created during the pilot study so that the student teachers' experiences and development of expertise could be covered without omission. The interview guides were then re-examined during the study before each interview and adjusted based on the participants' journal entries, my observation of their microteaching or my field notes, considering the courses that they enrolled in or activities and tasks in which they participated both in and outside the ITE curriculum. I also asked questions that were not included in the interview guide as the need arose and the overall interview process was flexible, allowing the student teachers to freely frame and explain their thoughts and views. I tried to be open to digressions, building some flexibility into the interviews and letting the student teachers lead the way.

The initial interview with each student teacher was conducted at the start of the spring term in 2009. The main purposes of the initial interview were to collect factual information, such as the age at which interviewees began to learn English or their current TOEIC scores, as well as to analyse their experiences and thoughts about learning and teaching, often influenced by their former teachers because of the long-term unexamined experiences of 'apprenticeship of observation' (Lortie, 1975). The questions included 'What do you think a good teacher is?' and 'What has influenced your English language learning and teaching?'.

The second interview with each student teacher took place at the end of July or early August of the same year. The main purpose of the second interview was to explore their perspectives on their overall expertise development, particularly the influence of the ITE coursework during the first term. The questions included 'In the spring semester, what did you learn for your teacher expertise development through taking the Methods course?' and 'In the spring semester, what influenced your teacher expertise development outside the ITE programme?'. The questions that I found in their journal entries during the spring semester, such as what type of PCK they specifically learned in a methodology course, were clarified during the second interview as well.

I conducted the third interview with each student teacher at the start of the autumn term in October 2009. The main purpose of the third interview was to enable the student teachers, using a card-sorting exercise, to engage and reflect more on their perspectives on what a good English teacher is. The nature and the process of the card-sorting exercise will be elaborated on later in this chapter.

During the fourth interview, conducted at the end of the autumn term in January or February 2010, I asked each student teacher to view his or her own filmed microteaching in Methods of Teaching English course II and evaluate it using the stimulated recall task, which will also be explained later in this chapter. Subsequently, the second card-sorting exercise was conducted in order to examine their perspectives on what a good English teacher was. After the stimulated recall task and the card-sorting exercise, I then asked the student teachers to respond to questions such as 'In the autumn semester, what did you learn for your teacher expertise development through taking the Methods course?' and 'In the autumn semester, what influenced your teacher expertise development outside the ITE programme?' and discuss their perspectives on their overall expertise development. The questions that I found in their journal entries during the autumn semester, such as what sort of feedback they received on their microteaching, were clarified during the fourth interview as well.

Prior to school-based training in the spring term of the 2010 academic year, the fifth semi-structured interviews were conducted with each student teacher in order to explore their expectations, concerns and perspectives on teaching practice as well as to find out their school contexts. The questions included 'During the teaching practice, what kind of English lessons are you planning to conduct?' and 'What are your concerns now and how are you going to tackle them?'.

The final interviews were conducted in July or August 2010 after the teaching practice in order to investigate the student teachers' specific experiences with the teaching practice as well as their perspectives on their overall expertise development. In Mari's case, it was in early October because she did her teaching practice in September 2010. The third card-sorting exercise was conducted during the final interview as well.

It has been pointed out that there may be a gap between what people do and what they think they do. Interviewees may try to show themselves in a better light or be unable to articulate their thoughts and feelings, producing an insufficient amount of verbal data (Dörnyei, 2007). In fact, this latter case was observed in my data collection during the pilot study. I accept this as a limitation of qualitative interviews. It also needs to be recognised that interview responses are interviewees' interpretations of reality and the interpretation of interviewees' accounts may also be influenced by researchers' bias and subjectivity (Cohen et al., 2000). Thus, the accuracy of what the student teachers recorded needed to be ensured by using other research tools, such as participant observations, which give us more direct access to their experiences in order to examine how the participating student teachers applied their theoretical understanding to actual teaching practices, obtain further insights about each student teacher and triangulate them with the interview data.

Card-sorting exercises

At the start of the third interviews, the first card-sorting exercise was introduced in the manner described by Kettle and Sellars (1996), based on the concepts that recursively emerged in participants' journal entries and the two previous interviews in spring 2009. The purpose of this exercise is to investigate more deeply the student teachers' perspectives on expertise development, particularly the structure and reorganizing process of their expertise. The data of their journal entries between April and July 2009 as well as the first two interviews were first coded, focusing on how they viewed a good English teacher. As a result, 18 principles in total were found in their data, meaning that they either stated it during interviews or wrote it in their journals at least once. Seven key principles of a good English teacher were commonly identified among more than two participants' data, and these were placed on cards (see Table 5.4). Next, during the interviews, the participants were first asked to look at the cards, eliminate unnecessary ones and add new ideas if necessary. Then, the

Table 5.4 Seven key principles in becoming a good English teacher

A good English teacher is one who ...	Chie	Saori	Yurika	Aya	Kento	Mari	Nana
uses various teaching techniques and activities.	X	X					
relates to individual students.	X				X	X	X
is enthusiastic about English language teaching.	X						
teaches English in an easy-to-understand manner.	X		X			X	
changes approaches suitable for students' language proficiency levels, interests and needs.	X		X	X			
makes students think on their own.			X				
teaches English in a student-centred approach.				X	X	X	

participants were asked to prioritise, group and label them. As Kettle and Sellars (1996: 4) explain, data from this exercise were expected to 'allow the construction of a taxonomy graphically detailing the attributes of an individual's meaning system'.

At the end of each card-sorting exercise, the participants were also asked to explain how the principles they selected and prioritised were related to their perspectives on English language teaching. The card-sorting exercise was conducted three times during the study, in conjunction with the third, fourth and final interviews.

Stimulated recall

During the fourth interview at the end of the autumn term in January or February 2010, in addition to the second card-sorting exercise, participants were asked to evaluate their own microteaching too. According to Friedman (2012: 90), qualitative interviews can incorporate a stimulated recall task in order to allow participants to 'provide interpretations of their own or others' actions'. In this study, the stimulated recall task is employed to prompt the participants to further reflect on their own teaching, to clarify their thinking processes and to further analyse their perspectives on their cognitive strategies and actions during their teaching and the interactive relationship between the two (Hatch, 2002; Lyle, 2003).

At the start of the fourth interview, the participants were first asked to view their filmed microteaching, which was conducted in the Methods of Teaching English II courses, and to stop anywhere at will in order to make comments on their own thoughts and actions. This procedure was similar to an introspective verbal report on their thinking, such as a think-aloud protocol (Stromso et al., 2003; Wade et al., 1999), or a recall protocol (Connor, 1984; Lyle, 2003), often used in the field of second/foreign language acquisition, particularly in reading research. In these approaches, readers are generally asked to make reports on their own thinking while reading or after reading, in order to illustrate their reading processes and to justify their thinking, the use of strategies and reading behaviours.

Interviews with ITE lecturers

Since some of the student teachers enrolled in the Methods of Teaching English courses I/II taught by other lecturers than me, I decided to interview the three lecturers in the study in order to further understand each student teacher's context of learning to teach. Each of the participating lecturers and I negotiated to find space in their tight work schedule in order to conduct an interview; Lecturers A and C were interviewed in October 2009, whereas Lecturer B's interview was conducted in November 2009. All the lecturers chose their mother tongue (Japanese for Lecturers A and C, English for Lecturer B) so that they were able to express themselves fluently. An interview schedule was developed beforehand, which was given to each lecturer in advance so that they had time to reflect on their own courses and their overall teacher training practices at the institute. The questions included 'What are the goals for your method course I and II?' and 'What do you think is a role of theories in ITE?'.

Journals

Another data collection tool employed in this study is reflective journals. In a qualitative study, participants may keep a journal in which they write accounts of events and activities in their everyday lives (Brown & Dowling, 1998). One of the advantages of using instruments such as reflective journals is that in writing things down, participants can 'process and reflect on experiences in different ways than thinking about them or discussing them with others' (Hatch, 2002: 140). Journals are also a useful tool for documenting participants' activities, even when a researcher is not around to observe them (Friedman, 2012). Thus, journal entries allow researchers to access participants' first-hand experiences and voices and capture individual perspectives (Bailey, 1990; Bailey & Ochsner, 1983; Tsang, 2003), which are difficult to obtain using other research tools such as observation. In one sense, as Dörnyei (2007: 157) asserts, the participants become 'co-researchers as they keep records of their own feelings, thoughts, or activities'. In this study, keeping a journal provides them with an opportunity for self-awareness of the teacher development process in which they are involved.

One of the problems in using a journal as a data collection method is that it is almost impossible to display long samples (McDonough & McDonough, 1997). Participants are usually asked to keep a journal for an extended period of time and using short extracts taken from the original data may not be adequate to fully describe the changes in the participants over time. It should be kept in mind that the journal data are 'selective and subjective' (Friedman, 2012: 190) and they show a participant's perspective of an event, but not the event itself. Furthermore, as keeping a journal is very demanding on participants, the quantity and quality of journal entries usually show considerable variation (Dörnyei, 2007). The participants may simply forget to write down their thoughts or they may be too tired to write down an entry. By the time they find time to write down an entry, they may be unable to fully recount the event. Thus, any segments from the journal data should be appreciated as belonging to 'a broader temporal and contextual picture' (McDonough & McDonough, 1997: 123) and reading and re-reading the journal data allows me to notice important themes. Also, in addition to journal data, applying more than one research method and source of data to the analysis is essential (Friedman, 2012) to reveal a full picture of a case or a system.

In this study, the journals are used to understand how the participants experienced the process of learning to teach, alongside how they synthesise the knowledge and information they acquire across and beyond the curriculum. In this study, the participants were asked to keep focused journals, rather than free and open-ended writing, from April 2009 till January 2010 during the first and second terms of the 2009 academic year. Focused journals in this study imply that the participants were given a list of possible topics and they freely articulated their thoughts and views on these topics (Johnson, 1994). For example, the participants were asked specifically to describe their daily experiences of learning to teach, not only in the courses in the ITE programme but also in their everyday life such as working as a private tutor at *jyuku* (a preparatory school for secondary school students), or as a volunteer teacher in a nearby school, or in other courses outside the ITE programme at the research site. The focused journals were used in this study to provide the participants with some structure and choice in terms of the issues they wrote about, rather than constraining their freedom to express their thoughts or limiting them to specific topics. This was considered necessary since the participants in the study were not familiar with keeping a log of their learning experiences and may not have known what to record.

During the first interview, each participant was provided with a small notebook as well as a prompt for keeping reflective journals. The topics offered in the prompt included factors that may affect the participants' notions of what a good language teacher is and teacher development, their thoughts and experiences of learning and teaching in courses in and outside the ITE programme, as well as their feelings and experiences with former teachers, current teachers, peers and mentors. The prompt also indicated that the participants were allowed to make entries at their leisure and the length/amount/frequency of their writing was left to their discretion. During the first term in 2009, the journals were collected weekly regardless of the amount of journal entries, so that the participants could plan their time accordingly (Hatch, 2000). In the autumn term, however, their journals were collected at longer intervals because by this time the participants presumably had become accustomed to writing their reflections and needed less intervention by me. In addition, as the participants in Lee's (2007) study claim, some participants in this study also found it challenging to find time to write; thus, in order to reduce the participants' burden, they were asked to submit their journals every two or three weeks instead of every week. In addition, a choice of language (Japanese or English or Japanese and English) as well as methods for submitting a journal were offered during the first interview. As a result, initially, all the participants chose to write in Japanese by hand and submit a hard copy rather than via email. Later in the process, one of the participants, Kento, asked me for permission to type his journal up and submit it electronically in order to reduce his workload, which was, of course, allowed. All the other journal entries that were handwritten by the participants were typed by me for later analysis.

The participants kept their journals for two consecutive terms in 2009, while during school-based training in 2010, the participants kept teaching logs, instead of reflective journals, which was a requirement of the ITE programme. Student teachers in ITE in Japan are usually required to keep a teaching log provided by HEIs during their teaching practice in order to keep a record of and reflect on their teaching practices. Supervising teachers usually give written feedback, and upon completing the teaching practice, the logs are submitted to HEIs, and are used for evaluation. The participants were not asked to keep reflective journals for this particular study in order to lighten their workload during the teaching practice. This is because creating the required teaching logs is usually a heavy workload and from previous experiences as a tutor, I understood that the logs usually describe their experiences during the school-based training quite well. These logs are usually prescriptive and thus may be less reflective, and are kept every day in Japanese on every aspect of their practical training, such as constructing lesson plans, observing supervising teachers and cohort student teachers, teaching and getting feedback, conducting student counselling and guidance, as well as commenting on extracurricular activities. Supervising teachers at the local schools provide written comments every day, as well. However, this teaching log was used for the course assessment of the teaching practice. Although the grade was given by a supervising teacher at a local school, this may have influenced what and how the participants wrote in their logs; thus, although the teaching logs during the teaching practice were collected soon after their teaching practice, the data obtained were used in order to understand what student teachers actually experienced during the teaching practice and used as supplementary data for triangulation, which means applying multiple research methods and sources of data to the analysis (Friedman, 2012) so as to reveal a full picture of a case or a system. It should be pointed out, however, that in the case of Yurika, who was not good at verbalising her reflections (see Chapter 6: Section 6.2), the entries in her teaching practice teaching log were frequently used as the data, with her permission.

In analysing the data from their journal entries, I needed to be aware of 'observer effects' (Brown & Dowling, 1998: 65), since the participants may try to respond to my or the mentor's expectations and express only idealised stories of what they do and think. As Hatch (2002) suggests, making reflective journaling interactive by responding to participants' journal entries may also change the nature of the data. Therefore, commenting on the participants' writing was avoided; however, I tried to acknowledge their time and effort in writing, and follow-up questions were asked during the interviews when there were unclear statements in their journals in order to understand their meaning-making processes. In addition, these potential drawbacks of journals were reduced by 'clearly communicating the expectation that the participants' genuine perspectives and reactions are what is interested in, that whatever level of reflexivity participants are capable of is just fine, and that entries do not have to be of a certain length' (Hatch, 2002: 142).

Journal writing in the Japanese context

In addition to the general value of using journal writing as a research tool, it is essential to discuss the meaning of journal writing that is specific to Japanese culture. Kawaura *et al.* (1998), for instance, explain that the origins of diary writing date back to the Heian and Kamakura period (from the latter half of the 12th century to the first half of the 14th century) when diaries were kept both for recording facts and for expressing personal thoughts and individual conditions as literature. Even today, as Suzuki (2013) as well as Miura and Yamashita (2007) argue, personal diary keeping, including keeping a personal blog in more recent years, is a common practice in Japan. For example, elementary school students are often assigned with diary keeping, while posting personal diaries on the internet has also gained popularity. According to Kawaura *et al.* (1998), in interdependent Japanese culture in which one needs to cooperate with others, writing one's personal affairs and showing them to others serve the purpose of self-disclosure, and writers want to reveal their inner self in their journals and expect readers to have sympathy for what they write. Therefore, in this study, journals are expected to provide rich data of the participants' expressions and thoughts.

Classroom observations

In addition to observing microteaching in the Methods courses at the HEI, I visited each school once during the school-based training in order to find out school contexts and observe each participant's demonstration lesson. As was noted earlier, student teachers usually give a demonstration lesson called *kenkyujugyo* towards the end of their teaching practice, which is open to other student teachers, teachers and the school principal, and ITE tutors. At the research site, tutors are expected to visit only student teachers who do their teaching practice in a certain area near the research site. Only Kento's school was located in this zone. However, I made efforts to visit *all* the participants' schools with permission from both the ITE programme and the teaching practice schools, viewing this as an opportunity to observe how the participants were teaching in general, to see their relationship with their mentors, to converse with the mentors and get their insights, to see their relationship with students and to understand the school contexts. Straight after the demonstration lessons, I had a meeting with each participant in order to discuss their teaching, sometimes attended by the mentor and other times not. In case the mentor was present and assuming that the participants may hold back their feelings and ideas, the questions regarding this study were left unasked until the final interviews after the teaching practice.

Straight after each observation, I recorded what was observed as field notes, particularly on the above issues. The questions that arose during the observation were asked for clarification in the interviews. Field notes were also kept after conversing with the participants during everyday life, such as a discussion with them in the hall or during face-to-face counselling on teaching in the office. My own reflections were kept in order to keep track and make sense of the research experiences as a researcher as well as a teacher trainer.

Table 5.5 shows how often I was able to observe each participant's teaching during the study.

The accuracy of the interview and journal data is a challenge because participants may or cannot really do what they say they do. In order to avoid this problem, I supplemented interviews and journals with classroom observations in this study, since observation often permits a better understanding of the social phenomenon from the perspectives of the participants (Hatch, 2002). As Hatch (2002) further argues, to be there in the actual social setting and to keep a good and careful record of what participants say and how they behave, allows a researcher to make better sense of how the participants understand the setting. Therefore, the use of observation as a supplementary research tool contributes to creating a more complete, maybe not *true*, description of the social phenomenon being studied.

On the contrary, a major drawback to observation as a qualitative research tool is what is called the 'observer's paradox' (Friedman, 2012: 187). This means that the presence of an observer can change the

Table 5.5 Observations of the participants' teaching

Participants	In Methods course	In other ITE courses/ voluntary practice	School-based training
Kento	Three times (2 + 10 + 40 min)	Once (50 min)	Once (50 min)
Aya	Three times (2 + 10 + 40 min)	Once (50 min)	Once (50 min)
Chie	Once (40 min)	Once (50 min)	Once (50 min)
Mari	None	Twice (50 + 50 min)	Twice (50 + 50 min)
Yurika	Once (20 min)	Once (50 min)	Once (50 min)
Nana	Three times (2 + 10 + 40 min)	Once (50 min)	Once (50 min)
Saori	Once (20 min)	Once (50 min)	Once (50 min)

participants' behaviour. It is impossible to avoid the problem entirely; however, one way to alleviate it is to let the participants become used to the presence of an observer. In this study, the problem was also mitigated over time as the participants were willing to be observed and provided with feedback from me as well as their peers regarding their teaching skills. Another drawback is, as McDonough and McDonough (1997: 115) state, that an observer is a 'human instrument', which means that an observer also has a perspective. Thus, it needs to be kept in mind that a whole picture created in a qualitative research study is based on multiple perspectives, including that of the observer.

In addition, all related documents were also collected: documents that the participants developed during the coursework such as lesson plans, class materials and quizzes, and teaching logs that the participants kept during the school-based training. The documents were photocopied for later analysis. For example, these supplementary data were later triangulated with the two main qualitative data sources of the interviews and journals; however, they were mainly used for reference and clarification of the participants' meanings, and I did not intend to directly draw meanings from them.

Data organisation and analysis

The unit of analysis in this study is each individual participant, an EFL student teacher learning to teach in an ITE programme in Japan. Each data unit includes the following elements:

(1) six semi-structured interviews;
(2) the results of three card-sorting exercises;
(3) journal entries over two terms (spring 2009 and autumn 2009);
(4) teaching logs during the teaching practice period (spring 2010);
(5) the transcripts of verbal reports on their own microteaching;
(6) observation and field notes;
(7) written texts produced by the participants as a part of the coursework.

After working on the data collection for a year and a half, I had accumulated a huge amount of data from the seven participating student teachers. My next task was to organise and manage the data, which would help me develop a better understanding of the whole picture of their professional development in ITE.

According to Patton (2002: 447), organising data by cases can lead to 'comprehensive, systematic, and in-depth information about each case of interest'. In this study, I first organised each individual student teacher's data into one composite file. Each file included data from the seven sources listed above, such as journal entries (which had been typed) and the interview transcripts (which had also been typed). I then read all of the data material thoroughly, making notes of my interpretations. I would like to mention here that my thesis supervisor frequently said to me, 'By being immersed in the data, themes and patterns emerge from there'. Thus, while reading through the data, I waited until the data spoke for themselves, and then I did some preliminary coding of the data material by highlighting and tagging features of the data material. The preliminary codes included categories such as 'perspectives on a good teacher', 'experiences as a language learner' and 'factors that affected teaching', for instance.

Then, as I used a case-study approach, I tried to construct case profiles for each participating student teacher. In order to do so, I focused on the data fragments that arose in one singular case at a time. While reviewing the data of one case, I made further notes regarding my interpretations and tagged the major features of each case. I became particularly interested in Chie's and Kento's cases and decided to complete these two case profiles first, as I felt that these two cases would present interesting contrasts with respect to their 'perspectives on a good teacher' between 'subject-matter teaching' and 'holistic teaching'. The construction of these two case profiles and the identification of the thematic categories of being a subject teacher and a holistic teacher became a useful starting point for further analysis. At this point, I decided to return to the raw data again in order to further understand the distinctive and unique features of each case, and to formulate and synthesise more generalisations within and across the cases.

As the results were compared within one data unit generated by different data collection methods, as well as across the cases, several categories were added and refined in an attempt to accommodate all of the data. For example, the following two subcategories, 'emulation' and 'peer learning', were added under the category 'factors that affected teaching' at the later stage of data analysis in order to explain that the participants' emulation of experienced teachers and learning with one another may become an effective mediational learning process. This process of continually assessing and modifying the coding system was repeated several times until all of the data could be accounted for. In the end, the result was a systematic and holistic classification of the major categories.

To ensure the validity of the qualitative data, I also used the triangulation method throughout this study. In fact, the comparative method of moving from small to larger data sets and constantly testing out emerging themes and hypotheses is one way of increasing the validity of qualitative data. Another type of triangulation involves triangulating data sources, such as journal entries, interviews and observations. As many researchers assert (Patton, 1980, 2002; Silverman, 2000, 2001), the use of multiple research methods and data sources contributes 'to overcom[ing] partial views and present[s] a more complete picture' (Silverman 2000: 122). In this study, the two main research tools used were interviews and journals. However, individuals may not always be willing to share what they have on their mind through interviews and journal writing. Thus, as supplementary qualitative data, observation of the participants' teaching was added in order to observe what actually and more naturally occurred in the classroom. For example, Saori frequently mentioned in her journal and interviews that she believed in the importance of 'communicative language teaching', which is one of the major themes in this study; observation of her teaching, then, allowed me to look at what was actually going on in her teaching and provided important insights and additional evidence for the study (see Chapter 7: Section 7.1). Furthermore, when I found some disconfirmatory evidence or information, I shared the text with the participants during the interviews, whenever possible, and encouraged them to make comments. I then tried to reconsider the implications and incorporate them into the analysis and writing of the study.

6 Preservice Teachers' Perspectives on Teaching

> Although my goal is to become an English teacher, I clearly understand that student guidance is also an important task for junior-high-school teachers.
> Yurika, log entry, 27 May 2010

As Chapter 3 discussed, many researchers in the field of teacher education and development have used various terms and constructs to describe the professional expertise that teachers should attain (Borg, 2003, 2006; Elbaz, 1981; Richards, 1996, 1998; Roberts, 1998; Shulman, 1987; Wallace, 1991). For example, Tsui (2003) defines one such term, *teacher expertise*. She explains that the development of teacher expertise is an interactive process of 'the theorization of practical knowledge through reflection and conscious deliberation and the transformation of "formal knowledge" into practical knowledge' (Tsui, 2003: 261). This indicates that both *formal* and *practical* knowledge bases are essential constructs in becoming a good teacher and a student teacher must make *conscious* efforts to become professional. The necessary 'formal knowledge' offered to English as a foreign language (EFL) student teachers, mainly through initial teacher education (ITE) coursework, consists of seven dimensions often discussed in the language teacher education literature (Pachler *et al.*, 2007; Roberts, 1998; Shulman, 1987): content knowledge (CK) (i.e. knowledge of the target language system, knowledge on how the target language is learned, knowledge on strategies to learn the target language); general pedagogical knowledge (GPK) (i.e. classroom management, behaviour management); curriculum knowledge; pedagogical content knowledge (PCK) (i.e. knowledge that guides teachers' actions in making methodological choices such as inductive or deductive approaches, or when to use or not to use metalinguistic descriptions); knowledge of learners; knowledge of educational contexts; and knowledge of education ends and values. As was already discussed, the following two kinds of knowledge bases, CK and PCK, are of particular interest in this study.

In the following sections, the two research questions that guided the case studies of the six participating student teachers will be revisited: How do student teachers perceive theory and practice in their training?

How do student teachers' perceptions of theory and practice change over time? Each individual case study focuses on how the participants perceived the development of their teacher expertise as well as any changes, and failure to change, in their professional development as a language teacher.

6.1 Teacher as a Subject Specialist

As Moore (2004) argues, teachers are situated within contexts; thus, concepts of being a good language teacher and the process of how novice teachers try to become one vary from time to time and from context to context. Even within one cultural context, teachers develop their expertise in different ways depending on their individual contexts. In this section, the data collected from the four participating student teachers, Chie, Aya, Nana and Mari, will be presented as unique individual cases. Upon graduation from the university in March 2011, the first three went into teaching at public junior high schools; Chie and Nana held tenured positions, whereas Aya was hired on a fixed-term appointment. Mari was a would-be high school English teacher; therefore, despite a number of common features, her process of teacher socialisation slightly differed from the other three cases. Mari became a part-time English instructor at a private high school after graduation. The data on Saori will occasionally be referred to throughout this chapter. Saori, a returned student from New Zealand, was not able to obtain an in-depth understanding of English language teaching (ELT) at junior high school level in an EFL context. Therefore, she ended up not fully participating in this study. However, her comments gave the researcher many valuable insights, and thus, will be occasionally used for comparison.

The three participants, Chie, Aya and Nana, showed some transformation in the constructs of their teacher expertise over time differently from the others; in their cases, being a subject teacher gradually became more important and dominant. In the process of teacher socialisation in Japan, particularly in the case of junior high school teachers, subject knowledge is usually considered less important since teaching at this level is considered more of a holistic undertaking (Shimahara, 2002) in comparison with high school teachers. However, Chie, Aya and Nana were different in that they tried to improve their PCK and emphasised the development of their expertise as subject teachers.

Chie: *Kaizen*

At first, Chie was very keen to express her views in general terms about learning to become a *classroom teacher* rather than a *subject specialist*. This was mainly influenced by her experiences with former teachers. However, becoming an English language teacher gradually became more prominent in her reflections regarding expertise development. All the participants were undergraduate students in the Department of English Studies at the research site, while they were also registered in the university-wide ITE programme. Therefore, they were required to take linguistics and education, literature and culture, communication studies or international relations in the department, depending on their areas of concentration. In addition to the courses in the department, they took ITE courses by choice. In Chie's case, she was largely influenced not only by the courses taught in the ITE programme but also by some of the content courses offered in the Department of English Studies.

The following example illustrates how some university courses made an impact on Chie's teacher expertise as a subject teacher. In the second interview, for example, she stated that the textbook analysis task in the Methods course was beneficial in that the analysis of vocabulary items and grammar elements used in one English textbook made her aware of the importance of utilising this kind of knowledge in lesson planning as a foreign language teacher. This suggests that Chie came to understand that the choices that teachers make in lesson planning need to be underpinned by theoretical knowledge, particularly CK and PCK.

On the one hand, this initial transformation of Chie's perspectives is congruous with the idea that student teachers are influenced by ITE coursework to a certain degree, as some scholars and practitioners have argued. For example, Richards *et al.* (1996) posit that when trainees found that there were conflicts between their pre-training perspectives and practical experiences, they attempted to tackle the problem by applying what they acquired as theoretical knowledge, such as teaching skills and methodologies, through their coursework in higher education institutions (HEIs), although they interpreted the theoretical knowledge differently through the filter of their own assumptions. On the other hand, at the time of the second interview, Chie showed an awareness that she still lacked practical teaching experience and confessed that she was still not confident in how to appropriately adapt the theoretical knowledge that she learned in the university coursework to a particular teaching context. In other words, she was clearly aware of the gap between theory and practice and was not sure yet how to internalise scientific concepts. Chie's experience was in line with the idea that professional education at HEIs cannot be the only influential factor on the professional development of EFL student teachers. For instance, Cabaroglu and Roberts (2000) claim that experiential and reflective components are necessary in ITE, although in Chie's case, she reported in the second interview that she felt a need to first observe experienced teachers as one solution to narrow the discrepancy prior to more practical experiences at school.

The reasons why Chie needed to have a role model of experienced teachers before her own practical experiences can be explained as follows. In the autumn semester of 2009, Chie volunteered to work as an assistant English teacher at a junior high school in order to informally gain some practical experiences that she had not had so far. Her reflections on this experience in her journal and interview data reveal that two factors were important in her professional development: emulating experienced teachers (a mediation activity) and understanding actual classroom conditions (knowledge of educational contexts). Firstly, through observation, Chie was not only able to observe how the teaching techniques that she learned in the ITE coursework were actually used by experienced teachers in a classroom, but she also learned other teaching skills and tasks that were unknown to her then; one example is a bingo game in groups that created a competitive atmosphere among students and another is the use of presentation slides enabling less-able learners to view what they were learning more visually (Journal entry, 26 October 2009). In the post-teaching practice interview, Chie further explained this point by stating that she would first emulate these craft skills in her teaching in the same way as the teachers used them. As she had not yet established her own teaching style, she believed that actively looking for models and first emulating how model teachers taught would be a solid base for her expertise as a good language teacher. This implies that Chie believed in the importance of emulating various teachers to provide her with a springboard to explore and further develop her expertise. For example, she tried to emulate how the teacher that she worked with used the bingo game in one of the microteaching experiences in the ITE courses. As she reflected later in her journal on 27 November 2009, while she was satisfied with the way the activity went, some of her peers criticised her teaching, saying that having fun through a game may not lead to understanding a language element. This incident of peer feedback, according to Chie, gave her a new insight that a task that meets the needs of one situation may not fit another teaching context properly.

Secondly, in the fourth interview, Chie remarked that she gained better understanding of actual classroom conditions through observation while working as an assistant English teacher, which she formerly lacked. For example, the awareness of less-able learners who were struggling to learn English was particularly new and significant to Chie. By observing how the teacher dealt with these students, she came to understand the importance of grasping students' proficiency levels, characteristics and learning environments beyond the classroom. In this way, Chie's informal experiences as a volunteer teacher assistant prior to the teaching practice helped mediate her perspective changes from being a classroom teacher to more of a language teacher, particularly learning CK and PCK as well as knowledge of learners and educational contexts. Since the length of the teaching practice in Japan is quite short, as opposed to other ITE contexts such as the Post-Graduate Certificate in Education (PGCE) in the UK (see Chapter 2: Section 2.4 for more details about the length of school training), Chie's case suggests that additional informal teaching experiences where student teachers examine theories provided by HEIs in a pseudo environment could benefit them greatly.

The following example more specifically illustrates how observing experienced teachers influenced Chie's teaching. Earlier in the study, Chie stated that she believed in learner-centred education and communicative language teaching (CLT) in ELT (Third interview/Journal entry, 7 December 2009) based on the formal knowledge she acquired in the coursework at the HEI. She commented that, in this approach, learners could experience a stronger sense of achievement and this would lead to them having an increased intrinsic motivation to learn a foreign language. During the card sorting task in the third interview, prior to the volunteer teaching experiences, she explained why she chose learner centeredness as the second most important element in becoming a good English language teacher as follows[1]:

> I reckon that students learn English best when they are centred in a classroom, not as passive learners, and think and work on a task together. I chose learner-centeredness as the second most important element since students' motivation is highly valued in such a teaching approach. (Third interview)

However, following her informal experiences of observing and assisting junior high school English teachers, Chie realised that even a student-centred classroom should be controlled to some extent by the teacher, especially at junior high school level. In an English class at a public junior high school in Japan, students' proficiency levels are greatly mixed and Chie found that there were quite a few students with low academic abilities who found that working on language tasks on their own was challenging. This slightly differed from what Chie previously learned about learner centeredness in the university coursework. The following quote is taken from the fourth interview in which Chie explained during the card sorting task why learner centeredness was ranked lower than before:

> I previously thought that it is ideal to create a lesson together with students who actively express their ideas. Teachers shouldn't be the centre of a classroom, you know. But, as I observed experienced teachers and as I made lesson plans [in the Methods course],[2] I came to understand that [in order to make a student-centred approach successful] students need to possess a certain level of knowledge [of the English language] first and a teacher also needs to instruct or make suggestions to a certain degree; otherwise, it is as if a teacher threw the weight of responsibility only on students ... For example, if I were a junior-high-school student and my English teacher let us work totally on our own, we would probably get lost. If a teacher first teaches [a grammatical structure] in a

> teacher-centred manner, and then, tells students to work on their own and use the target structure ... For example, if a teacher says, 'Let's make a similar sentence by yourselves [using the grammar structure we learned] like this example', and then, students can have some confidence in doing so since they already made the sentence together with the teacher. They can feel more comfortable to work on their own. (Fourth interview)

Chie's quote indicates her growing understanding that a good language teacher needs to adjust and alter their teaching approaches by first understanding actual students' proficiency levels and teaching contexts, a part of knowledge of learners and educational contexts.

What is far more interesting is that Chie's perspectives on learner centeredness showed another shift back and more towards her previous perspective due to the teaching practice experiences. In the post-teaching practice interview, Chie noted again that she found it most significant to teach English using a student-centred approach. At this stage, she understood that using this approach students could collaborate with peers, learn from each other and enjoy the freedom to practise using the English language, which she believed would lead to gradually fostering their communicative competence and individual learner autonomy:

> During a group activity [that I did during the teaching practice], of course there were some students who were unwilling to participate in a language task, but most of the students actively participated in the task by sharing roles. I reckoned that both lower-proficiency-level and higher-proficiency-level students were able to work together. ... During the teaching practice, I found many students unable to think and focus on the given task individually. In that case, I found it more effective to provide a group activity through which they were able to think together and learn from each other. When they work individually, they are afraid of making a mistake in front of a class, but when they create an answer and make a mistake as a group, it seems less stressful [for them]. With regard to this point, it would be great if students can first nurture the ability to learn through group work and eventually can think independently. (Final interview)

Here, Chie explained her growing awareness of the concept without referring to the teacher's control over students, unlike before. Through teaching practice at a junior high school, Chie came to notice that a teacher needed to see language learners' growth as a longer-term process. Teaching in a learner-centred approach cannot be achieved in a single lesson. Becoming an autonomous language learner is a long process that a learner-centred classroom helps to develop. The modulating perspective of Chie's suggests that she was trying to continuously mitigate the discrepancy between theoretical knowledge and practical experiences;

theories and concepts that a student teacher first internalises in the ITE coursework are externalised by observing and emulating experienced teachers, sharing ideas with them and actually practising the ideas, and it is a continuous process of positioning themselves professionally, even in pre-service experiences.

This resonates with what many scholars have argued with reference to the dialogical nature of the process of professional development (Korthagen et al., 2001; Tsui, 2003). It also indicates that student teachers try to create meaning through their interactions with others and with their environments, not an individual process; as a sociocultural theory suggests (Johnson, 2009; Johnson & Golombek, 2011), social interactions greatly mediate student teachers' learning. In Chie's case, by understanding the needs of a specific teaching context and the students through observation, emulation and practice, she tried to adapt, refine and reframe the concept of learner centeredness that she formerly acquired in the coursework at the HEI. What is notable in Chie's case is that, in order to adapt and refine abstract concepts, it was essential for her to interact with others in her teaching context, and then to produce and accumulate improvements, *kaizen* in her words, better fitting for the actual teaching contexts, the term that Mari also frequently used in her reflection. *Kaizen* is a Japanese word that is now also used in English, meaning 'making continuous improvements', particularly in management practices. A famous example of a Japanese company that advocates *kaizen* is the Toyota Motor Corporation. *Kaizen*, according to Chie in the post-teaching practice interview, was possible as a result of first emulating experienced teachers' craft skills in her own teaching. This suggests that the teacher expertise model proposed by Tsui (2003) does not fully capture some of the important characteristics of novice English teachers in Japan. While Tsui strongly emphasises that reflection and deliberation on teaching actions are the elements that link theory to the practice of teacher expertise, the findings of the study suggest that some novice teachers ought to first have a model to emulate and experiment with before they can individually problematise their own teaching behaviours. The importance of emulation, and as a result, making improvements in student teachers' professional development will be further elaborated in Chapter 8.

In this section, Chie's perspective in shifting from thinking about classroom teaching to subject teaching was discussed. Based on the knowledge bases provided by the coursework at the HEI, such as CK and PCK, Chie attempted to link theory and practice. However, due to curriculum constraints that did not provide formal practical training until towards the end of ITE, she first actively sought informal practical experiences where she utilised two mediational activities of observation and emulation and gained better understanding of theories and actual teaching contexts. These informal practical experiences, particularly observation and emulation, helped her narrow the gap between formal and practical knowledge in school-based training, transform scientific concepts such as a learner-centred approach into more generalisable understanding as a subject teacher and make improvements to her teaching.

Aya: *Hikidashi*

Aya was a participant whose perspectives changed from that of a language *learner* to a language *teacher*. Mainly influenced by peer learning and experimentation on her own, one of the salient characteristics that Aya showed in her professional development was a shift in perspectives regarding her personal theory of a good English lesson.

Regarding the concept of a good English lesson, learning from negative experiences of her student days in an English classroom, Aya stated in the third interview that she considered a 'fun' class far more important than a class conducted in the grammar-translation method where students passively listen to what teachers say, typical of many secondary school classrooms in Japan. When asked to make a further comment on this point during the interview, she defined a 'fun' class as a learner-centred class in which a teacher interacts with students by asking and responding to questions, not as accurately interpreted as Chie.

Aya's perspective on the learner-centred approach, however, was largely modified due to microteaching and peer learning. For example, after microteaching in an ITE course at the HEI, Aya reflected in her journal on what could make her teaching more effective rather than what would make her class fun (Journal entry, 9 November 2009). The reflection resulted from her peers' questions and advice on the activities that she was planning to use in her microteaching. In the lesson plan that she created during the Methods course, she included some of the language activities that she learned in the coursework. However, her peers commented on her lesson plan, saying that the purposes of using the particular activities were not clear, particularly which language skills were supposed to be developed through the activities. Aya explained that her peers' comments made her notice more as a language teacher that a learner-centred class would be successful if the teacher could stress both the development of individual students' language skills and the interaction among students.

What was unique about Aya's professional development was the degree to which she valued emulation. As opposed to Chie, Nana and Mari who believed that emulation was an important mediational activity for their professional development, Aya found it less valuable to have a model of an experienced teacher to emulate even at the initial stage of her development. Instead of emulating experienced teachers' craft knowledge as it was, Aya often reported that she tried to be creative and devise novel techniques based on what she acquired in the ITE coursework, in reference books, as well as her own previous teaching experiences; she was more willing to self-direct her learning and teaching, which is in fact an essential quality of teacher autonomy (Smith & Erdoğan, 2008). When Aya found some discrepancies between her perspectives and theoretical knowledge on ELT and the actual conditions of a classroom in school-based training, she reported that she was willing to observe experienced teachers or peers to improve her teaching; however, they were to be used as a reference, not as a target of emulation, according to Aya (Journal entry, 16 December 2009). In contrast to Chie, Aya believed that to emulate how others teach was not a solution; what she thought more significant was to be inventive and devise her own methods when faced with a challenge in the classroom. Observing others worked as a way of making Aya recognise her own teaching patterns, which, she confessed, also made her feel that she needed to break out of them and reach beyond her current limits as a language teacher.

In order to be inventive, however, Aya was clearly aware that she needed to expand and appropriate her knowledge base such as CK and PCK (Shimahara, 1998; Shulman, 1987) in her practices. In other words, she valued experimenting with her personal theory and craft directly in practice, as Tsui (2003: 227–228) argues that expertise is characterised as 'engagement in exploration and experimentation, in problematizing the unproblematic, and responding to challenges'. For instance, Aya commented on her teaching in the teaching log as follows:

> It is truly a challenge to teach what I have already acquired [as theoretical knowledge] to students who know nothing; I am never satisfied with how I teach, no matter how many times I do it. (Log entry, 16 June 2010)

This entry was written after Aya had used a language game in a class she taught, in which students had to work in a group and compete with each other to accomplish the task, and one of the less-able learners with lower motivation later commented in self-evaluation, to her surprise, that he was able to enjoy the class owing to the game on that particular day. For Aya, making lower-level students motivated to learn was a major challenge, and this entry shows that Aya learned by way of students' direct reaction towards her own teaching.

Through experimentation and reflection, Aya came to notice that a language teacher needs to have a variety of ideas and teaching techniques that can satisfy students with various levels and needs. The following teaching practice teaching log on 11 June 2010 also supports Aya's belief: 'Although I thought I understood what I had learned in the ITE programme at the HEI, I realised that I needed more skills and abilities to actually act and teach effectively'. Aya often described this point of having many teaching competences by using a metaphor of 'having plenty of drawers' (e.g. Journal entry, 10 November 2009). Aya often used the expression *hikidashi-o-motsu* in Japanese to describe a good language teacher with wide knowledge. *Hikidashi* literally means 'drawers' in English, whereas a verb *motsu* means 'to have' and a particle *o* is added right after an object of a verb and before a verb. In order to bridge the gap between theoretical knowledge and practical knowledge, Aya stated that language teachers need to be open to new ideas and techniques that they should store in 'drawers' and to experiment with them in order to suit the needs and interests of a particular group of students, rather than emulating others' teaching.

As Shulman (1987: 13) rightly argues, 'sound reasoning requires both a process of thinking about what they are doing and an adequate base of facts, principles, and experiences from which to reason'. Aya was not fully ready to use her knowledge base to provide the grounds for her actions; yet, her case illustrates that she was eager to struggle with the transformation of her knowledge base to suit particular teaching contexts and become a better language teacher. Unlike Chie, Aya's case is quite similar to Tsui's model of the professional development of more experienced teachers in that she attempted to link practice to theory by self-directing actions and experiments and reflecting on them without first emulating others' teaching. The differences between Chie's and Aya's professional development will be further discussed in the following chapters.

Nana: Seeking a model for emulation

Nana was different from the other participants, even from Chie and Aya, in that she had experienced a longer teaching practice of teaching English at a primary school prior to joining the ITE programme at the research site. In the teacher training programme that Nana previously attended, she learned to teach as an English teacher for younger learners at private schools and institutions, not as a certified primary school teacher. Therefore, even at the very beginning of the investigation period, Nana was more aware of the importance of being a subject teacher, rather than a classroom teacher.

Her views on language teaching underwent a few stages of development during the investigation. Originally influenced by her previous teaching practice experiences at a primary school, Nana argued in the first interview that, as a language teacher, she found it important to teach students that learning English was fun and useable, similar to Aya, although in Nana's case, this reflected her understanding of the goals of ELT laid down in the national curriculum guidelines for primary education. The goals of ELT in primary education, which were revised and implemented in the 2011 school year, are currently threefold: (1) to form the foundation of pupils' communication abilities while familiarising them with the sounds and basic expressions of foreign languages; (2) to develop the understanding of languages and cultures through various experiences; and (3) to foster a positive attitude towards communication (MEXT, 2010b). As these goals show, the main purpose of ELT at the primary education level is not to master the English language, but rather to provide learners with an environment where they become familiar with the language and its culture. However, Nana was aiming to become a lower secondary school teacher, and the goals at the lower secondary school level differ from those in primary education, where the focus is more on the development of 'basic communication abilities' in the English language (MEXT, 2010c). This implies that Nana still lacked the knowledge base of educational ends and values, the seventh dimension of Shulman's (1987) teacher knowledge mentioned at the beginning of this chapter.

After joining the ITE programme at the HEI, Nana came to value abstract theory that she learned in the university coursework, particularly in terms of CK and PCK. For example, in the 2009 spring semester, Nana frequently jotted down her thoughts in her journal on what she learned in the Methods course or one of the content courses on applied linguistics in the Department of English Studies, such as the age factor in foreign language acquisition, theories on testing and teaching grammar.

However, later on in the same semester, there was growing evidence that her informal practical teaching experiences at *jyuku* had a crucial impact on shifting her views of being a language teacher. *Jyuku* is a Japanese word for a cram school or a preparatory school that provides additional after-school instruction to improve the probability of students getting into secondary schools and universities. Many student teachers in Japan teach part-time at *jyuku* in order to gain practical work experiences informally. In Nana's case, for instance, she discussed in her journal (e.g. 25 November 2009) and in the second interview that an English language teacher should encourage a sense of mastery of the English language among learners, not just teaching the fun of learning. At *jyuku*, Nana was teaching junior high school students who had already learned English to some degree in primary education. As the aforementioned goals of ELT in primary education indicate, they previously learned English through fun and experiential activities that they enjoyed very much, while in junior high school, they were to learn the English language system and how the language is used, which they found quite challenging. Nana's experience at *jyuku* made her aware that she had to teach the English language utilising CK and PCK, differently from ELT in primary education. This view was further reinforced by her experiences of microteaching and peer feedback in the Methods course. By the fourth interview, she came to believe that a good language teacher needs not only to enhance learners' English language skills but also to make them retain what they learned through in-class tasks and assignments beyond the classroom. Such continuous transformation of Nana's perspective on a language teacher indicates that she was very much informed by informal practical teaching experiences and peer learning in ITE in addition to theoretical intervention in the university coursework.

As noted above, one of the significant factors that had a major impact on Nana's learning-to-teach process was the participants in the context of her professional community; namely, her fellow students in the ITE programme and experienced teachers during the teaching practice at a primary school. Many teacher educators advocate peers as an important mediational tool in the process of learning to teach. For example, Johnson (2009) argues that trainees are temporarily affected by peers who help trainees verbalise and externalise their thinking and co-construct the meaning in learning to teach. In Nana's case, the role of peers was particularly crucial in her professional development. Nana viewed them as the ones who could give her honest criticism without feeling intimidated. Sharing comments and ideas with peers for a better language lesson helped her reframe the theoretical knowledge she acquired in university courses and broadened her outlook on ELT. Additionally, Nana often sought a model for emulation in her microteaching, and through observation and emulation, she noted that she learned teaching skills and knowledge that she had not been previously aware of, and became more successfully able to bridge the discrepancy between what she had already known as abstract theory and what she had never practically experienced (for example, second and fifth interviews, as well as teaching log on 17 June 2010).

Seeking a model for emulation, however, sometimes caused Nana a problem; without a model to begin with, it was challenging for Nana to create a lesson from scratch on her own. For example, during the teaching practice at a junior high school, when Nana's supervising teacher asked her to teach a reading passage, she faced difficulties creating an effective lesson. Teaching reading skills is an important element in PCK, usually taught in one of the ITE courses at the HEI, and Nana had some theoretical understanding of how to teach reading effectively. However, as she explained in the final interview, the difficulty was mainly due to a lack of opportunity to observe how experienced teachers would typically teach a reading element in a textbook, as opposed to how they taught grammatical elements, which she observed well enough and was thus able to emulate. This implies that too much dependence on emulation may hinder some student teachers from becoming professionally independent. On the one hand, emulation is an effective mediational tool, as has been discussed in this section, which can work as a springboard for novice teachers without confidence and enough teaching experiences. On the other hand, Nana's case indicates that student teachers also need to eventually learn how to move away from emulation in internalising theory and self-directing their learning and teaching.

During the post-teaching practice interview, Nana maintained that she learned greatly from practical experiences as well. For instance, what struck Nana most was the fact that students' scholastic abilities and learning environments were greatly mixed, currently typical in a public junior high school in Japan. As a result, she found it important to have a good grasp of a teaching context prior to lesson planning and teaching, and then to devise ways in which no students would be left behind. In other words, at the final stage of her ITE experiences, Nana found knowledge on learners and knowledge of educational contexts (Shulman, 1987) beneficial in reshaping and reframing her teacher expertise.

Both Nana and Aya became aware of the importance of being flexible about changing lesson plans depending on the needs and interests of a particular group of students during the teaching practice. In Nana's case, based on her previous teaching experiences as well as a knowledge base she built in the university coursework, she was originally keen to invest time and effort in planning a lesson: for instance, as she noted in the fourth interview, preparing clear instructions and in-class tasks for newly introduced grammatical points. However, school-based training made her more certain about the importance of flexibility in changing plans as the lesson had to proceed so as not to leave any student behind. In order to be successful in doing this, Nana discussed in the final interview that it was essential to grasp each student's conditions including both cognitive and affective factors, which Chie also came to understand during the teaching practice. Nana further illustrated this point by giving an example of when she conducted a lesson based on the same lesson plan to two different classes; things went rather smoothly in one of the classes, while they did not in the other. This resulted from the fact, Nana stated, that each class consisted of students with various contexts and competences. In order to tackle this issue, Nana had to change her lesson plans by, for instance, lowering the levels of her explanations by using more non-verbal cues and adding extra visual aids so that all the students could follow her explanations and would not feel discouraged to learn the target language. This suggests that EFL student teachers at the final stage of their ITE experiences learn greatly from more practical teaching experiences, as the vast research literature in teacher education has already discussed, where they not only experiment with their personal theory and craft, but also learn through understanding the actual conditions of classrooms and learners, although at earlier stages, other interventions like theory and members of their learning community contribute more to their professional development.

As the findings of the study so far suggest, for some novice teachers in ELT like Nana, being on their own without a model to emulate could become a major challenge, particularly with a language skill that they have never taught before and with a large class with mixed levels of abilities and motivation. The three cases of Chie, Aya and Nana suggest that to seek a model and/or to work with peers are significant interventions for novice teachers in the earlier stages of expertise development. As Chie argued, they would help them reshape their theoretical knowledge base and make it more solid as a language teacher, while they should also have ample practical experiences at the later stages to learn actual teaching contexts and experiment with their own ideas, like Aya, so that they can eventually learn to tackle new situations and tasks without help from others, being free from control by others.

Mari: Being an upper secondary school teacher

Mari showed large shifts in her professional expertise over time during the study from a language *learner's* perspective to that of a professional language *teacher*. Originally influenced by her prior experiences of an 'apprenticeship of observation' (Lortie, 1975) as a student, Mari often discussed in her early journal entries what a good teacher should be like, rather than a good EFL teacher; however, she gradually developed teacher expertise as an EFL teacher over the year-and-a-half investigation period. She was probably the most successful participant in the study in that she was eager to learn from abstract theories, appropriate theories and emulate experts' techniques in practical contexts, reflect on her own teaching and then try out new methods in her teaching. Though similar shifts were commonly found in other participants in this study, such as Chie, Aya and Nana, for different purposes and regarding various constructs of professional expertise, it was more obvious in the case of Mari probably because she was a would-be high school teacher. As opposed to lower secondary schools, teachers are expected to be more of a subject specialist at the upper secondary school level in Japan.

Two elements showed distinct shifts in Mari's development as a subject teacher; one was how to transmit expert knowledge on the subject matter (CK) to students, while the other was how to teach a language class smoothly and effectively (PCK). It should also be noted that some particular factors, such as observation and emulation of experienced teachers and her peers, were crucial in mediating these shifts.

Initially, Mari was very particular about how she was viewed as an English language learner. EFL student teachers in Japan cannot cease to make an effort to develop their knowledge and skills of the English language, since most are non-native speakers of English. For example, at the start of the investigation, Mari frequently stated that her major concern was a lack of English language ability. This was observed in Mari's initial description of professional expertise that mainly consisted of the following two elements in CK (Shulman, 1987): knowledge of the English language system and fluency in the English language. She was particularly concerned about her pronunciation of the English language, frequently commenting on this throughout the study. One of the reasons why she often pointed out her imperfect pronunciation as a concern was because of the following belief: as a teacher, she wanted to be observed as a fluent speaker of the English language by her students.

Mari also frequently used the expression, 'to convey (equivalent to *tsutaeru* in Japanese) information' about the subject. For example, during the first interview, she stressed the importance of transmitting CK, particularly about the English language and its culture, to her prospective students. A verb, *tsutaeru* in Japanese, often implies one-directional communication, typically observed in a Japanese classroom in which the teacher is the authority who is likely to pass on information to learners without much interaction with them. Influenced by this cultural norm as well as her former experiences as a student, Mari at first believed that a language teacher ought to possess sufficient CK as a well-informed professional, in addition to a high level of proficiency in the target language to teach.

One of the changes that Mari made in her professional development over time was her perspective on how to 'convey' her CK to students. Eventually, Mari started to mention more frequently that she wanted to involve her students more in her teaching rather than to teach in a unidirectional way. Observing experienced teachers' filmed teaching in the ITE courses at the HEI as well as reflecting on her teaching experiences at *jyuku*, Mari became more concerned about PCK, such as how to involve and make every student understand explanations, particularly those who were less motivated and slower at learning, than her being a fluent speaker of English with ample expert knowledge. For example, she stated in the fifth interview that one-way explanations in fluent English from a teacher to students was not a solution; instead, she needed to be able to teach in an easy-to-understand manner by employing more teaching techniques such as paraphrasing and eliciting students' responses by asking questions appropriately and effectively. Thus, she noted that she tried to observe peers and experienced teachers in order to improve these skills. In addition, through observation of experienced teachers' teaching during the teaching practice, Mari reported in the final interview that she became more certain that adequate lesson preparation as well as sufficient knowledge about the language were important factors in providing clear and intelligible explanations.

Mari also became more fully aware of the expectations for high school English teachers in Japan. The interview data at the later stage clarified that her own English language proficiency was one of her concerns not only because of her perspective as a language learner, but also due to the newly-implemented curriculum for upper secondary schools in Japan, which is a part of the knowledge of educational ends and values (Shulman, 1987) that she learned in the university coursework. The new curriculum, implemented in the academic year 2013, stated for the first time in Japan that the medium of instruction for high school English classes should be the target language, English. Mari maintained in the fourth interview that she was clear about this imminent change in the educational policies, and as a prospective English teacher, she wanted to be ready for teaching English in English. She firmly believed that high-level proficiency in English, which would enable teachers to effectively teach in English suitable for students' linguistic level, should be an essential construct of language teacher expertise.

Another change observed in Mari's perspectives was how to teach a foreign language class smoothly. Originally, Mari explained in her first interview that a lack of experience of teaching a large mixed-ability class led to her concern about how to teach it effectively. Although she had taught at *jyuku*, she only taught smaller classes, which were grouped based on students' academic abilities. Without ability grouping, she was not sure how to involve all the students, particularly those with lower motivation and proficiency levels, while teaching English effectively and meeting their needs. As a solution to this challenge, she was able to point out a few mediational activities during the second interview: observation of experienced teachers and peers, peers' feedback on her microteaching and emulation of experienced teachers' and peers' teaching. Through observation, for example, Mari stressed that the imbalanced image of ELT that she previously held as a language learner would be corrected and she could discover newer ways of teaching. Observation of others' teaching also provided her with a model of a good language teacher, and she could improve her teaching by emulating this and later reflecting on it. This in fact contradicts what her ITE tutor at the site, Lecturer C, believed. According to the interview data, her tutor contended that she would never encourage her student teachers to emulate a model since she believed that they should progress through trial and error by themselves in creating their own styles without emulation.

In the fourth interview, Mari further elaborated on this point by saying that 'stealing' somebody else's craft skills was culturally endorsed. *Nusumu* is the actual word she used in the interview, which means literally 'to steal' or 'to emulate'. The word was also frequently used by Lecturer A during the interview, who encouraged her student teachers to emulate experienced teachers.

Through observing experienced teachers' teaching in the Methods course as well as her peers' microteaching in ITE, Mari became aware of many unknown skills that she could employ in her own teaching, such as how to effectively use teaching materials, how to inform students of the purposes of tasks and activities and how much English should be used as a medium of instruction. Mari maintained that what she and others believed to be a good language class may differ, but they shared an ultimate goal in common: to promote learners' English language proficiency. In order to achieve this goal, she became convinced through observation that there was much more variety in teaching methods and techniques than she had expected in ELT, which she hoped to experiment through emulation.

During the teaching practice, Mari continued to observe teachers, particularly her supervising teacher, and emulated what she thought was effective in her own teaching. In the final interview, Mari showed her understanding that she could not exactly emulate how her supervising teacher taught since she was not as experienced; thus, although she emulated his basic teaching techniques, such as how to call on students, how to treat errors or how to jot down on the blackboard, or activities he employed, she mentioned it was difficult to emulate how he elicited his students' responses and reactions, and how he timed his lessons. Mari noted that she was aware she was not yet ready to emulate these advanced skills. However, employing some of his basic teaching techniques gave her teaching more *merihari* in her words, which means being 'well-modulated' in English. She further mentioned that mere emulation of experienced teachers did not improve her teaching. In order to improve her teaching, she needed to first try to emulate them, and then try to make improvements, *kaizen* in Japanese, similar to what was mentioned by Chie, by linking various constructs of her professional expertise, to fit a particular classroom context. This resonates with what Tsui (2003: 58) argues, 'the boundaries between these knowledge bases … constantly intermesh in practice', since it often involved other constructs in professional expertise than merely CK.

Overall, Mari's data indicate that she was quite successful in developing her expertise as an EFL teacher. She was able to change her perspective from that of a language learner to that of a language teacher in her ITE experiences. What helped her develop her teacher expertise was complex mixtures of various mediational tools: theories of CK and PCK, observation and emulation of others, practical experiences, reflection and experimentation. Additionally, as many qualitative researchers state, participation in a research study can often increase a sense of self-understanding as personal self-benefits. The very first quote of Chie's at the start of Chapter 9 indicates a similar belief in the benefit of participation in the research study. In this study, Mari's high motivation to become a high school English teacher and her active participation in the study were, as a consequence, linked with a positive outcome, as opposed to Yurika, who as I will describe in the following section, was unable to cultivate her critical reflective skills even by joining this project.

6.2 Perspectives on Holistic Teaching

Compared to Chie, Aya and Nana, who developed a more advanced understanding of being a language teacher through pre-service experiences, Kento and Yurika found themselves leaning more towards being a classroom teacher. As discussed in Chapter 4, teaching is often considered a holistic undertaking. This is particularly true of primary school teachers in Japan; junior high school teachers in Japan are also responsible for inclusive and whole-person education, which is deeply engrained in the teaching culture in Japan (Shimahara, 2002). For example, extracurricular club activities, student guidance and moral education are important areas of holistic teaching to understand for junior high school student teachers in Japan. Furthermore, as Ito (2011) discusses, there is a classroom-homeroom teacher system in elementary and junior high schools in Japan, in which students study in the same classroom, which is called a 'homeroom', and occupy their assigned seats all day long, and the homeroom teacher is responsible for 'guiding students in their class in areas of academic, personal-social, and career development' (Ito, 2011: 43). The following cases of Kento and Yurika describe how some student teachers valued GPK (Roberts, 1998; Shulman, 1987) and struggled to become a good *homeroom* teacher despite the fact that they were EFL student teachers, in addition to what hindered their development as subject teachers.

Kento: The importance of student guidance

The concept of teaching as a holistic undertaking was deeply reflected in Kento's perspectives from the very beginning of the investigation period and he did not make large changes regarding this point over time, but rather strengthened it due to the following three factors: ITE coursework, other members of the learning community he encountered and practical experiences. He explained in the first interview that one of the chief reasons for becoming a junior high school teacher was to serve as a coach of a basketball club, rather than becoming a subject teacher. In fact, it is not uncommon for student teachers in Japan to state such things as the reason for becoming a teacher, very often based on their broader interest in social aspects of being a teacher than the subject as a discipline. Kento was also greatly inspired by one of the ITE lecturers at the HEI who taught courses on the principles of education. Under his influence, Kento joined the circle of in-service teachers who regularly gathered outside school in order to discuss issues on student guidance and learn from local input. He then started his own circle among student teachers at the HEI, through which he and his peers discussed various educational issues in Japan, such as declining academic abilities and the problem of bullying, reflections of which he sometimes jotted down in the journal for this study.

Therefore, Kento's journal entries were predominantly focused on holistic teaching rather than subject pedagogy, which provided a clear view of his perspective on the social aspects of being a teacher. For example, after taking an ITE class on general education at the HEI, he reflected on the course content and stressed the importance of holistic teaching in his journal in late October 2009, saying that in every aspect of students' school life it was essential for teachers to clearly understand students' developmental stages in guiding them. He further stated that a better understanding of children's development and the underpinnings of learning theory were extremely important for him as a student teacher. This shows that, at earlier stages of professional development, learning a conceptual framework in general pedagogy was of considerable significance for Kento in terms of holistic teaching, but not subject teaching.

Kento's stance that practical experiences were marginal for his professional development changed over time, however. In the final interview after the three-week teaching practice, when asked about the most valuable element in his pre-service experiences, Kento responded, 'the teaching practice', without hesitation. During the teaching practice, he found it difficult to put his theoretical understanding of student guidance into practice. Kento, for example, originally did not want to show his anger when disciplining his students, since he learned in the ITE coursework that to suppress students by raising his voice and showing a dominant and authoritative character was not effective in student guidance. However, his supervising teacher was not satisfied with the way Kento disciplined his students during the English class because his level of anger was too low and thus she thought it ineffective. What Kento found through observing experienced teachers at the teaching practice school was that many of them were likely to get angry with and talk over the students, instead of properly guiding them depending on the situation as he had learned in the coursework at the HEI. Through practical experiences during the teaching practice, Kento became aware of the discrepancy between theory and practice in holistic teaching, particularly actual conditions of junior high school classrooms where student guidance was not performed as he had expected.

During the post-teaching practice interview, Kento stated that he still believed in the importance of holistic teaching, although he also mentioned that he valued the importance of trying out and internalising theories and scientific concepts in practices and evaluating his own teaching more than before. He elaborated on this point as follows:

Kento: The core principles [regarding holistic teaching] remain unchanged [through the ITE experiences], but, you know, as I experienced the teaching practice, I became sort of greedier. I mean, [prior to the teaching practice] my understanding about teaching was all in my brain or from reading books, but I went to the teaching-practice school and experienced teaching there, and the questions that I had [in my brain] were actually a little resolved.

C³: What were your questions like?
Kento: For example, what is an actual classroom like, how does a teacher teach, can I teach it in this way or not, and so on. These questions were little by little clarified during the teaching practice by understanding actual teaching contexts. Furthermore, I tried out the theories that I had learned in my teaching, and received various feedbacks, and I was able to evaluate myself [as a teacher]. So now I feel that I want to teach this way or that way [depending on needs and situations]; that's why I said I became greedier. (Final interview)

What this quote suggests identifies with what Tsui (2003) argues, that language teachers develop their expertise through dialogical interaction between theory and practice by way of reflections, although in Kento's case, this more concerned holistic teaching.

Although Kento did not make major changes in his perspective on the importance of holistic teaching, he did show a shift in reframing some constructs in ELT. One major concept was learner centeredness and the other was ability grouping. First of all, in learner-centred pedagogy, learners are placed at the centre so that they are the ones who think and use the target language and take control of their own learning, eventually leading to learner autonomy (Benson, 2001; Nunan, 1988). Kento explained in the first interview that he initially took passive learning for granted. The approach was mostly encouraged by his own experiences as a secondary school student, typically found in the grammar-translation method. However, through taking the advanced-level English courses at the HEI, Kento became convinced that it was important for him as a language learner himself to be able to express his ideas in the target language. Since most EFL student teachers in Japan are not native speakers of the English language, they do not stop being a language learner even after the teacher socialisation process begins. Kento also learned the effectiveness of using group work in a foreign language classroom in one of the content classes at the HEI that he attended as a student. According to Kento, these classes were not ITE courses; the former ones were English for academic purposes courses while the latter ones were content-based courses on foreign language education. Both were courses offered in the Department of English Studies where this research study was conducted. Thus, he came to believe that group work was one of the essential teaching methods in ELT that would lead to a more communicative and student-centred classroom. Kento stated in the second interview that in such a classroom, learners could practise expressing their voices in the target language.

The following journal entry, however, indicates that perspective shifting on the learner-centred approach did not result in a successful performance of ideal teaching behaviours in microteaching at the HEI:

> I made a lesson plan for microteaching in an Advanced-level Student Guidance course. I'm thinking about using many activities and group work in my lesson, but couldn't think of the right ones. I think I should study more about various kinds of activities and group work and when and which ones are possible and effective. (Journal entry, 23 October 2009)

This quote indicates that Kento had a good understanding of the learner-centred approach, but he had not yet internalised it sufficiently to effectively adjust his teaching performance. According to my field notes while observing his microteaching in the autumn semester in 2009, Kento tended to monologise by providing lengthy explanations without eliciting responses from the students. He also provided only one short pair-work activity within a 50-minute lesson. In the fourth interview, he attributed the failure to a lack of former experiences as a student, without which it was a challenge for him to incorporate various theoretical elements that he acquired at the HEI, including PCK, into his teaching. The very first quote by Kento provided in Chapter 1 clearly illustrates his feelings then. As he noted in the fourth interview, '[i]t was difficult to theorise what I have never experienced'. He further stated that observation of others' teaching and more practical experiences would lead to developing his PCK, *hikidashi*, the term also used by Aya, of ideas and activities in his words, which would allow him to adapt to sudden changes in circumstances.

In the fourth interview, he further said that in a classroom where learners were encouraged to freely express their ideas, the teacher's main role should be to facilitate learning and give assistance as the need arose, rather than the teacher who encourages passive learning and regulates and dominates talk. This perspective change implies that the student teachers' process of learning to teach is complex in that they internalise their own current experiences as a language learner, their experiences as former students, their experiences in becoming teachers, in addition to the theoretical knowledge base that they acquire at HEIs.

In the fifth interview just before the teaching practice, Kento postulated that during the teaching practice he wanted to teach English using a learner-centred approach without dominating the classroom communication. Through the teaching practice, however, Kento realised that his ideal approach did not always function well. What he experienced was the realities of *gakkyu-hokai*[4] and less-able learners. In the final interview, Kento tried to analyse and make sense of the difficulties of implementing a learner-centred approach in his class. What was first needed, according to Kento, was to discipline his students rather than to encourage them to exchange their ideas in English. Using the knowledge base of PCK he acquired at the HEI, he prepared a lesson plan with some language activities where his students could use English and share some information;

however, what Kento found was that the students threw themselves into the fun part of the activities, and as a result, did not learn much English through engaging in the activities. According to my field notes on 28 May 2010 after observing his *kenkyu jugyo* called a demonstration lesson[5] at the practice teaching school, although Kento was observed to have made a great effort to involve his students, using pair work and showing visual aids, he seemed to have difficulty in attracting all the students' attention, and thus could not get them to play active roles in their own learning. Kento later agreed that this incident influenced him greatly in building a firmer belief in being a holistic teacher before being a good English teacher.

This incident also had a significant impact on Kento's perspective shifting on the issue of ability grouping in a foreign language classroom. Ability grouping, *shujukudo-betsu-shido* in Japanese, is also called 'differentiation', the method of using some forms of grouping such as banding and setting (Ireson & Hallam, 1999). In ability grouping, students are placed in classrooms or small groups according to their abilities in order to reduce frustration and increase students' academic motivation (Danzi *et al.*, 2008), a method used not only in Japan but also in the United States and the UK. Sato (2004) states that *ability grouping* in primary and junior high schools in Japan spread rapidly in the early 2000s after the term was first introduced by the Ministry of Education, Culture, Sports, Science and Technology (MEXT) in 2001, in response to the first strategy of the Rainbow Plan (Chapter 2: Section 2.2), which was to improve students' basic scholastic ability through easy-to-understand classes. The main purpose of this instruction is that individual students acquire the basic knowledge and skills mentioned in the course of study, and it is usually conducted for maths, Japanese and English classes in Japan.

Heavily influenced by the ITE lecturer, as previously noted, Kento was originally opposed to proficiency-dependent teaching. In the second interview, by quoting what the lecturer said in class, Kento claimed that 'ability grouping will not lead to *ningen-keisei*. Students need to meet various perspectives and values in a mixed-level classroom in order to grow'. *Ningen* is a noun in Japanese that literally means 'human beings' and *keisei-suru* is a verb that means 'to build or form something'. Thus, *ningen-keisei* is equivalent to 'character formation' in English. This excerpt shows what Kento understood as the essence of the inclusive approach to teaching, stressing the importance of growing up together holistically in a mixed-ability classroom, rather than prioritising the acquisition of the target language.

Kento's experience as a volunteer teacher assistant at an evening high school also reconfirmed his belief in the drawback of ability grouping. At this school, he assisted an English teacher in a classroom where the students' English language proficiency levels were quite low and the students were not motivated to learn English at all. Kento noted in his journal that in such a case of the lowest proficiency-level group, it was a challenge to teach, even though the students were at a similar proficiency level, which usually makes it easier for a language teacher to focus on one proficiency level (5 October 2009). Kento's concern with ability grouping resonates with previous research studies in other EFL settings in East Asia. For example, Kim (2012) posits that in South Korea, although a proficiency-dependent teaching policy has been implemented by the government, many junior high school teachers and students have raised their concerns about students' emotional problems and mixed attitudes towards ability grouping.

On the other hand, partially because of Kento's part-time teaching experiences at *jyuku* where he met some more low-level learners, he started to question in his reflections on teaching a large class of 35–40 students with mixed proficiency levels (e.g. Journal entry, 26 April 2009). This was in fact a common concern typically observed among many participants in this study – Chie, Aya and Nana. Wavering between these two approaches of ability grouping and mixed-ability grouping, Kento finally reported in his teaching log during the teaching practice that he experimented with various methods including group tasks and communicative activities in his teaching to examine what worked best in a large class. With more than a few less-able learners among 40 students in his classroom, Kento confessed during the final interview that he had not come to any conclusions on whether it was more effective to place them together or divide them into ability groups according to their English proficiency levels. This means that he was not able to conduct his classroom practice with the theoretical underpinning he then possessed. He was not satisfied with how he taught since he could not effectively encourage higher-level students to learn English, while he had to pay more attention to less-able learners and less-motivated students. According to Kento, what he found important through this practical experience was the disciplining role of the teacher in order to make classroom teaching more effective.

Why did Kento not make major changes to his perspective of being a holistic teacher and remained less focused on subject teaching? His supervising teacher's attitude is certainly another cause of this problem, in addition to the existence of less-able learners. During the final interview, Kento complained that his supervising teacher at the teaching practice school was not creative or passionate about ELT. All she did was follow the teacher's manual and teaching routines that she had established over time. Kento described her teaching as *tantan-to-shiteiru*, literally meaning being emotionally intact and distant. This implies that the supervising teacher followed regular teaching routines but did not try to devise any creative or ingenious ways of communicating effectively to best accommodate her students' needs and interests. This resulted partially from the fact that the role of supervising teachers during the teaching practice is not clearly defined in ITE in Japan, as discussed in Chapter 2, and it certainly does not specify the role of being a mentor, an essential function of which is to actively assist student teachers (Tomlinson, 1995). As the following quote indicates, Kento was in fact first trying to actively seek a role model during the teaching practice who could effectively teach English using group tasks, since he had never experienced group-work tasks in ELT as a junior high school student, but he soon gave up looking for an appropriate model to observe and learn from:

> When I was a student, teachers taught English only based on textbooks, so I've never experienced group-work activities in English classes until I entered this university. So, the activities I used in my teaching were my original ones … I heard that the teacher who taught second graders there taught using group activities, which I thought sounded more similar to my ideal approach, so I really wanted to see his teaching, but, unfortunately, I could not due to time constraints. (Final interview)

The supervising teacher's feedback on Kento's teaching, according to Kento, focused on how to manage a classroom smoothly, such as disciplining students, making students listen to him or giving attention to those who were doing something irrelevant. With no good model of ELT to follow or to be inspired by during the teaching practice, Kento failed to transform subject knowledge into appropriate practical experiences. The teaching practice experiences only reconfirmed his belief in the importance of a disciplined classroom as the basis for effective ELT.

Yurika: Surviving as a teacher

Yurika was not very successful in enhancing her reflective skills throughout the investigation period and thus could not fully develop her teacher expertise as a subject teacher; rather, her practical experiences made her 'imitate' her supervising teacher's teaching in order to survive the teaching practice, and reinforced her belief in holistic teaching. Reflection may be challenging for some student teachers and Yurika was certainly one such case. For instance, her journal entries were usually very short and descriptive, rather than critically reflective, and her interviews with me were always the shortest among the participants. Yurika was also the only participant who revealed that the main reason for becoming a public school English teacher was gender equality in school teaching as opposed to in companies, rather than a passion for learning or teaching English or interests in the cultures of English-speaking countries, as she explained in the first interview.

As is the case with Kento, Yurika strongly believed in the importance of being a holistic teacher, rather than a subject teacher. Yurika's journal entries and the interview data indicate that she could not recall how her former teachers taught English in detail, while she was more anxious about how to praise and motivate students. She stated during the second interview that her informal teaching experiences at *jyuku* contributed to her anxiety. At *jyuku* where Yurika taught part-time, individual and small-group tutoring was offered. She tutored one student with low motivation to learn English who often fell asleep during a tutorial session, tired from club activities. In order to deal with this student, Yurika noted that, informed by GPK she acquired at the HEI, she started to praise him more. This gradually had an effect on the student and he seemed to become motivated to learn English, according to Yurika (second interview). It was possible for Yurika to motivate the student because the tutorial was conducted at the individual level and the purposes of *jyuku* teaching were very clear; to teach students so that they can obtain high grades on tests. As a result of this experience, Yurika stated that she started to feel anxious about teaching at school where she had to face a larger class with students with mixed proficiency levels and to teach so that every student understands easily and develops their overall English proficiency.

Not well informed by CK and PCK acquired in the university coursework, Yurika had a firm belief that she could only develop her teacher expertise with practical experiences. This was congruent with her tutor's (Lecturer B) belief in ELT, who described the process of learning to teach by using the metaphor of coming to play tennis well and noted that 'what learners do reinforces what they learned earlier' during the interview with the researcher (Interview, 9 November 2009). Influenced by the tutor, Yurika also often maintained in her journal that the theoretical knowledge she acquired in the coursework about ELT should be tested in practice in order to judge its effectiveness (e.g. Journal entry, 26 May 2009).

However, during her microteaching in the Methods course in autumn 2009, which I observed, Yurika failed to transform the theoretical knowledge she learned in the ITE coursework into actual teaching. Moreover, she avoided verbalising and analysing what exactly happened in her teaching. The following illustration based on field notes tells exactly what happened during her microteaching on 3 December 2009 in the Methods course. She was originally assigned to microteach listening skills to junior high school students. According to the syllabus for this course, the role of schemata in teaching listening and reading skills was discussed earlier in the course. Known as schema theory in language teaching, learners often bring their own prior knowledge and experiences about the world to a classroom (Brown, 2007b). However, without introducing either a content topic and background knowledge, which was 'cool biz'[6] in summer in Japan, or new and key vocabulary to help students comprehend the content, Yurika started her teaching by playing a CD of the script twice, and then providing her classmates, who acted as her students, with a handout of a list of comprehension questions written in Japanese. Then, she orally asked them the questions on the handout, which they were allowed to answer in Japanese. Although she frequently commented in her journal as well as in the interviews that teaching in a lucid manner was important, my field notes indicate that she taught a lesson one-sidedly without activating her students' schema, and her classmates, feeling lost, did not have to utter almost anything in English. Yurika did not later write down any reflections regarding this particular microteaching in her journal, whether positive or negative, which most of the participants in the study often did on their own microteaching. This example implies that, prior to the formal school-based teaching practice, Yurika was not quite ready to try out a train of events in the dialogical process of theory and teaching actions with the help of reflection, although this is the process that the vast literature on teacher education, including Korthagen et al. (2001) and Tsui (2003), has suggested to be effective in teacher development.

Through the three-week teaching practice in 2010, her views on inclusive education did not show a major shift, but rather were further reconfirmed. In the teaching log during the teaching practice, she frequently mentioned the importance of student guidance, one important aspect in holistic teaching. For instance, after observing one English class in the first week, Yurika felt the difficulty of motivating students and wrote as follows:

> Although my goal is to become an English teacher, I clearly understand that student guidance is also an important task for junior-high-school teachers. (Log entry, 27 May 2010)

In this context, what Yurika meant by student guidance was simply dealing with students with behaviour problems in a classroom, although LeTendre (1999) argues that it usually includes more demanding responsibilities beyond the classroom and the school curriculum. This shows that Yurika did not yet fully understand the complexity of GPK, one of the seven dimensions of teacher expertise according to Shulman (1987), though she stressed that she continued to value it highly in her expertise development.

In as much as Yurika mentioned subject teaching in the teaching log during the teaching practice, such as how to deal with students who disliked English, and how to deal with differences in students' proficiency levels, the final entry in the teaching log indicates that she was greatly influenced by her teaching practice supervisor who attached great importance to holistic teaching. She illustrated her point with a quotation from the supervising teacher's comments in the teaching log: 'Teachers need to study theories more, while student teachers as well as teacher educators at HEIs should understand the issues and challenges of student guidance in a language classroom; otherwise, theory and practice will never be linked' (Log entry, 11 June 2010). As if to respond to her supervising teacher's comment, Yurika wrote at the end of the teaching log as her general impression of the teaching practice that student guidance was essential in lower secondary education. As she stated earlier, she believed that teacher expertise could be enhanced by experimenting through practical experiences, but what she mainly tried to test was GPK (Roberts, 1998; Shulman, 1987) including student guidance in a classroom, rather than the CK and PCK of the subject matter.

However, some minor changes were observed in Yurika's perspectives on ELT, and one example is her understanding of the concept of learner-centred pedagogy. Prior to the teaching practice, Yurika defined the concept in interviews, as noted below, as an approach in which a teacher prioritises students' needs and abilities over other issues. For example:

> It is important to teach English clearly by understanding students' situations first. (Third interview)

> I should teach carefully based on an assumption that students do not know much about the target language yet. (Fourth interview)

Lecturer B's comment during the interview with the researcher supports her idea: '[w]e should think of students first because they are the learners who should be mainly concerned [in a language classroom]' (Interview, 9 November 2009). However, as was discussed earlier, the observation of her microteaching in the Methods course in autumn 2009, in which she taught a lesson one-sidedly where her students had to say hardly anything in English, indicates that her understanding of learner-centred pedagogy in a language classroom was partial. To be more specific, based on the observation of her microteaching, her teaching lacked the idea of putting students in the centre so that they are the ones who use the English language and negotiate the meaning, and take control of their own learning, gradually leading to learner autonomy (Benson, 2001; Nunan, 1988).

Through the teaching practice, however, Yurika showed a slight shift in this regard due to observing and working with the supervising teacher and an assistant language teacher (ALT).[7] According to Yurika (Teaching log, 28 May 2010), she observed that the supervising teacher devised various ways to teach English and often approached her students and asked questions. With this role model that Yurika found possible to emulate, she came to understand that eliciting students' voices would make them think, as opposed to Kento who found it quite difficult to implement a learner-centred classroom where discipline was a major issue with less-able learners. I observed Yurika's *kenkyu jugyo*, a demonstration lesson, towards the end of the teaching practice, and the field notes then indicate that she seemed successful in approaching and encouraging her students to use and answer in English, in a similar way to her supervising teacher.

Yurika's experience could be understood in Furlong and Maynard's (1995) five stages of student teachers' developmental process stated in Chapter 3. They maintain that student teachers typically go through five stages in school-based training. In their framework, Yurika was at the third stage of surviving as a teacher, when student teachers begin to make sense of what is going on in a classroom, and very often, in order to deal with difficulties, they try to emulate, or '"mimic" what they believed to be teachers' behaviour' (Furlong & Maynard, 1995: 82). Without understanding how complex teacher thinking behind the stage is, they could 'at least adopt the outward appearance of being a teacher' (Furlong & Maynard, 1995: 82). This means that emulating teaching behaviours without a full appreciation of the theoretical knowledge that underpins them will confine student teachers to one approach, and cannot lead to solutions to the problems they face in a classroom.

What Kento and Yurika had in common and what also differentiated them from the four participants in the previous section, was the influence of their supervising teachers on their professional development. At the beginning of the investigation, both noted that they prioritised GPK over CK and PCK (Roberts, 1998; Shulman, 1987) in teacher expertise. In Kento's case, his supervising teacher placed importance on student guidance, one element in GPK, while she valued subject teaching less. This led Kento to reconfirm his perspective on the importance of student guidance and a disciplined classroom even in ELT in lower secondary education. On the contrary, in the case of Yurika, her supervising teacher emphasised the importance of student guidance; however, she also served as a role model as a subject specialist who could teach in a learner-centred approach. Although Yurika did not fully cultivate the ability to reflect on her teaching in her pre-service experiences, she managed to imitate her supervising teacher and survived the teaching practice. Her perspectives on learner-centred pedagogy in ELT were reconceptualised by practical experience to a certain degree, but she had a long way to go before fully developing autonomy as a professional EFL teacher.

6.3 Theory and Practice: Evolving Student Teacher Perspective

This study initially began with the following two research questions: How do EFL student teachers in Japan perceive theory and practice in their pre-service training? How do their perceptions of theory and practice change over time? The profiles of the six participants depicted how their perspectives towards professional expertise, especially on theory and practice, shifted and developed.

The value of theoretical knowledge for student teachers

The six case studies in the previous sections reveal that most of the participating student teachers valued the importance of theory in their teacher expertise development. The cases also show that the knowledge bases they valued covered a broad range of topics, including subject-matter knowledge, pedagogical knowledge and a knowledge base on being a holistic teacher.

First of all, most of the participants in this study highly valued the importance of theory in their expertise, particularly at the beginning of the investigation because they were acquiring a theoretical base at the HEI. As Eraut (1989) and many other researchers in teacher education have previously argued, the absorption of theoretical knowledge takes place at the HEI. The knowledge base acquired in the ITE coursework allowed the student teachers to feel confident, and this confidence underpinned their lesson planning and teaching. The conceptual and theoretical knowledge also helped the student teachers to organise concepts of the subject, English in this case, and to identify potential difficulties in their students in learning English, as Pachler et al. (2007: 57) argue that 'pedagogical, methodological and disciplinary knowledge obtained from background reading, be it empirical, theoretical or professional, can help foreign language teachers construct, articulate, test out and modify personal theories of teaching'. It should be pointed out though, that in the case of Japan, due to the balance between theory and practice in their ITE experiences, which is seven to one (see Chapter 2 for more explanation on this issue), student teachers are in one sense confined to theoretical knowledge, be it good or bad, since they do not experience formal practical experiences until the seventh semester upon matriculation.

The findings in this study further indicate that not only was the value of theoretical knowledge acknowledged by the participants, but also that the kinds of knowledge the participants valued were multifaceted. Using the labels of the seven dimensions of teacher knowledge suggested by Shulman (1987), one dimension that many of the participants (Aya, Chie, Nana, Mari) mentioned is CK, and the data in this study have shown that it included second/foreign language acquisition theory, and pronunciation and grammatical structures of the target language. The second label, GPK, was valued by two participants, Kento and Yurika. This included behaviour management and ability grouping in this study, for instance. Examples of PCK in the study, the third dimension, further varied: for example, textbook analysis, materials development, teaching methods, how to teach vocabulary, how to teach reading skills, how to instruct effective and fun activities, evaluating attitude and setting standards. Again, four participants (Aya, Chie, Nana and Mari) stated that they acknowledged the influence of this knowledge on their expertise development. The following dimensions, curriculum knowledge (e.g. newly revised Course of Study, newly introduced English activities in primary education), knowledge of learners (e.g. less-able learners), knowledge of educational contexts (e.g. team teaching, ALTs, *gakkyu-hokai*) and knowledge of education ends and values (objectives of the newly revised

Course of Study), were also frequently mentioned by most of the participants in this study.

Some of the participants valued the knowledge base not directly related to ELT; although they were EFL student teachers, some of them, especially Kento and Yurika, were very eager to develop a knowledge base on being a holistic homeroom teacher, such as behavioural management, even before they actually encountered classroom issues and problems during the teaching practice. This study found that it was mainly as a result of the cultural characteristics of teaching at junior high schools in Japan. Junior high school teachers in Japan are responsible for whole-person education, while they specialise in particular academic subjects (Ito, 2011; Shimahara, 2002; Shimahara & Sakai, 1992). The perspective of an inclusive approach in junior high schools in Japan is often emphasised in some ITE courses at HEIs outside the core courses on CK, as Kento reported that he was very strongly influenced by one of the ITE lecturers regarding this matter.

The improvement of the target language abilities

Furthermore, what was also unique about the case studies was that the participants in this study were not only eager to establish a knowledge base about the target language, English in this study, but they themselves wanted to develop *their* target language abilities in order to become good English teachers. Many discussed their experiences as learners in the English language classes in the first and second years of their undergraduate study at the HEI, very different from their high school classes, as well as their impact on professional development.

For instance, in Mari's case, she wanted to develop knowledge of the phonological structures of the English language and use this knowledge in her teaching; at the same time, she considered that being a fluent English speaker with proper pronunciation was a must for a good English teacher, and therefore, she herself wanted to improve her own pronunciation. As Pachler *et al.* (2007) rightly posit, a good and secure grasp of the target language promotes student teachers' confidence, especially when they ought to give instructions and interaction in the target language, as they can provide a good target language model themselves.

In Kento's case, he had never experienced discussion activities in English classes in high school. Thus, Kento's personal theory of learner-centred pedagogy was influenced by the tasks that he experienced in one of the English classes he attended as an undergraduate student at the HEI. As Almarza (1996: 70) argues, teacher trainees reflect 'not only on their activity during teaching practice but also on their own language learning experiences. These reflections provide them with a springboard to explore the theoretical aspects of the profession in ITE, without necessarily having to postpone it until they are full-fledged classroom teachers'.

However, the cases in this study indicate that one of the characteristics of their professional development is that while they were EFL student teachers, they never ceased to be English language learners at the same time, and thus, attempted to incorporate their experiences as language learners in reconceptualising their personal theories. What is usually considered in the existing literature is that student teachers are influenced by their former experiences as language learners; in the case of EFL student teachers in Japan, their experiences as language learners are not in the past tense, but rather, are influential on language teacher development as an ongoing experience.

The role of practical experiences in teacher development

In contrast to how the participants responded to theory in their professional development, how did they view the role of practical experiences? One thing to note here is that the relatively short period of school-based practical teaching experiences is one of the problems that confronts ITE in Japan. Therefore, as the results of the study indicate, at the initial stage of the study and particularly in the spring and autumn semesters of 2009, the participants did not have many chances to experiment with their personal theories unless they actively sought opportunities to go into a classroom beyond the ITE curriculum. For instance, Chie, Nana and Kento worked as volunteer teacher assistants at nearby schools. All the participants, except for Chie, also taught English at *jyuku* as their part-time jobs to explore classroom teaching. All the participants except Kento fully realised their lack of practical experience as a weakness, which they believed should be eventually remedied. Aya expressed the point in the second interview: she understood that practice teaching experiences, although quite short, would be a place where she could 'put together' what she learned at the HEI and test it out in order to develop her expertise. Yurika also agreed in her journal that she had a strong belief that the abstract theory that she learned in ITE at the HEI should be tested first in practice in order to understand its effectiveness (Journal entry, 26 May 2009).

On the other hand, Kento, whose initial stance was that practical experiences were marginal for professional development in comparison to abstract theory, also changed his perspective on practice over time. In the post-teaching practice interview, he noted that the most valuable element in his pre-service experiences was the teaching practice. During the student teaching, he found it extremely difficult to put his theoretical understanding of student guidance into practice. The three-week exposure to actual classroom contexts introduced him to a number of issues relevant to teaching that he further needed to address.

As a number of researchers and teacher educators have argued (Borg, 2003, 2006; Korthagen *et al.*, 2001; Roberts, 1998; Tsui, 2003), the student teachers in the study also recognised both professional coursework and classroom practice as significant elements in language teacher expertise. However, the process of expertise development was not that simple. Many of the participants noticed, earlier or later in their developmental processes, that there was a gap between their theoretical knowledge and actual practical experiences. As Borg (2003) notes, in order to examine the effectiveness of teacher education, while it is important to discuss the content of student teachers' cognitions and related elements, the processes of cognitive development should also be investigated. Thus, Chapter 7 will address what specific factors were involved in the EFL student teachers' processes of narrowing the disparity between theoretical knowledge and practical experiences.

In this chapter, the reported processes of each student teacher's professional development were presented as individual cases. All participants were aware of the importance of theory and practice as essential elements in developing their teacher expertise, although the kinds of knowledge bases they valued differed. The participants also actively sought chances to go into a classroom beyond the ITE curriculum, since they were aware that lack of practical experiences was a weakness. In addition, in the final interviews, many participants reported that they perceived some changes in their perspectives about ELT, from that of a language learner to a language teacher or from that of a homeroom teacher to a language teacher. Some greatly benefited from having a good model to emulate or having peers who could give honest and constructive criticism. On the other hand, some cases suggest that they were not able to perceive radical changes in their expertise. For example, they were not able to critically reflect on their teaching behaviours due to lack of reflective skills or lack of an expert model.

Every student teacher's process varied as each case has described. The factors that influenced or challenged the participants to become more professional varied too. What is still not clear is why some participants were more successful in developing their expertise in this study, while others failed to transform their perspectives and become more professional EFL teachers. To further examine this issue, the major factors that influenced these student teachers to become more professional or hindered them from developing their expertise will be explored in the next chapter.

Notes

(1) The interview data and the journal entries originally produced in Japanese were translated into English by the author. The author checked the translated version with each participant for its accuracy. Since subjects and objects of verbs are often unsaid in Japanese when they can be clearly interpreted from contexts, when necessary, the author added them in brackets. Also an ellipsis (...) in transcripts indicates that text has been omitted because of relevance and space.

(2) The extra information in some of the brackets in quotes was also obtained directly from each participant during the later interviews.
(3) C stands for Chitose, the first name of the researcher.
(4) *Gakkyu-hokai* is an expression widely used in the late 1990s in Japan. It means breakdown in classroom discipline in primary and lower secondary school classrooms.
(5) A student teacher usually provides a demonstration lesson towards the end of the teaching practice, which is observed by a head teacher, a supervising teacher and other teachers across disciplines as well as other student teachers who are doing their teaching practice at the same time, in order to demonstrate his or her teaching and to receive feedback for future improvements.
(6) 'Cool biz' is a governmental campaign in Japan that promotes a business style to deal with global warming, which enables us to feel cooler and more comfortable when working in offices in summer.
(7) An ALT refers to an assistant language teacher who is a young overseas graduate recruited by the Japan and Exchange Teaching programme in order to assist foreign language education in elementary, junior and senior high schools throughout Japan. More information is available from http://www.jetprogramme.org/e/introduction/index.html

7 Factors that Affect Initial Teacher Education

> In the spring semester, I could not explain well why giving clear explanations was important … When I did microteaching the other day, my cohort students gave me feedback [on giving explanations]. … This made me think more about [how I can give] clearer explanations in teaching.
>
> (Nana, Fourth interview)

Chapter 6 depicted the reported processes of each participant's professional development as individual cases. Each story was different, while some common issues emerged from the interview and journal data, particularly in terms of factors that influenced professional development, both positively and negatively.

This chapter further discusses the two guiding research questions: Do student teachers perceive a gap between theory and practice? If student teachers see this as a problem, how do they mitigate the disparity between theory and practice? In order to respond to these questions, the chapter first explores the factors that influenced the student teachers to become more professional or hindered them from developing their expertise. The main factors discussed in this chapter are: schooling experiences, theoretical knowledge base and informal teaching experiences.

Examining the growth of the English as a foreign language (EFL) student teachers in initial teacher education (ITE) in Japan, close analysis of the interview and journal data has identified the following mediational tools that influenced, mediated *and* challenged the teachers' early professional learning: previous and current experiences as learners, theoretical knowledge that they acquired in ITE coursework and practical experiences both in formal and informal settings. These factors influenced the development of the student teachers' professional expertise at various stages for different purposes. The fact that the student teachers were learners of English at the same time also made the process complex and multifaceted. It should also be emphasised here that student teachers in ITE are still at an early stage of their professional development, where the foundations of their future development are being built. Without realising that the process of developing teacher expertise takes time, some student teachers such as Saori and Kento in this study possessed unrealistic and inadequate expectations of teaching, which resulted in the struggle to link theoretical knowledge and practical teaching experiences, especially when there was not enough support from the pre-service training programme.

This chapter explores elements in the dialogical process whereby student teachers develop their expertise: schooling experiences as a learner, theoretical learning in ITE coursework and informal teaching experiences. These aspects were beneficial in novice teachers' professional development, although in this study they were not necessarily well connected to their teaching practices without mediational activities and human mediation.

7.1 Previous and Current Experiences as a Learner

This study finds that at an early stage of the student teachers' professional development, all participants drew heavily on their own experiences of being taught English in the past, at least to a certain degree. This is congruent with what Furlong and Maynard (1995: 75) call the stage of 'early idealism', in line with other previous studies in ITE (Borg, 2005; Cabaroglu & Roberts, 2000; Kagan, 1992; Pajares, 1992; Richardson, 1996). In the early part of the first phase of the main study, the participants tended to be informed mainly by their prior knowledge and experiences as a student, which they established through 'apprenticeship of observation' (Lortie, 1975), discussed in Chapter 4. This was due to lack of theoretical knowledge about English language teaching (ELT) to draw upon or lack of opportunity to formally practise teaching at that stage of the study, as we shall see in the following examples.

As Borg (2003: 277) argues, previous schooling experiences usually provide student teachers with 'first-hand encounters with the realities of life in schools and classrooms', and some participants in this study were positively influenced by previously encountered teachers in pursuing a career in teaching and becoming like them. In the first interview, for example, Chie explained how much she was influenced by one homeroom teacher in her junior high school days. Her former school was located in the suburbs of Tokyo and had a welter of problems due to the variety of students, but the teacher never gave up on facing each student and bringing them together as a group. Influenced by this teacher, Chie wished to become a good *homeroom* teacher like him in the future, someone who can create a positive learning environment. Unlike Chie, Aya and Saori reported that they were positively influenced by their previous English teachers in becoming a *subject* teacher. In the first interview, Aya stated that owing to an English teacher in her junior high school days who employed a communicative approach, she chose a career as an EFL teacher and wished to be like her in the future, although she did not elaborate on how effective the teacher's teaching was on the development of her own English competences and English teaching abilities. Similarly, Saori stated in the first interview that because of her experiences of learning English as an English as a second language (ESL) student in New Zealand, through observing her teachers, she became convinced of the importance of students' autonomy as well as communicative language teaching (CLT), and wished to actively involve students in learning as her teachers did. This will be further discussed in the next section.

These examples indicate that participants' own teachers in the past influenced them in deciding how they wished to manage students and teach English in the future. However, at the stage of the first interviews, they were still unable to analyse how the thinking behind their teachers' behaviours shaped their actual teaching and student management, without enough theoretical knowledge to draw upon or opportunities to practise teaching and reflect on it. As Borg (2005) argues, their perspectives were only built around what teachers do in class and they were not able to observe what was going on behind the scene of teaching such as thinking, planning, preparing and reflecting. Similar to many of the previous studies in ITE, the participants individually formed their perspectives of what made a good teacher through 'apprenticeship of observation' (Lortie, 1975), based on the observable behaviours of a teacher's job. The following cases of Saori and Kento illustrate what Furlong and Maynard (1995: 75) explain, that these student teachers at the stage of 'early idealism' cannot evaluate their teachers 'in terms of their effectiveness as *teachers*' as to CLT.

Saori: Communicative language teaching

Although Saori did not fully participate in this study, her case is worth noting because she clearly expressed her thoughts on the impact of her former teachers, which unfortunately did not contribute to her successful professional development. As Cabaroglu and Roberts (2000) discuss with regard to the impact of ITE on student teachers, their pre-existing beliefs are often not changed drastically by pre-service teacher training. Many student teachers use theoretical knowledge that they acquire in ITE at higher education institutions (HEIs) or actual practical contexts in which they teach to confirm their beliefs, rather than reconstructing or correcting them. The following example of Saori also indicates that her understanding of one of the theoretical concepts in language teaching, CLT, did not change much because she was unwilling to evaluate the theoretical knowledge that she possessed then and the practical teaching situations where she taught; rather, she seemed vulnerable to critical feedback and was stubbornly attached to her pre-existing perspective of CLT, influenced by her experiences as an ESL learner with her former teachers in New Zealand.

In the first interview, Saori stated that she left her former public high school in Japan because she did not find any meaning in the exam-oriented education there. She subsequently moved to New Zealand, where she attended a high school and learned ESL. While studying there, she observed her ESL teachers and became convinced of the importance of CLT in ELT. CLT is an approach that focuses on learners as well as developing their communicative competence (Savignon, 2005). In CLT, the role of a teacher is more of a facilitator, whereas students are expected to actively engage in interaction with other students and collaboratively construct meaning in the target language (Brown, 2007b). Saori showed a clear understanding of CLT in the first interview, stating that a language teacher needs to value the autonomy of individual students and to actively involve them in learning so that they can engage in interaction and use the language.

Saori conducted a 20-minute microteaching in the Methods II course on 11 November 2009. Although she was able to articulate what CLT was in the first interview and thought she understood it, the following description of her microteaching indicates that she did not necessarily grasp the approach from a teacher's point of view. According to my field notes, the target audience of her teaching was first graders of a lower secondary school and she conducted all her teaching in English, though the two preceding student teachers taught almost entirely in Japanese. She started her teaching by first reading aloud a short text for her students. Then, breaking the text into shorter chunks, she asked them to repeat after her. Without the text in front of them, the students listened to what she said and immediately repeated it. This procedure was repeated a few times, and chunks that Saori provided at one time progressively lengthened as she continued; as a result, the students were asked to repeat at the sentence level in the end. This shows that she was unable to incorporate the concept of CLT into her own teaching. In this teaching process, her students did not have many chances to interact with each other, but rather had to 'parrot' Saori's words.

After the microteaching, there was a feedback session with her classmates where she received critical feedback on her teaching approach. Many of the criticisms focused on her teaching not matching the level of her future students, particularly because it was all conducted in English and the text was provided only orally. Some of the criticisms also reflected the fact that she did not encourage her students to interact with each other. She could not embrace the criticism well and wrote a journal entry on this incident as follows:

> They commented [that my teaching approach] was not appropriate for the level of my [future] students, but, if so, then it is impossible to teach English in English. I don't want to teach English in the grammar-translation method, which was a reason why I quit high school [in Japan]. ... I have

doubts about 'passive learning' and ... I felt I was not suited for teaching at public schools. (Journal entry, 12 November 2009)

This excerpt indicates that Saori was unwilling to objectively analyse and evaluate her teaching with the help of theoretical knowledge or peer interaction. In fact, she only had a partial understanding of CLT and did not actively involve her students in learning, which is one of the features of the CLT approach, as noted earlier in this section. As the Course of Study (MEXT, 2010c) states, English language teachers are required to devise teaching methods and approaches such as pair work and group work as appropriate in order to gain facility and confidence in using English and to cultivate students' communicative ability. She could have, for example, employed some strategies to prepare her students to engage more actively in language tasks and these teaching strategies could have been provided by ITE coursework. Instead, she showed an incomplete understanding of CLT in her teaching, which was to teach entirely in English and have students say sentences aloud in English, without trying to understand the actual teaching conditions at secondary schools in Japan. To put it another way, she was unable to reconstruct her pre-existing experiences of CLT, and this finding is in line with Cabaroglu and Roberts (2000).

Even at a later stage of this study, during the teaching practice, Saori discovered a gap between her ideal teaching approach of CLT, which she established through observing her previous ESL teachers in New Zealand, and the reality of an EFL classroom in Japan. Saori faced a classroom situation with behaviour problems during the teaching practice, and without much support on ELT from her supervising teacher, she lost her interest in further pursuing her career as an EFL teacher in Japan. She was unable to analyse the causes of the problems utilising the theoretical knowledge that she then possessed and to reflect on her own teaching, but rather became discouraged in pursuing her career as an EFL teacher, as she stated in the final interview. When asked about her future plans in teaching in the final interview, Saori responded:

> I want to enjoy teaching, and I mean it. I wish to teach students who want to learn, not the ones who are forced to. ... Also I want to think together with students, and develop my own materials from a scratch. [I wonder if] it might be more enjoyable to teach in developing countries. I've never been to any, but it seems more interesting to begin teaching from nothing. Not to teach in a fixed [curriculum], but, yes, introducing activities and thinking [on my own]. I have no intention of teaching in Japan now. (Final interview)

Some student teachers like Saori think that they know more than they actually know and can do more than they actually can; when they find their understanding still partial and incomplete, they express their frustration by not being sure how to take any step forward. When Saori found the gap between her experiences of CLT as an ESL student and the actual EFL classroom contexts, she showed her vulnerability and was unable to find a way to promote her learning. However, it should be emphasised again that student teachers are still at the very early stage of their professional development and should be supported within an ITE process so that they can overcome issues they face. In the case of Saori, more chances to practise, critically reflecting on her pre-existing beliefs and analysing classroom situations and learner needs, in addition to fostering a more positive attitude towards collaborative support by others in the same learning community, could have resulted in more effective development of her expertise as an EFL teacher.

Kento: Communicative language teaching

What differentiated this study from the other studies in ITE was the dual identities of the participants as English language teachers as well as English language learners. During the study, participants often reflected on their experiences as language learners with their current teachers at the university, not just on their former schooling experiences. All the participants in this study were undergraduate students in the Department of English Studies. In order to satisfy the requirement of the curriculum, they were still taking English language courses (English for academic purposes: EAP) in addition to courses in their focus areas, as well as ITE courses outside of the department.

For example, as was discussed in Chapter 6, Kento was greatly affected by his English teachers at the university. Kento recalled in the first and second interviews that his EAP teachers employed CLT and that their teaching differed greatly from the teacher-fronted classes of his high school days. For instance, in CLT, learners are considered agents who interact and co-construct meanings by using the target language (Nunan, 1999). Thus, in the EAP classes in which Kento enrolled, students were often asked to engage in small-group discussion through which they had to form and express their opinions, receive criticism and make rebuttal statements in English. His teachers also often assigned group roles to the students to help them develop learner autonomy. He confessed that it was the first time he had experienced this kind of opinion-building practice in English classes. Through these communication-oriented activities, he came to realise that to be able to express one's ideas in English and to work collaboratively with peers in a group were essential elements in CLT, as he stated in the second interview. He also commented that this approach would contribute to creating a more communicative and student-centred classroom in his own teaching.

In this way, Kento gradually developed his understanding of the concept of CLT, influenced by current experiences as a learner prior to his practical teaching experiences; however, similar to Saori, he was not sufficiently prepared to employ this approach appropriately in his informal teaching. In the Methods II courses, Kento conducted his 20-minute microteaching in December 2009. My field notes indicate that the target audience of his lesson was the second graders of a lower secondary school and the topic of the unit was Easter Island, a Polynesian island in the south-eastern Pacific Ocean. Kento focused on one of the new grammar structures that he found in the text; the usage of a verb, *call*, when it is used as 'call + an object + a complement', as in 'We *call* him Bob'. This is one of the typically taught grammatical structures at the lower secondary school-level in Japan. Kento started his teaching by writing down a few examples with the target structure on the blackboard, and then spent quite a long time one-sidedly explaining the examples. There was little student–student interaction and it was far from CLT, although he explained later that he meant to introduce an information-sharing task through which the students were expected to practise using the structure by asking their classmates' nicknames for each other. During the fourth interview, he watched his filmed teaching and was asked about his teaching approach. He responded that the reason why he gave a lengthy explanation of the grammatical structure was because he wanted to make sure his students clearly understood how to use it. At the same time, he also stated that he was aware that his students remained silent and looked bored, but he did not know how to engage them during his grammar instruction. Without referring to his partial theoretical understanding of the concept of CLT, he further commented with regard to an increase in student interaction as follows:

> To increase interaction was difficult. I mean, the differences between simply chatting or effectively interacting [with students], I found it difficult to differentiate them. When I broadened the topic, then, hmmm, [I thought] I was just chatting, this is not [effective] teaching. Or [in other occasions I thought] I should broaden the topic more and interact more [with students]. It requires quick decisions, which was still difficult for me. (Fourth interview)

This interview excerpt indicates that Kento's confusion was caused by the gap between his experiences of his current EAP teachers, who were more experienced than Kento, and his partial understanding of CLT as well as his teaching competences, which were still not fully developed. Thus, Kento could not adjust the CLT approach to meet the levels and needs of his students and increase student interaction. His understanding of CLT was also partial because he stated in the interview that interaction was for a teacher and students, not between students, although his view on CLT was informed by his current teachers who employed a great amount of group work to increase student interaction and improve students' communicative ability. To put it another way, Kento's pre-existing experience of CLT that learners should be placed at the centre of interaction and they are the ones who should develop their agency and communicative ability did not result in successful application to actual teaching.

As Lortie (1975) rightly posits, these examples of Kento and Saori in this study imply that observing former and current teachers did not contribute to the successful professional development of dialogically linking theoretical knowledge and practical experiences. As they were still in the middle of developing a sound basis for the early stages of professional development, the participants could have been encouraged to explore alternative ways within their training to deal with the struggle and confusion. As noted earlier, the impact of former teachers was observed at early stages of this study; how other elements and tools influenced, mediated and challenged the participants' professional development will be discussed in the following sections.

7.2 Theoretical Learning in ITE Coursework

The theoretical principles that student teachers acquire in the ITE coursework are often criticised as being ineffective and irrelevant (Peacock, 2001; Richardson, 1996). However, the findings of this study show that they were an influential factor for participants to an extent, which changed their pre-existing perspectives established through 'apprenticeship of observation' (Lortie, 1975) and helped develop their expertise as a teacher, similar to some studies in ITE. For instance, MacDonald *et al.* (2001) conducted two surveys (pre-training and post-training) on beliefs and cognition on second language acquisition (SLA) theories with novice teachers in initial teacher training, and found that there were some statistically significant differences between their pre-existing and post-training perspectives, although, as they observed, no data from classroom practice were used in the study.

As with MacDonald *et al.*'s study, the results of the present study show that theoretical knowledge influences the participants to a certain degree, although dimensions and degrees varied depending on the participants. In addition, student teachers' theoretical knowledge in itself did not have a major impact on advancing their professional development. For instance, Chie, Aya, Nana and Mari found theoretical knowledge significant in changing their views from the perspective of a foreign language learner to that of a foreign language teacher, but what enabled them to realise this was actual classroom contexts. These cases, both the successful and the unsuccessful ones, provide valuable insights regarding which elements of training can contribute to laying the foundation for early professional development in ITE in Japan. The following example illustrates how theoretical knowledge of SLA theory influenced Mari's professional development.

Mari: Second language acquisition theory

Chie, Aya, Nana and Mari found content knowledge (CK) and pedagogical content knowledge (PCK) (Shulman, 1987) particularly important in transforming their perspective of being a language learner into that of being a language teacher. To give one successful example, in the final interview after the teaching practice, Mari explained how her understanding of one of the teaching skills, reading-aloud tasks, developed due to the theoretical knowledge of affective filter (Krashen, 1985), both of which she learned in the coursework at the HEI. The affective filter is a hypothesis developed by Krashen (1985, 2008), who explains that the affective filter must be weak in order for optimal learning to occur in language learning. Mari states that before the teaching practice, she was planning to use reading-aloud tasks in her teaching because her former teachers often used this teaching activity. Through the coursework, she understood that the benefits of using these tasks were to increase the amount of student output and give them an opportunity for pronunciation practice. However, in the reality of the classroom during her teaching practice, she discovered that her students did not have much confidence speaking in English. According to Mari during the final interview, this reminded her of one of the SLA theories that stresses the importance of lowering the affective filter of learners for effective instruction in a classroom. As a consequence, unlike Saori (explained earlier in the chapter), who failed to analyse the appropriate use of a reading-aloud task, Mari decided to use a reading-aloud task to lower her students' filter prior to a small-group discussion activity, instead of using it to simply increase the amount of output. She explained that the reading-aloud task could lower her students' affective filter since they did not have to produce their own utterances in English and negotiate meaning with each other by using their own words. She changed the task instructions accordingly as follows:

> Because [students] did not have [much] confidence [in their English], I provided a model first and [they] could imitate and follow me. Also, with regard to a reading-aloud task, when [they] listened to others around themselves, [they could notice that] there weren't that many who were very good at pronunciation, so they could feel relaxed and wouldn't lose confidence. Well, yes ... if [they can] feel a sense of achievement at least once in one line [during the task], that will do, I guess. (Final interview)

In this example, Mari used both CK (affective filter hypothesis) and PCK (how to instruct a reading-aloud task effectively) as 'guidelines for understanding particular situations' (Elliott & Labatt, 1975: 59) in making professional choices and taking concrete action in her own classroom.

This was a successful case of connecting student teachers' theoretical learning to practical teaching situations. To put it another way, practical teaching experiences and an actual teaching context were essential in making meaning out of Mari's theoretical understanding and further developing her expertise.

Kento: Learner-centred pedagogy

Although the previous example shows that some student teachers in this study were able to utilise their theoretical knowledge and adjust their practical teaching behaviour, not all the participants were able to do so. Kento, who found general pedagogical knowledge (Shulman, 1987) more beneficial for becoming a good *homeroom* teacher, was one such example. As Chapter 6 (Section 6.2) already discussed, through the coursework at the HEI, Kento gradually developed his perspectives on a learner-centred approach in ELT, one of the concepts in PCK. He understood that in such an approach, learners are placed at the centre and practise expressing their ideas in the target language to learn (Second interview). However, he failed to employ the approach successfully in his microteaching at the HEI in December 2009. He reflected on his teaching and explained in the fourth interview that the failure partly resulted from a lack of former experiences as a student, without which it was difficult to internalise his theoretical understanding in his own teaching. This implies that Kento believed he first needed to learn how to teach in the learner-centred pedagogy through observing experienced teachers as a model, as the following quote indicates, 'it was difficult to theorise what I have never experienced [as a student]' (Fourth interview). In fact, this view of the necessity of having a good model to create a good lesson was observed among other participants such as Nana (Chapter 6: Section 6.1).

During the teaching practice, Kento faced the realities of *gakkyu-hokai*, a breakdown in classroom discipline and management in translation, and found it challenging to teach using a learner-centred approach, which he was hoping to employ in his teaching during the school-based teaching practice. Based on the knowledge base of PCK that he possessed, he developed a lesson plan in which his students could practise using English through an information-sharing task. However, he soon found that his students were not able to perform the task well, since they had poor concentration and could not stay focused. Although he had a good knowledge base of the approach, he stated in the final interview that he failed to adjust it to an actual teaching context and put it into practice.

Kento could have more actively sought some mediation to link his theoretical knowledge to actual teaching contexts; for example, with the help of a supervising teacher as a model, he may have had a better understanding of how to adjust his teaching approach and make his teaching more learner centred accordingly. Kento noted that his supervising teacher during the teaching practice was not too influential as a subject teacher. Reflecting on his teaching practice in the final interview, Kento stated that his teaching practice experience made him more aware of the importance of behaviour management at the lower secondary school level, rather than subject teaching. This case indicates that correct understanding of a theoretical concept in itself does not necessarily result in successful application to a classroom setting.

As Furlong *et al.* (2000) point out, theoretical studies can give student teachers opportunities to sort out their own perspectives and values and reflect on the practical situations they encounter, which Kento did to a certain degree. However, Kento could have developed his expertise as a subject teacher in a more balanced way and narrowed the gap between theoretical knowledge and practical contexts in different ways, if he had received more support on ELT from others or had been given more chances to experiment with his ELT skills by way of various mediational activities, as we shall see in Chapter 8. Pachler *et al.* (2007) also rightly posit that student teachers' expertise development is enhanced more effectively through actively engaging in social practices than at the individual level with the sole use of knowledge bases acquired at HEIs.

7.3 Practical Learning in Informal Settings

Many previous studies on ITE have suggested that some form of practical experience in a classroom is a vital element in the development of student teachers' expertise. In fact, in response to the criticism that there is too much emphasis on theoretical learning at HEIs, longer school-based training was introduced, for example, in the UK. Regardless of the fact that ITE in Japan still offers only a relatively short period of practical teaching experiences, all the participants in this study agreed that practical teaching experiences were essential for developing their expertise. Kento was the only participant who reported in the early phase of the study that he found theoretical knowledge more significant for the development of his expertise; however, after the practice teaching, he also agreed that practical experiences were necessary for his professional development. Two weeks for upper secondary schools and four weeks for lower secondary schools is a minimum requirement as school-based training in ITE in Japan. What emerged from the data, however, was the student teachers' struggle to find an opportunity to apply their theoretical knowledge to real teaching contexts, due to the imbalance between theoretical learning at the HEI and practical experiences at schools. The participants were certainly aware that a few-week teaching experience was not sufficient to internalise their teacher knowledge and connect it to actual teaching contexts. Thus, all the participants, except Saori, reported in the data that they actively sought more informal practical learning opportunities prior to the teaching practice, which is not observed much in previous studies in ITE in Japan. Their informal practical experiences included teaching at *jyuku*, microteaching in the ITE courses and volunteer teaching at nearby schools. The results of this study imply that their informal practical experiences made them more aware of the divide between theory and practice, but did not always function well for mitigating the gap between the two; as a result, as we shall see in the next example, during formal practical learning, the participants actively sought mediational activities in order to further narrow the gap between them.

Nana: Giving clear explanations

By the latter part of the first phase of this study, the participants' expertise was shaped by informal practical experiences to a certain degree. As with the aforementioned two constructs of former experiences as a student and theoretical knowledge acquired in ITE, however, informal teaching experiences made student teachers aware of the importance of other mediational tools that could connect theoretical knowledge and actual teaching practices more effectively. For example, worried about a lack of practice, Chie volunteered to work as an assistant teacher at a nearby junior high school. Her reflections on this experience reveal that she learned significantly through observing experienced teachers and understanding real classroom situations. However, she was only allowed to take a role as a support person for students or to co-teach with the experienced teacher by leading one language activity at a maximum, and as a result, she felt a more urgent need to actually teach on her own and experiment with her knowledge and teaching skills.

Teaching at *jyuku* was another informal practical teaching situation that many of the participants in the study found useful. For example, in the second interview, Aya discussed how she attempted to solve the problem of teaching a mixed-ability group at *jyuku* through observing one experienced teacher. Aya found that he communicated well with his students, which made them look up and listen to him carefully. According to Aya, she still could not teach well like him even after observation, which is natural since she was still developing her foundations for early professional expertise. At least teaching at *jyuku* provided her with opportunities to reflect on her own teaching and analyse somebody else's teaching.

Similarly, microteaching in ITE courses, particularly the Methods courses, was another opportunity for the participants to directly apply their knowledge base to practice. In some recent studies in ITE, microteaching is considered an effective mediational tool that provides an opportunity for novice teachers to 'trial, analyse and revise' and involve themselves in active learning (Fernandéz, 2010: 351). For example,

Nana's reflections on her own microteaching accounted for a substantial proportion of her journal entries in the autumn semester of 2009. Her comments ranged from time management and non-verbal delivery to teaching materials, lesson plans and language activities, but the focus in this section is on giving clear explanations (PCK) as this was rated highly by Nana during the second card-sorting exercise in the fourth interview. The following illustration of Nana's case on giving clear explanations indicates that the informal teaching experience in itself is not influential enough in student teachers' development of expertise.

Nana commented on how she gave grammatical explanations in November 2009, after her 10-minute microteaching in the Methods II course:

> I did 10-minute microteaching today [in the Methods course]. I had to introduce 'be going to ~' so I made three kinds of example sentences with the names of the teachers that [learners] were familiar with. But by making the sentences appear authentic, I ended up using difficult words. My classmates gave me feedback [after teaching] and I realised I need to use already-taught vocabulary words more. (Journal entry, 16 November 2009)

This journal entry indicates that her informal teaching experience, with the help of peer feedback, made her realise the importance of using understandable *teacher talk*, which is one of the crucial factors that help a teacher to formulate an effective approach to teaching beginners (Brown, 2007b). In the fourth interview, Nana cited her awareness of less-able students as one of the reasons for rating clear explanations more highly than in the spring semester. She explained as follows:

> In the spring semester, I could not explain well why giving clear explanations was important ... When I did microteaching the other day, my cohort students gave me feedback [on giving explanations]. For example, 'your explanations were too difficult for students at a certain school' or 'too easy' and so forth ... This made me think more about [how I can give] clearer explanations in teaching. (Fourth interview)

Nana further mentioned that because of her informal teaching experience, she realised that giving clear explanations was more difficult than she had thought, especially when there were so many other issues she had to consider in teaching. This example implies that Nana tried to reflect on and analyse her microteaching with the help of peers and came to realise what issues and challenges she still had to work on in developing her expertise further, with which many of the participants in this study also agreed.

7.4 Reflections on Case Studies

Both previous and current experiences as a learner of theoretical knowledge influenced the participants to a certain degree; however, each factor in itself did not have a major impact on shaping their professional expertise. Thus, as noted above, in this study most of the participants attempted to gain some informal practical teaching experiences, leading to an awareness of actual educational contexts and the student teachers' teaching abilities at the time.

Such experiences sometimes caused a feeling of anxiety in some participants such as Aya, Nana, Kento and Mari, because when they discovered what issues needed further work and improvement because of reflection, they did not have an opportunity to fully practise what and how they wanted to teach prior to the teaching practice. As we saw earlier, Furlong and Maynard (1995) discuss five stages in the development of student teachers on their school experiences: 'early idealism', 'personal survival', 'dealing with difficulties', 'hitting a plateau' and 'moving on'. In a sense, even with informal practical learning experiences, the participants were still at the first stage of their five-stage professional development without full teaching experiences in a real classroom setting. Before the teaching practice, the participants may have been allowed to teach for a relatively short amount of time or for one classroom activity only during volunteer teaching. They may have had a very small group of students at *jyuku*. Or, they may have taught in a hypothetical situation in ITE courses in which university students were the audience instead of actual students. To put the point differently, informal practical teaching experiences enabled many of the participants in this study to have clearer purposes when interacting with experienced teachers, students and peers later in the training, and in further developing their expertise. They raised their awareness of the challenges and issues that needed to be tackled prior to the teaching practice.

However, without much opportunity to fully practise teaching, the participants did not have much confidence in directly experimenting and individually solving the problems based on their own teacher expertise, but rather, as we shall see in Chapter 8, first employed mediational activities in order to narrow the gap between their theoretical knowledge and practical teaching.

8 Mediational Tools: Narrowing the Gap between Theory and Practice

> The best thing [about observation] is student teachers can learn the techniques they've never used, which I believe is not useless. So, [they should] observe many teachers and find out what they can emulate and develop [in their own teaching]. If they think 'I can use this technique myself' and take an interest in it, it's great, so I should show them various models of teaching ... They can develop the hints and the tips they get, so observing teachers is not a waste at all, I believe.
> (Lecturer A, Interview, 9 October 2009)

> [W]hat I changed most in the autumn semester was I tried to 'steal' good teaching skills of peers and emulate them in my own teaching. I knew this was effective, but it was probably the first time that I actually did this.
> (Mari, Fourth interview)

In this chapter, two kinds of mediational tools for narrowing the gap between theory and practice are discussed. Human cognition emerges out of participation in social activities, and as Johnson (2009) discusses from a sociocultural theoretical perspective, tools that mediate teacher learning can include cultural artefacts and activities, scientific concepts and social relations. In this study, the following two tools, mediational activities (observation and emulation) and social relations (learning from experienced teachers and peers), supported the developmental process of the student teachers and enabled them to narrow the gap between theoretical knowledge and practical experiences. In some studies, such as Nagamine (2008) and Poehner (2011), the above elements are required components of the initial teacher education (ITE) curriculum. In Collins *et al.*'s (1989) cognitive apprenticeship model, imitating teachers' thinking processes is utilised as part of the process of learning. Instead, the participants in this study spontaneously sought mediational tools in order to fill the gap, as the situation demanded. In the following sections, how these tools mediated their process of learning to teach and why they depended on these tools will be further delineated.

8.1 Observation and Emulation

In this study, the findings indicate that the following mediational activities – observation, emulation and peer learning – were actively used by the participants as a way of shortening the gap between theory and practice. For example, Chie, Nana, Kento, Mari and Yurika frequently mention in both the interviews and journals that they actively seek role models of experienced teachers and peers, observe how they teach and emulate their methods of teaching in their own teaching. The successful example of Chie that follows, shows that some student teachers in the study are able to make the transition naturally from a language learner to a language teacher by critically observing and emulating experienced teachers, unlike school pupils who observe their teachers uncritically without understanding what the teacher is actually thinking (Lortie, 1975). Furthermore, peers served both as a provider of critical and honest feedback on their teaching in a non-threatening manner, as well as a role model who could provide craft skills, which were challenging but possible to replicate. It should also be noted that some student teachers are not as gifted and do not necessarily have the natural skills to fill the gap between theory and practice. As Kento's case in this chapter indicates, the failure to find an appropriate role model for observation or emulation may result in their failure to make sense of their expertise as a subject specialist. Also, as can be seen in Yurika's case in this chapter, the inability to critically reflect on theory and practice may lead to mere imitation of teachers in order to survive the teaching practice (Furlong & Maynard, 1995) when there is no proper support through ITE.

Chie: A successful case

In foreign language teaching, it is generally accepted that the learner-centred approach has attracted attention and is certainly one of the areas taught in ITE courses at the research site. In foreign language learning, learners are at the centre of active learning: they think and use the target language and take control of their own learning (Benson, 2001; Nunan, 1988). In this study, the interview and journal data show that Chie and Mari are the two cases that articulate the concept of learner-centred pedagogy in English language teaching (ELT) more successfully and in a more balanced way compared to the other participants. What makes these participants more successful is mostly their active use of the observation and emulation of experienced teachers, as we will see in the following example of Chie.

In the third interview, Chie's understanding of the concept of the learner-centred approach in ELT was still somewhat inaccurate: prioritising students' needs over teacher needs, and planning and monitoring students' progress from their perspectives. As my field notes show, the third interview with Chie was conducted before she began to regularly visit a nearby junior high school as a volunteer teacher assistant. Thus, what she noted during the interview was not yet underpinned by formal practical experiences.

However, mainly through further observation and emulation, she developed her understanding of the concept. For example, Chie wrote in her journal about her volunteer teaching experiences, explaining how group tasks were effectively used by experienced teachers: 'The students during group work were thinking hard and worked very actively. I found it important to give an opportunity for moving their seats and discussing with their classmates' (Journal entry, 7 December 2009). With regard to what exactly happened to the students, Chie stated in the fourth interview as follows:

> This is a technique that Mr. Yamamoto was using today, and, for example, he asked a volunteer teacher like me to introduce myself [in English] first. And then, he asked the students to listen to me, and then to think of what they wanted to ask me and put [questions] into English. Then, they discussed by rows for about three minutes and they made questions in English. Hmmm, for example, they asked me questions like 'Have you been to the US?', 'What is your favourite school lunch menu?' They thought by themselves and made questions [together] about what they wanted to ask, and since [the teacher said] it is ok to make mistakes, so, their words were sometimes grammatically in the wrong order, but [he said] it is important that what you want to ask gets through [to a listener], and as they discussed together, well, they were discussing like, an interrogative word comes first and what word should be next, I thought such an activity is very effective to promote their autonomy. (Fourth interview)

Mr Yamamoto is a pseudonym given to the teacher whom Chie mainly worked with as a volunteer teaching assistant. He was an English teacher with five years of teaching experience, who happened to be a graduate of the same ITE programme. Chie went to the junior high school once or twice a week in the autumn semester of 2009, where she also had some opportunities to work with other English teachers. As noted earlier in this section, in the third interview, Chie defined the concept in a somewhat undeveloped way. However, the previous quote shows that, due largely to observing the experienced teacher, her understanding of learner centeredness was gradually changing more towards having students work on their own and use English to express their ideas, closer to how the pedagogy is usually defined in ELT.

Chie's perspective on learner-centred pedagogy continued to transform; during the fourth interview, she further explained her understanding of the pedagogy, then based on observation of Mr Yamamoto's teaching:

> What I thought ideal before was, well, [a] student-centred [approach] where students actively volunteer their opinions and [a teacher and students] establish a lesson together, not so teacher-dominant, but, well, [I saw] actual classrooms, and in addition, I made lesson plans myself [in the Methods course], and now I feel, unless [a teacher] teaches a certain degree of knowledge [first], or gives explanations [to students] to do this or that, it's kind of like [a teacher] abandoning [his responsibility]. Ideally, [a teacher should] provide a topic and let students work on their own, but in fact, if I were a junior-high-school student and [a teacher] told us to work [on our own right away], then we would say, 'I don't know what to do', or 'I don't want to do this'. To some extent, a teacher [should] teach in a teacher-centred way, then tell students, 'now you are ready to do this by yourselves,' or 'make sentences on your own which are different from the model I gave you'. Then students can have some confidence since they did it once already [with the teacher]. This will raise students' motivation, too. (Fourth interview)

This excerpt shows Chie's understanding of the concept; in order to make a learner-centred class successful, a lesson should be carefully sequenced with ample staged tasks appropriate for students, while a teacher must give proper instructions so that students will feel safe enough to actively participate in a group task. Chie became aware that the degree of learner centeredness should be controlled by the teacher depending on factors such as contextual constraints and learner disposition and competences, which is in line with what Hedge (2000) asserts in her study on language teachers with some experience. Similarly, Chie came to notice through observation that a teacher did not simply hand over their responsibilities to learners and learners were not always ready to make responsible decisions on their own.

At this phase, however, Chie had only a few opportunities to emulate what she observed in her own teaching. In order to further develop her perspectives on learner-centred pedagogy in ELT, during the teaching practice she actively used observation and emulation. Chie was asked by her supervising teacher to observe how experienced teachers taught English in the first week of the three-week teaching practice. The following quotes from the teaching log indicate that in observation, Chie paid close attention to specific teaching skills that she could later emulate in her own teaching, though no specific objectives or behaviours on which to focus were provided in advance by the supervising teacher:

> Third-year, Class 4 — [The students were] preparing for an interview with an ALT. The teacher provided an in-class handout which was made to suit the students with the lower proficiency level. [They were to] choose questions to ask [during the interview] from the handout. I understood well that [the teacher was trying to] give them support

according to students' levels so that they could use English actively. (Log entry, 27 May 2010)

Second-year, Class 4 — I found the first activity of a crossword puzzle effective in that [the students were asked to] not only fill in blanks [with verbs] but also change them into the past tense by themselves ... In a translation task, the teacher very effectively and adequately led [the students] to an answer. I've seen many times that even the students who first said they didn't understand could get to the answer on the teacher's hints. I would like to emulate this and teach in such a way that I could lead them to answers. (Log entry, 28 May 2010)

These quotes show that Chie did not observe experienced teachers' teaching behaviours uncritically, although many researchers in the past have criticised the impact of the implicit process of 'observation of apprenticeship' (Lortie, 1975); rather, she tried to analyse why some tasks worked well and which teaching skills she could later emulate in her own teaching. The first excerpt shows that Chie came to notice that providing support appropriate for students' proficiency levels is essential to facilitate an interactive task. The second excerpt also indicates that Chie paid attention to how the teacher's support could lead students to forming answers in English. As Bandura (1977: 22) argues, as a process of human learning, by nature, people learn observationally and form an idea of how new behaviours can be performed; Chie also tried to examine how she could use the model as 'a guide for action' in order to promote student-centred learning.

During the post-teaching practice interview, Chie stated that at the start of the teaching practice, she attempted to look at how the lessons flowed and emulated exactly how her supervising teacher taught because she had not yet established her teaching style. The following quote indicates that even in emulating routine tasks such as giving instructions for a reading-aloud activity, Chie found it difficult to perform well and give as clear instructions for her students as her supervising teacher did:

Every time [I taught], I emulated how the supervising teacher taught, but, since [the students] have done this [before] in every lesson, so [I thought they] must be fine [with the procedure], so I just said, like 'then, let's practise reading. OK? Start'. And then [the students said] 'are we doing this in a pair?' or 'up to what point are we reading?' Without specific instructions, [the students] became worried even with what they do in every lesson. So, I should give specific instructions, like 'today, this, tomorrow, that', and so forth. (Final interview)

Later in the teaching practice, Chie was able to observe and emulate more extensively how her supervising teacher taught, and later reflected on how it went. The following quote shows that Chie tried to emulate not only the routine tasks but also more complicated teaching craft that needed deeper teacher thinking behind the stage:

> First of all, [as for] the lesson flow, in the very beginning [of the teaching practice] I was asked by Ms Imada to emulate how she taught, so I thoroughly observed her teaching style, and additionally, I tried to observe particular skills. For example, when she asked questions, how she elicited answers from the students, or who answered the questions, [I observed] these points. Also, how she dealt with the students when they had a lapse in concentration, and from [how she dealt with the students] I gathered some hints and then emulated it in my teaching. While I observed her, I myself walked among the students, like [as if it were] in team teaching. This way, I learned by closely observing how the students perceived the teacher and how they became focused, or how they learned. (Final interview)

Ms Imada (a pseudonym) was Chie's supervising teacher during the teaching practice. She was a female English teacher with about 20 years of teaching experiences in the suburbs of Tokyo. As the foregoing quote indicates, Chie came to understand how observation and emulation were beneficial for her in developing her reflective skills as well as teaching skills.

According to one of the few studies on English as a foreign language (EFL) student teachers in ITE in Japan, Nagamine (2008) observed a common value among the participants, that they found it essential to emulate experienced teachers' teaching to become better at teaching English, especially at an early stage of their development, in order to make up for their anxieties about their lack of content knowledge (CK) and pedagogical content knowledge (PCK). Some participants in his study, however, experienced difficulty and reservation in imitating experienced teachers. They stated that it was 'dangerous' (Nagamine, 2008: 181) to emulate others without analysing the situation and teacher thinking behind the stage. This suggests that some student teachers may imitate experts uncritically, which will not contribute to their professional development. As we shall see later in this section, this is similar to Yurika's case.

In contrast, what made Chie more successful in effectively using emulation was that she emulated experienced teachers with some clear purpose in mind, which she explained in the final interview (see the preceding quote). Joining this study and keeping reflective journals for two consecutive semesters prior to teaching practice was certainly one reason for providing her with a sense of purpose; in addition, her informal practical experiences as a volunteer teaching assistant beyond the curriculum had a strong impact on Chie. In the final interview, when asked about the beneficial factors of the mediational activities she utilised, Chie stated:

As I observed how Mr. Yamamoto taught English [prior to the teaching practice], although there were differences in their lesson flows because [Mr. Yamamoto and my supervising teacher] had different teaching styles, I was able to notice that they had many common points such as how to plan and conduct lessons within fifty minutes, so I should admit I learned a lot [from observing Mr. Yamamoto]. (Final interview)

Towards the end of her ITE experience, Chie was able to articulate her reconstructed idea of the learner-centred pedagogy in comparison to the start of the study. During the third card-sorting exercise in the final interview, Chie stated that what is important in a learner-centred approach is to pay attention to individual students and to adjust teaching accordingly. In her understanding, a teacher needs to grasp each student's levels and interests first so that he or she can provide appropriate tasks and support, with which students can actively engage in learning. Active interaction with each other on language tasks will eventually lead to forming their own ideas and taking responsibility for their own learning, which she believed is an ultimate goal of ELT.

Chie's case implies that in ITE at higher education institutions (HEIs), more opportunities to observe and emulate others' teaching, particularly with specific purposes and goals, could be useful. Through this mediational task, student teachers can practise drawing on their emulated actions using theoretical underpinnings. They can also make up for the short period of teaching practice in the case of ITE in Japan. It should also be noted that the failure to find an appropriate role model for observation or emulation may result in the failure to make sense of teacher expertise as a subject specialist. As opposed to Chie's case, in the cases of Aya and Nana, without an appropriate model, they found it harder to create a lesson on their own.

For instance, in Nana's case (see also Chapter 6: Section 6.1), at first glance she successfully used observation and emulation in developing her teacher expertise. For example, in the post-teaching practice interview, Nana stated that she was very comfortable emulating her supervising teacher during the teaching practice since her supervising teacher had a similar teaching approach to her ideal way of teaching, such as teaching grammar in inductive ways by first giving familiar examples embedded in contexts rather than explicitly providing rules (Brown, 2007b). As Clarke *et al.* (2014) argue, the degree of influence of supervising teachers depends on the degree of congruence of values of a supervising teacher and a student teacher.

However, when Nana was asked to teach reading during the teaching practice, she noted in the post-teaching practice interview that she found it challenging to plan and conduct a lesson from scratch without a good model to emulate. Not knowing what to do, Nana further explained during the same interview that she first introduced new vocabulary words, and then asked her students to read aloud and translate one line at a time, a typical technique in the traditional grammar-translation method. As we saw in Chapter 6, this is the same method she commented that she disliked as a student. Without a good model to emulate, Nana simply followed how her former teachers taught English. She instead could have taught reading, for instance, by having students read paragraphs together and discuss what each paragraph meant in groups in a more top-down approach by using background knowledge and knowledge of the world; however, without appropriate PCK to implement such a learner-centred class, she claimed that she needed a model first that could show her how to adapt the concept into practice. Nana's case, and Aya's case as well, gives an indication that having an appropriate model to observe and emulate can help student teachers link their theoretical knowledge to practical experiences more effectively.

Kento: An unsuccessful case

In contrast to Chie's case, the following case of Kento further illustrates that an understanding of theoretical principles alone does not result in effective teaching without a good model to underpin the teaching. The second interview with Kento reveals that his initial understanding of learner-centred pedagogy was informed by one of the content courses on applied linguistics he joined in the Department of English Studies in the spring semester of 2009; this was to have students think on their own and express their ideas, and the role of the teacher in such an approach was to make appropriate judgements in deciding when to give hints and when to watch without support. According to Kento, he had never learned the concept before. Furthermore, he was informed by English language courses he took as an undergraduate English major student where his teachers usually had students discuss many issues in English. Through taking these courses, he stated in the second interview that he learned that teaching in the learner-centred approach was what he wished to aim towards as an EFL teacher who makes students work in a group and express their ideas in English. In the autumn semester 2009, however, he put more stress on the theory he was then learning in general education courses; with regard to learner-centred pedagogy, for example, he made comments such as 'a learner needs to grow so that he will not say yes all the time to adults' and 'he has to have his own ideas and express them clearly and listen to others' (Third interview). This indicates that his understanding of the concept was fluctuating between the one relevant to being an EFL teacher and that of being a homeroom teacher.

During the teaching practise, Kento was supervised by Ms Matsuda (a pseudonym) who was a female English teacher with about 20 years of teaching experience in junior high schools in suburban areas in Tokyo. Kento stated in the final interview that during the teaching practice, he first attempted to look at Ms Matsuda as a model in order to improve his subject teaching skills; but this soon turned to disappointment since the supervising teacher was not a good model of a subject teacher:

> It was helpful to see how Ms Matsuda used flashcards and picture cards. I thought writing down [new words] on the blackboard was a lot of work but Ms Matsuda used the flashcards and later stuck them up on the blackboard. I found it less stressful. Yes, picture cards. [Ms Matsuda] used them just as the teachers' manual tells you to do. (Final interview)

As Kento explained in the final interview, some basic craft skills such as using flashcards and picture cards were easy to emulate in his teaching, but he could not see Ms Matsuda as a model of learner-centred pedagogy. Through observing her, Kento realised that she did not devise various teaching strategies or make informed choices, which he thought were essential for making a more learner-centred English class. He found instead that many of the students looked as if they had been thinking and engaging in classroom activities, but in fact they were just zoning out or gave up studying English. Also, during the group tasks, he saw that some students just left it to other group members without any appropriate support from the teacher. Although Kento theoretically understood that to be able to express ideas in English to others should be one of the foreign language learners' long-term goals, with no good model to underpin his ideal teaching, he could not make it happen in his own teaching. Here, I refer back to the very first quote of Kento's provided in Chapter 1:

> Making a lesson plan using content-based instruction was extremely difficult for me. No matter how much I thought, I couldn't make any progress, only time passing by. What you have never experienced as a student is very difficult to master, I guess. (Kento, Fourth interview)

As Kento's quote indicates, he gave a similar comment on content-based instruction during the fourth interview.

Kento's case is in one sense similar to many practical learning contexts in ITE, such as Holligan's (1997) case study. Holligan (1997: 548) argues that student teachers are often implicitly forced to conform to 'implicit professional norms governing acceptable thought and behaviour expected of teachers' through contact with school teachers. Similarly, without a model to critically observe, analyse and emulate, he was unable to make further meaning of a learner-centred pedagogy in ELT, but was forced to imitate his supervising teacher's basic craft skills. Unfortunately, throughout his study in the interviews and journal entries, Kento did not mention using other mediational activities much, such as working with peers and co-constructing meaning with them as being influential on his professional development. Perhaps with the systematic support of providing more interaction with peers, he could have connected his theoretical understanding to an actual teaching context more successfully in becoming a subject specialist.

Yurika: Uncritical examination

Finally, the results of the study indicate that some student teachers in the study merely imitated teachers' teaching skills in order to survive the teaching practice, which Furlong and Maynard (1995) refer to as the third stage of survival as a teacher. As Yurika's case indicates (Chapter 6: Section 6.2), what differentiated unsuccessful cases from successful ones was the inability to reflect on theory and practice.

In contrast to Kento's case, Yurika, who was poor at reflection and originally had a strong belief in being a good homeroom teacher, in fact had a good model of a subject teacher during her teaching practice. At the start of the investigation, when asked what she meant by a student-centred classroom, she answered as follows with no indication of theoretical intervention:

C: Can you give me an example of a student-centred classroom?
Yurika: Well, to teach in an easy-to-understand manner, I think.
C: A teacher teaches in an easy-to-understand manner. This is equal to a student-centred class?
Yurika: … that's what I think. [Third interview]

In this excerpt, Yurika could not elaborate on what learner-centred pedagogy means, reflecting on what was presented in ITE courses with regard to a learner-centred approach in ELT. Later, during the fourth interview, Yurika discussed one of the journal articles that she was reading in a content-based course on foreign language learning and teaching, and 'being able to teach clearly' was raised again by Yurika as an important element of learner-centred pedagogy. Asked to elaborate on what she meant, she responded as follows:

C: Could you explain more about teaching in an easy-to-understand manner?
Yurika: Well, hmm …, in the book [that I read in the course], when teaching English, a class which encourages students to have interests in English is a class easy for students to understand.
C: A class which makes students become interested in English. That's what you mean by a class which is easy for students to understand?
Yurika: Yes … [Fourth interview]

However, while I observed her microteaching in the Methods course, her teaching was far from being learner centred and easy to understand, the details of which were elaborated on in Chapter 6. In her case, she was unable to refer back to theoretical knowledge, analyse and underpin her own teaching actions using her theoretical knowledge and make sense of her teaching in order to further improve it. As Funaki (2008) discusses, many student teachers in ITE in Japan lack problem-solving abilities due to lack of proper training for reflective teaching and support; Yurika is certainly one such example.

During my observation of her demonstration lesson in the teaching practice, however, Yurika actively interacted with her students and more or less successfully taught English. Prior to the teaching practice, Yurika noted that she wanted to teach in a learner-centred approach, which she defined as an easy-to-understand manner in the third interview. Returning back to the HEI after the teaching practice, she stated in the final interview that she tried to teach using a learner-centred approach. She was asked to cite a case and gave the following examples: asking her students to translate example sentences into Japanese in explicit grammar instruction and providing explanations in English so that they could think about what she was saying. She stressed that in both cases, she emulated how her supervisor taught and tried to encourage them to think on their own. Her understanding of learner-centred pedagogy showed a slight change; however, it was still far from the real sense of the term and, during the interview, again, she did not refer back to theoretical principles to analyse her teaching and support her understanding of the pedagogy.

During the final interview, Yurika also stated that, lacking confidence in her CK and PCK, it was good to have a model, her supervising teacher, with which to begin. As Borg (2003) posits, it should be stressed that her superficial behavioural changes did not necessarily mean that her teacher cognition was fully developed. As was previously discussed, emulation has often been criticised in the literature in ITE (Alexander, 2002; Furlong & Maynard, 1995; Roberts, 1998), as student teachers may be confined to a particular model of certain techniques or a particular school context without much difference in their teacher cognition. As opposed to Chie, who was able to experience a 'creative form of imitation' (Dunn, 2011: 56) because she tried to analyse her emulated teaching and make some improvements, *kaizen*, Yurika is certainly the case who was confined to what Furlong and Maynard (1995: 82) would call *stage three* of novice teachers' development: the stage of survival as a teacher. As the example indicates, without being able to make subject-related theories explicit and relate them to her teaching practice, she could only adopt 'the outward appearance of being a teacher' by uncritically imitating her supervising teacher's teaching behaviours in order to survive as a teacher.

Observation and emulation are one kind of mediation in human learning (Rogoff, 1995) through which novice teachers can transform from external and social interactions to internal and psychological elements (Johnson & Golombek, 2011). Why did most of the participants in this study resort to the mediational activities of observation and emulation to link theoretical knowledge to teaching practice, rather than directly experimenting in actual classroom practices with the theoretical principles they had acquired? Firstly, it should be pointed out again that there is the problem of the balance between theoretical and practical elements in ITE in Japan. The participating student teachers entered the ITE programme and began their coursework upon matriculation. The core courses on teacher knowledge in ELT, 'Methods Course I and II', were not offered until their third year, which they were required to register for two consecutive semesters prior to teaching practice.[1] The teaching practice was conducted during the spring semester of the fourth year, lasting only three weeks on average. As was previously mentioned, in comparison to the Post-Graduate Certificate in Education (PGCE) in the UK, where the ratio of theoretical and practical components is one to two, that of ITE in Japan is, roughly speaking, seven to one. This imbalance usually leads to student teachers' anxiety, since they obviously lack ample time for practical experiences, as many of the participants frequently stated during the investigation period. As a result, many participants in the study sought more informal practical experiences, such as volunteer teaching or *jyuku* teaching. The addition of informal experiences did not ease their anxiety, however. Their low confidence in teaching often resulted in seeking a model of an experienced teacher who they felt comfortable to emulate as a way to connect theory to practice, as also noted by Nagamine (2008).

Another issue that should be raised again regarding emulation is its positive cultural connotation in Japan. As formerly discussed, this is an approach deeply rooted in apprentice training in becoming professional in Japan. This practice is found not only in the industrial sectors and the traditional arts, but also in the teaching culture in Japan. In Japanese in-service teacher training, it is considered valuable to look for a model to further develop autonomy as a professional teacher. As Shimahara and Sakai (1992) point out, novice teachers in Japan are also expected to 'steal' ideas and skills from more experienced teachers by observing, emulating and interacting with them. Student teachers work through the process of emulation in personally meaningful ways 'in order to change the nature of their instructional activities' (Johnson, 2009: 39). This relates to what Chie and Mari mentioned as *kaizen* in Chapter 6, making improvements in their teaching after observation, emulation and reflection on emulated teaching. As the case of Chie's conceptual development of the learner-centred pedagogy shows, theoretical knowledge acquired at the HEI underpinned the participants' emulated teaching, leading to 'internalization' (Johnson, 2009: 18) and the establishment of a more solid foundation of teacher expertise. They made informed choices of what to observe and which skills to emulate, rather than merely imitating an implicit model, as was the case with, for example, the ethnographic study on student teachers in childcare by Alexander (2002). In this author's study, the participants developed a set of skills they saw and merely imitated in their specific settings due to the nature of competence-based training. As opposed to Alexander's study, many participants in the present study later reflected on their emulation and attempted to reconceptualise the teacher knowledge that they acquired at the HEI. This was also reflected in some of the ITE tutors' perspectives of professional development: Lecturer A who Chie took the Methods course from and the ITE lecturer who Kento admired. For instance, while observing Kento's microteaching on 5 December 2009, the ITE lecturer encouraged the student teachers during the feedback session to actively observe, emulate and 'steal' experts' craft in order to become more professional. Many of the participants in this study possessed this culturally endorsed value about the process of learning to teach in Japan.

Limitations of observation and emulation

As this section has discussed, most of the participating student teachers in this study attempted to employ observation and emulation as mediational tools to narrow the gap between theoretical knowledge and actual teaching practice and to make improvements in their teaching. The results indicate that observation and emulation are significant elements in the process of student teachers' early professional development in ITE in Japan. This is found to be consistent with what Dunn (2011: 56) calls a 'creative form of imitation'. However, as the cases in the study also indicate, willingness and capacity to critically observe and analyse others' teaching, make professional choices about which teaching skills to emulate and make continuous improvement are essential for developing their expertise. Without willingness or capacity, such as in the cases of Kento and Yurika, student teachers may simply copy others' teaching craft or may adhere to routines and continue traditional teaching approaches.

8.2 Impact of Peer Learning

Within the framework of sociocultural theory (Vygotsky, 1978), learning is conceptualised as participation, and social relations in the learning community are crucial for promoting learning. Similarly, in the present study, in addition to the mediational activities of observation and emulation, the role of other members of the learning community is significant as a 'mediational means' (Johnson, 2009: 25), and the student teachers in the present study are largely dependent on engagement with experienced teachers and peers. This implies that EFL student teachers' development of teacher expertise is achieved more effectively not only at the personal level through critical reflection on *individual* experiences

(Borg, 2006; Korthagen et al., 2001; Tsui, 2003), but also through social learning with *others*, members of the same learning community. *Others* in the present study include (1) former teachers (Chie/Nana/Kento/Mari); (2) experienced teachers in informal settings where they practised teaching as volunteer teachers (Chie/Kento); (3) experienced teachers in formal settings at the teaching practice sites (Chie/Nana/Kento/Yurika/Mari); (4) current ITE tutors and/or English teachers at the university (Chie/Kento/Mari); and (5) peers (Chie/Aya/Nana/Kento/ Mari). In this section, the focus will be on peer learning and the two functions of peers: co-meaning makers and model providers.

In Chapter 3, one of the major roles of peer learning in second language (L2) teacher education is explained that peers, who are not necessarily more capable experts, collectively go through cognitive struggles and develop collective identities as professional teachers (Nagamine, 2008). The findings of the study also indicate that the participating student teachers developed their expertise by actively observing and working with peers. The benefits of peers in the present study are twofold. Firstly, student teachers appreciate honest criticism on their teaching from peers, who are less intimidating than experienced teachers. This gives them opportunities to co-create meaning and reconstruct their theoretical knowledge prior to their practical experiences at school. Secondly, peers serve as a role model and as a resource for teaching skills of which they were not aware, and they are easier to emulate because they are at a similar professional level. Articulation and emulation can assist them to 'push the boundaries of their current state of cognitive development' (Johnson & Golombek, 2011: 8) and professional growth occurs through interactions with each other.

It should also be recognised that peer learning is found to be beneficial in the present study although it was neither explicitly incorporated in the curriculum nor forced by participation in this study, in contrast with some previous studies in which peer learning is more vigorously encouraged and incorporated in the curriculum. These studies report that it has beneficial effects on the professional development of student teachers. For example, in Nagamine's (2008) study, EFL student teachers are asked to keep a collaborative journal that helps them to reconstruct some of the theoretical concepts about language learning and teaching. In another study, Dunn (2011) concludes that the intervention of a workshop allows the trainees of L2 teachers to express newly learned theoretical concepts by connecting them with their personal experiences as well as sharing ideas with other trainees during small-group activities. Similarly, Childs (2011) argues that a support system in a master of arts in teaching English as a second language (MA TESL) programme, afforded through supervising professors and other trainees, mediates the trainees' conceptualisation of L2 teaching. Whether in writing or directly interacting, these studies indicate that cognitive and emotional support by members of the learning community, especially those who are similar to their cognitive, social and professional levels, can mediate novice teachers to conceptualise their learning and teaching more effectively (Murphey & Arao, 2001). What these studies do not fully reveal is how peer learning can be effectively facilitated when it is not explicitly incorporated into a curriculum, such as in this particular study. What the results suggest is that student teachers in ITE in Japan normally draw on peers and interaction with them; however, as Kento's case indicates earlier in this chapter, some student teachers do not take advantage of peers in mediating their learning-to-teach process.

Peers as co-meaning makers

Peers often serve as co-meaning makers who can provide constructive feedback in ITE. Johnson (2009: 25) also calls a peer in teacher education a 'temporary other' who can help a teacher or a student teacher verbalise and externalise his or her thinking and co-construct meanings in the process of learning to teach. In a similar way, the findings of the study suggest that all the participants found working with their peers, EFL student teachers in the ITE programme, as one solution to their problems. The benefits of having peers were mainly twofold. Firstly, the participating student teachers appreciated honest and investigative criticism from peers on their teaching. This is similar to what Clarke *et al.* (2014: 174) term 'providers of feedback', one way that supervising teachers participate in ITE. Feedback from peers differs from that of supervising teachers, however, in that there is no power relationship and thus it is less intimidating. Chie, Aya, Nana and Mari were particularly positive about the first kind of benefit of having peers in their learning-to-teach process. They believed that it gave them opportunities to co-construct their theoretical knowledge prior to their practical experiences at school. The following example of Nana illustrates how co-constructing meanings with peers and reflecting on their teaching contributed to her growth as a teacher.

Nana stated during the fourth interview that peer feedback often made her aware of others' ideas and perspectives that she lacked. For example, during her microteaching in autumn 2009, which I observed, she tried to implicitly introduce a new grammatical structure, *there + be*, using the names of fruits in English. According to Nana, since she assumed that her future students would not be familiar with the names of fruits in English, she first provided them with flashcards and stuck them on the blackboard. As she spent more time introducing the fruits than explaining the structure *there + be*, her peers commented later that the lesson was focused more on the introduction of the fruit terms and they did not have enough time to practise using the new grammatical structure, and thus, they did not feel that they had learned it. In this regard, Nana stated, 'it was illuminating for me' (Fourth interview) and it reminded her of the importance of *noticing* and *output* in second language acquisition (SLA) theory (Swain, 2005) that she learned at the HEI. She explained that in order for learners to pay attention to language form, the structure needs to be noticed and practised, which she failed to do during her microteaching. As this example shows, in the post-teaching practice interview, Nana stated that observing and discussing with her peers provided her with the opportunity to be aware of shortcomings in her knowledge base and enabled her to better clarify problems at an appropriate level. This is often observed in the case of peer learning in other disciplines, such as medical education training (Bulte *et al.*, 2007). Whatever the discipline is, according to Bulte *et al.* (2007: 583), the 'social and cognitive congruence' is important to peer learning and teaching because social and cognitive congruence enables student teachers to communicate with each other in a more informal way, coupled with an empathic attitude.

Aya also valued her peers' questions and advice. For example, her peers' feedback on the activities that she used in microteaching in autumn 2009, made her notice that a learner-centred class was one where students think on their own, with a minimum amount of teacher control, in order to promote learner autonomy (Fourth interview). During the microteaching that I observed, she team-taught with her classmate, one playing the role of a Japanese teacher while the other the role of an assistant language teacher. The game activity that they provided was fun, but there was no specific communicative purpose. This issue was later pointed out by her peers, which she reflected on during the fourth interview and commented that it gave her a chance to rethink the purposes and benefits of the learner-centred pedagogy. In the same interview, she also mentioned that she noticed through peer feedback that interaction with peers encouraged her to make clearer sense of the concept of learner-centred pedagogy.

Mari was another participant who positively valued her peers, who gave her honest criticism. The following example illustrates how Mari used her peers' criticism to make sense of her theoretical knowledge and grow as a subject teacher. In the second interview, Mari reported that she learned in the Methods course how teaching materials should be analysed, and that thorough materials analysis before lesson planning would lead to more successful teaching. This view was stressed again while observing experienced teachers' filmed teaching during the coursework; she noted in the second interview that in order to teach effectively, careful lesson planning and thorough preparation were essential, which in turn would contribute to students' effective learning. Thus, Mari stated that she carefully analysed teaching materials and planned a lesson before her microteaching in one of the ITE courses. During the feedback session after her microteaching, however, she received many critical comments from her peers despite her thorough lesson planning. As the following excerpt shows, her peers criticised her teaching by saying that it was lengthy and one-sided, and she looked more like a straight-laced teacher at a cram school, *jyuku*, which in fact reflected Mari's initial thought on her ideal teaching approach of conveying her CK to students:

> [My peers] gave me feedback, saying that [I] was fast-paced and seemed to be in a hurry. I didn't mean it, but ... if I spend more time [on each particular teaching point], I cannot teach [everything I planned] within 50 minutes. [Their comments reminded me that] I learned in the Methods course [before] there are some points you can [wait to] teach [till] later and other points you have to teach now. And I learned [from observing filmed teaching of an experience teacher] an experienced teacher can switch [between these two approaches] quickly. I quite agreed with [my peers' comments] and [they] made me think I need to have more practical experiences. (Second interview)

This excerpt indicates that Mari analysed her peers' comments on her teaching by referring back to what she gained in the coursework. She was able to positively reflect on her teaching based on her peers' criticism, since they shared similar backgrounds and experiences, rather than experienced teachers with more sophisticated teaching skills and longer teaching experiences. Mari's idea on peer learning also shows that she appreciated these sorts of co-learning experiences in ITE and she was encouraged to further explore her teacher thinking:

> I don' t [usually] teach in a context where I get such [critical] comments. This was the first time to be in an environment where [we] point out both negative and positive points with each other. Looking back, I mean, [my peers] tell me my good points, and as for negative points [of my teaching], they don't only point them out, but they tell me how I can improve them. It made a very positive impact on my [teaching], I believe. (Second interview)

Another example of the impact of peer learning on expertise development was Mari's case of using reading-aloud activities in microteaching. Reading-aloud tasks are very common language activities in ELT in Japan at the secondary school level (Tsuchiya, 2004), typically introduced to EFL student teachers as PCK in ITE. During the Methods course, Mari learned that there were numerous reading-aloud activities, which she decided to experiment with in her microteaching in the 2009 autumn semester. According to my field notes, she began a lesson with chorus reading as a class, then moved on to a task of reading aloud a text together slash by slash, called *chunk reading*. According to Tsuchiya (2004), chunk reading is a task in which students read sentences divided beforehand into smaller groups of meaningfully related words. Then, she provided another reading-aloud task called *chain reading* in which students took turns to read aloud the same text. Mari noted in the fourth interview after this microteaching experience that she voluntarily went to observe her supervising teacher's teaching prior to the teaching practice and emulated how her prospective supervising teacher taught using this chain-reading task. During her microteaching at the HEI, it was observed that she also rigorously followed the Ministry of Education, Culture, Sports, Science and Technology's (MEXT) new policy on the medium of instruction by teaching entirely in English, and used the approach in which she tried not to make her class too teacher dominant, since that was the main feedback she previously received from her peers.

According to Mari, the main reason why she used a series of reading-aloud tasks was to make her class more student centred since she believed reading-aloud tasks allowed students to use English. Contrary to her expectation, her peers gave critical feedback of her teaching again:

> [My peers] said, 'I didn't understand the purposes of doing these [reading-aloud] activities', or 'it wasn't clear whether you wanted to teach grammar, or to make [students] read intensively, or to focus on reading comprehension'. These comments made me rethink what I really wanted students to learn in this lesson. (Final interview)

As this excerpt illustrates, although Mari tried to reshape her teacher expertise by experimenting with what she learned and observed as PCK in her practice, her peers' sincere comments led to a new insight on how to use the tasks more effectively in actual teaching by clarifying the purposes of activities and using appropriate ones that meet the needs of a specific group of learners.

Mari valued the impact of emulating experienced teachers on her teaching in the post-teaching practice interview; she also valued working with her peers as a 'temporary other' (Johnson, 2009: 25). She equally valued observing her peers and being observed and given feedback by her peers, which provided her with further hints for making meaning of her own teaching. The supplementary data of the interview with Lecturer C support Mari's point. When asked about her perspective on peer learning on the process of learning to teach, Lecturer C responded that student teachers should be aware that there are other student teachers who can teach better than them, which should stimulate them to co-grow as a teacher. In other words, having a peer is essential in co-constructing the meanings of theory and alleviating the disparity between theory and practice, especially in the early stage of professional development. As Shulman and Shulman (2004: 267) rightly posit, student teachers learn to teach effectively when the process of learning to teach is supported by 'membership of a learning community'. As the examples of Nana, Aya and Mari indicate, in the case of the present study, cohort student teachers in the ITE coursework are certainly members of the learning community, in addition to former and experienced teachers.

Peers as model providers

With regard to the second function of peers, they can also serve as role models, a resource for teacher thinking and teaching skills of which student teachers were not previously aware. This is similar to what Clarke *et al.* (2014: 177) call 'modelers of practice', another way of supervising teachers' participation in ITE, although a modeller can be a peer in the present study, not only an experienced teacher. In having a peer as a model provider in their learning-to-teach process, two main benefits are observed in this study: while peers allow student teachers to have a third person's point of view, the skills of their peers are easier for them to emulate, since they are at a similar professional level. Peers are proximal and easier to identify with; thus, they can assist each other in making sense of their learning within each other's zone of proximal development (ZPD) more easily (Murphey & Arao, 2001).

Firstly, Chie and Aya occasionally reflected on how beneficial their peers were on their professional development, providing them with an opportunity to reflect on their own teaching with a third person's perspective. To cite an example, Aya stated in her journal that the existence of peers was motivating since they shared the same goal of becoming an English secondary school teacher, and that through observing and reflecting on how they taught, she could think about how she would teach and tackle problems in the same settings (Journal entry, 7 December 2009). Observing peers from an objective perspective was also mentioned by Chie. For example, in her journal, she argued that through observing her peers' microteaching, she noticed many issues in PCK, such as the volume of voice, how to summarise the main points and write them down neatly on the blackboard and how to teach grammar more effectively (Journal entry, 23 November 2009). She pointed out that being able to see teaching from a third person's viewpoint owing to peers was beneficial in assessing and correcting her own teaching behaviours as well as learning and integrating new techniques into her own teaching whenever they were possible for her to emulate. Chie made similar comments on the impact of peer learning in the fourth and fifth interviews as well.

The second benefit of peers as role-model providers is that their skills and thinking processes are easier for student teachers to replicate. As Weiten *et al.* (1991: 46) posit, in children's learning, emulation often takes place when there is somewhat of a similarity between a model and a learner, and when a learner sees emulating the model 'leading to positive outcomes'. For instance, children tend to imitate same-sex role models rather than opposite-sex ones. Similar phenomena were observed in other experimental studies of the impact of peers on learning (Bulte *et al.*, 2007; Johnston, 1992; Murphey & Arao, 2001). For example, on the basis of the ZPD theory (Vygotsky, 1962), Murphey and Arao (2001) argue that English language learners in Japan were encouraged to further learn English by peers close to their social level and/or age level with similar past and/or present experiences and whom they respect. This means that when learners observe peers who succeed in a task and when they see that they too have the ability to do similarly, they become motivated to emulate their peers' performance.

The foregoing studies imply that confident people can readily emulate models of excellence with highly skilful craft, whereas learners with less self-confidence and experience could also profit from observing same-level or slightly higher-level performances. As Murphey and Arao (2001) rightly claim, peers make student teachers aware that certain successes are possible in their teaching, which allows them to try certain teaching behaviours with hopeful expectations. Both Nana and Mari actively sought role models of peers as a way to narrow the gap between theory and practice and develop their expertise.

For instance, Nana stated in her journal that observing a student teacher of German who taught entirely in German encouraged her to use more gestures in her own teaching. She realised that gestures were helpful for junior high school students to learn vocabulary in context and understand the meanings of unknown words in English as well (Journal entry, 15 December 2009). She further commented in the same journal entry that she learned in a content-based class of SLA theory at the HEI that a teacher needs to help language learners associate new words with a meaningful context, to which they can apply them later on (Brown, 2007b), and she came to notice through observing her peer's teaching that gesturing was certainly an effective way of vocabulary learning. According to Mari, as using gestures in vocabulary teaching was easy enough for her to replicate in her own teaching, she emulated the technique in her own microteaching later on.

Reflecting on her professional development during the fourth interview, Mari also noted that 'what I changed most in the autumn semester was I tried to "steal" good teaching skills of peers and emulate them in my own teaching. I knew this was effective, but it was probably the first time that I actually did this' (Fourth interview). This excerpt shows that through observing peers' teaching, she came to realise her peers' teaching techniques and thinking processes were available for her to easily replicate. When asked to offer specific examples, she mentioned teaching skills such as how to give instructions for certain language activities or how to explain the purposes of them to students. For instance, she observed how one student teacher introduced a reading-aloud task during his microteaching. He read the text out loud together with the students, which she found encouraging, especially for less-able students. She thought it could lower their anxiety, which she learned as one of learners' affective factors (Brown, 2007a) in one of the content-based courses in SLA theories at the HEI. She understood that the factor of anxiety plays a major affective role in SLA. In fact, it can be said that the combination of theoretical intervention and peer learning contributed to her understanding of the benefits of a reading-aloud task. Regardless of her reconstructed understanding of the task, however, when she emulated his teaching skill during her microteaching, she expressed later in the fourth interview that she realised that the volume of students' voices was actually quite low and it was difficult for her as a teacher to assess how they were reading if she read the text together. Emulating her peer's teaching made Mari aware that she needed to lower her voice to assess students' chorus reading more effectively during the task. According to Mari, this is one of the *kaizen*s she was able to make through emulating her peers' teaching.

Limitations of peer learning

The examples in this chapter highlight one of the mediational means that the participating student teachers sought out to restructure their theoretical concepts and knowledge bases. What they mentioned was their cohort student teachers in ITE, other members of the same learning community. Without being forced to, most of the participants relied on each other since they were like-minded. Peers' sincere and critical feedback helped to facilitate learning and enabled them to articulate their underlying rationale for their teaching behaviour, without feeling intimidated. Most of the participants also showed a willingness to emulate each other's teaching behaviour, since they found it within the realm of possibility, and could reflect on it to internalise their thinking and make improvements in their expertise. As Johnson (2009: 23) argues, student teachers 'collectively struggle through issues that are directly relevant to their professional lives' and this research also suggests that peer interaction and learning is an important aspect in teacher education. The limitations of peer learning need to be discussed, however, in order to explain the unsuccessful cases of Kento and Saori.

In one major respect, peer learning in ITE could be limited. Since peer learning is not systematically provided by the ITE curriculum in Japan, in interacting with cohort student teachers who are at a similar professional level, student teachers may choose an inappropriate model or teaching skill to emulate. Their feedback may also be intuitive, not underpinned by theoretical knowledge, or simply inappropriately articulated. Feedback or role models provided by student teachers may simply depend on what they experienced themselves as learners with no real understanding of the underlying principles that inform them. Thus, as Kento and Saori's cases have shown, some student teachers may be reserved about simply imitating peers' teaching. As Nagamine (2008) points out in his study on student teachers in ITE, some have doubts about emulating others without analysing the situation and teacher thinking behind the stage. Some might also feel confused or vulnerable about peers' intuitive comments, as Saori's case indicated earlier in this chapter. This is largely due to student teachers not usually being explicitly trained to give constructive feedback and provide a model in the ITE curriculum in Japan.

8.3 Reflections on Effective Mediational Tools

This chapter highlights the major research findings of the study in presenting the mediational tools that affect the participants' professional development. The participating student teachers struggled to seek ways in which to develop their teacher expertise, mainly due to the imbalance between theory and practice in ITE in Japan. As the educational literature has already revealed, three factors – former and current experiences as a learner, theoretical knowledge acquired in ITE and practical experiences – are influential to a certain degree, but the present study finds that they did not function well in themselves. Instead, the participating student teachers in this study resorted to mediational activities (observation and emulation) and mediation by others (peer learning) to link theoretical knowledge and practical teaching experiences effectively.

As for Research Question 4 (Chapter 1: Section 1.3), 'Do student teachers perceive that there is a gap between theory and practice?', for the student teachers in the present study, this was definitely the case. All participants in the study continuously saw the divide between the two elements in ITE at different stages of their professional development. With regard to Research Question 5, 'If student teachers see it as a problem, how do they mitigate the disparity between theory and practice?', the teacher expertise models of teacher trainees, such as the studies of Borg (2003), Roberts (1998) and Tsui (2003), will be revisited first, in order to delve further into the complex processes of EFL student teachers' development in this section.

The literature on teacher education has told us that the process of learning to teach is, to a large extent, an *individual* process of cognitive development and behavioural change informed by various factors. The factors usually include student teachers' prior knowledge and experiences, drawing on both generalised knowledge, such as language acquisition or language learning and teaching in the case of ELT, and contextualised knowledge of school and classroom circumstances. Student teachers are also expected to reflect on their own teaching behaviours and explain their professional decisions in light of the aforementioned elements in order to reconstruct theories and improve practical skills. For example, Tsui's (2003: 261) empirical study on English as a second language (ESL) expert/non-expert teachers, argues that teacher expertise is a dialogical interaction 'between the theorization of practical knowledge through reflection and conscious deliberation, and the transformation of "formal knowledge" into practical knowledge', within a teacher herself or himself, and practical experience is essential for such interaction to take place. Based on the vast amount of literature on second and foreign language teaching, Borg (2003) also concludes that language teachers' cognitions and practices are mutually informed and transformed as they accumulate experience. In his framework, teacher cognitions are informed by teachers' former schooling experiences, professional coursework as well as contextual factors. In line with these two previous studies, Roberts (1998) describes a constructivist learning-to-teach model of typical ITE programmes for language teachers in the UK. In his model, student teachers are to make choices, test them out and reflect on their knowledge and practices, drawing on both decontexualised and contextualised knowledge bases. What all these models have in common is a highly self-exploratory and hypothesis-testing process in which teacher trainees are expected to reconstruct their theories and values through reflecting on their *own* knowledge bases and practices.

Such a constructivist and experiential process of language teacher education, however, does not fully tell us what it means to socialise into and become a member of the learning community of teachers and how other members contribute to novice teachers' socialisation into the community. In contrast, within the framework of sociocultural theory (Vygotsky, 1978), the present study has addressed that the personal pedagogical practice of teacher expertise should be reinterpreted more from the perspective of a 'social interactionist dimension' (Shulman & Shulman, 2004: 267), by adding another layer of observing and emulating *others* in the learning community and interacting with them in the process. These elements are particularly important in the process of learning to teach in ITE in Japan because of the curriculum constraints. As previously noted, the curriculum provides only a limited amount of formal practical training, the length of which is not enough for student teachers to dialogically engage in the interaction of theory and practice on their own.

In this qualitative study, examining the growth of EFL student teachers in ITE in Japan, it became clear that participants developed their expertise in distinctive ways, slightly different from novice teachers in the previous literature, which provided us with a new expertise development model (see Figure 8.1). In the early part of the first phase of the main study, without much opportunity to practise teaching, the participants were largely informed by their prior perspectives based on former and current schooling experiences as well as theoretical principles that they acquired in the ITE coursework. By the latter part of the first phase, their theoretical framework was further shaped by informal practical experiences, which in many cases they sought voluntarily, in addition to the aforementioned two constructs. At this stage, some of the participating student teachers actively sought a role model in experienced teachers or peers and experimented with emulation in their pseudo-teaching contexts, often with interaction with them to discuss and reflect on their teaching. Peers served as providers of critical and honest feedback on their teaching in a non-threatening manner, as well as being role models who could provide craft skills and thinking processes, challenging but possible to replicate because they were at a similar professional level (Murphey & Arao, 2001). In the meantime, the student teachers did not stop being English language learners (Kento in Chapter 6: Section 6.2, for instance), so they also learned from interacting with their own English teachers in an English for academic purposes (EAP) classroom at the university, which added an additional aspect to their identity as an English teacher who is a non-native speaker of the target language.

At the stage of teaching practice, which took place as the second phase of the main study, many participants had clear purposes when interacting with experienced teachers, largely due to informal practical experiences. Furthermore, through observation, emulation and reflection, most of them were able to further shape their theories and perspectives. In this new expertise development model, the following mediational means – observation, emulation and peer learning – were actively utilised as a springboard for connecting theory that they possessed to their practical teaching experiences.

According to Johnson (2009), there is increasing evidence of the role played by peers in the process of learning to teach in teacher education. In line with Johnson's theory, the results of this study also reveal that peers in the same learning community can help student teachers to verbalise and internalise their thinking and co-construct meanings in the process of learning to teach. Furthermore, Roberts (1998: 185) suggests that teacher trainees are supported by 'regular discussions with supervising teachers and peers' in the constructive model of learning to teach, while in this study most of the participating student teachers learned to teach not just through sharing ideas with others; the process was more complex, incorporating observation, emulation and discussion and reflection on their emulated teaching into teacher expertise. This implies that teacher expertise is developed more effectively not at the personal level through critical reflection on individual experiences, but through learning and interacting *with others*, the members of the same learning community. In line with Pachler *et al.* (2007), in relation to reflection, the findings of this study also indicate that an additional layer of reflection on the interaction of individuals within the professional community needs to be added to the more traditional teacher expertise models.

The new model of the development of student teachers' expertise in the present study is congruent with the sociocultural theory of learning, which considers learning as a socially mediated process that occurs as people participate in cultural and social activity (Johnson, 2009; Johnson & Golombek, 2011). Within this framework, the present study has found that learning to teach in ITE in Japan is a process that takes place as novice teachers participate both in pseudo and real teaching contexts with the assistance of more experienced teachers as well as peers at a similar professional level. This also implies that in both teacher education programmes and school settings, researchers and educators should create environments in which they support and accommodate student teachers and let them co-construct values, understandings, performances and reflections.

Figure 8.1 is a schematic representation of a dialogical process of the theory and practice of EFL student teachers in ITE in Japan. It represents an update on Figure 4.1 in Chapter 4 in five ways:

(1) it situates the theorisation of teacher expertise at the centre within a community of learners;
(2) it includes student teachers' prior schooling experiences as a student as well as on-going experiences as a language learner[2];
(3) it adds an element of *others* (experts and peers) to the stage of observation, emulation, discussion and reflection to reflect the fact that these mediational activities are often collaboratively done with *others* in the learning community[3];
(4) it adds practical experiences in a broader sense to the stage of observation to reflect the fact that student teachers find a model and learn from informal practical experiences prior to the teaching practice;

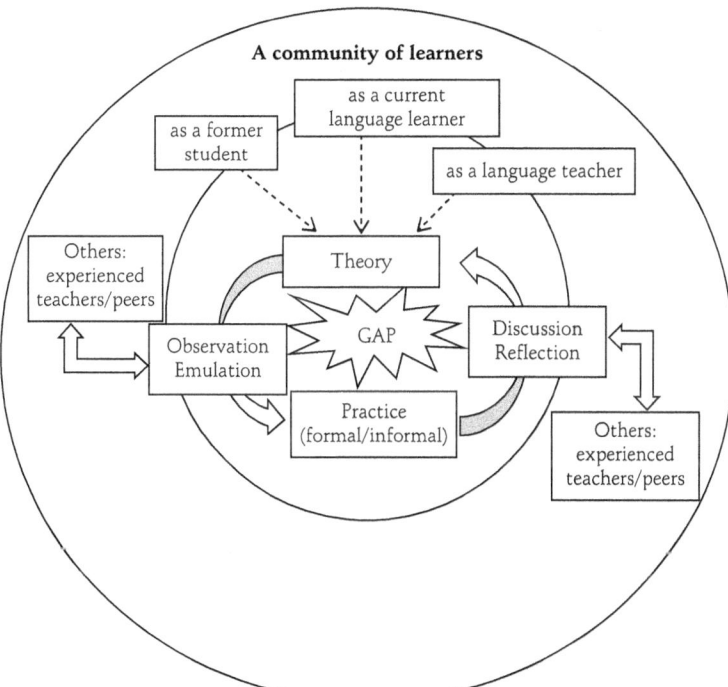

Figure 8.1 A dialogical process of theory and practice revisited

(5) it clarifies the most frequently used mediational means that connect theory and practice as observation and emulation of experienced teachers at both formal and informal settings as well as peers, and discussion and reflection on their teaching behaviours collaboratively done with experienced teachers and peers.

The relation between theory and practice in EFL student teachers' professional development processes is not straightforward. In the present study, since the participating student teachers were at the beginning stage of their professional careers, all of them experienced modulating perspective shifting in their expertise development. In addition, with the help of mediational activities such as observation, emulation and reflection, and temporary others, they struggled to make sense of their learning. In other words, they tried to continuously mitigate the discrepancy between theoretical knowledge bases and practical experiences; theories and concepts that the student teachers first acquired in the ITE coursework were externalised, and then internalised, by former schooling experiences, current experiences as a language learner, observing and emulating experienced teachers and peers, sharing ideas with them and actually experimenting with the ideas and skills in both formal and informal practical situations. The present study also reveals that EFL student teachers' process of learning to teach is a continuous and dialogical process of positioning themselves professionally in a 'community of practice' (Wenger, 2005) and a community of learners, such as cohort student teachers, supervising teachers and teacher educators. Membership of a community of practice enabled the participants to explore their expertise by interacting and sharing ideas with others; as a result, professional growth occurred through interactions with peers and experts, which is what Johnson (2009) describes as the interactive aspect of the ZPD. However, as the findings of the study also indicate, the process of EFL student teachers' professional development is not straightforward, as each mediational activity found in this study was not sufficient in itself, each had some limitations. Thus, it is necessary to re-evaluate the system of ITE programmes in Japan, which should provide a combination of various mediational activities and training systematically.

Notes

(1) The ITE curriculum at the research site was revised in the 2013 academic year and student teachers are now required to take three core courses (Methods I, II and III) on teacher knowledge.
(2) Dotted lines in Figure 8.1 indicate that the influence of these elements on student teachers' professional development is not as strong in comparison to the mediational activities of observation and emulation as well as interaction with peers.
(3) Double-headed arrows in Figure 8.1 show that they mutually construct assistance.

9 A Critical Reflection: Professional Development in Initial Teacher Education in Japan

> In writing journal entries [for this study], I was surprised to find out that there were many clues and hints [for improving my teaching] in daily living that I wanted to think and write about. Also, when I was interviewed [for this study], [I had an opportunity] to look anew at and express my thoughts on what kind of a teacher I want to become, which I found very rewarding. While expressing my thoughts, I realised myself that I wanted to become such and such a teacher, or when I sorted the cards [during the card-sorting task], [it turned out to be] an opportunity for me to think even more keenly on which qualities are important for me [as a good English teacher]. Well, participating in this project was like taking a one-year-and-a-half-long special course [of professional development]. I felt as if I took the [professional development] course on my own will in order to motivate myself and become a better teacher.'
> (Chie, Final interview)

This qualitative study began with the aim of exploring student teachers' perceptions and experiences during their initial teacher education (ITE) in becoming a more autonomous secondary school English teacher in an English as a foreign language (EFL) context in Japan. As the present study indicated, the quantitative imbalance between theory as represented by higher education institutes (HEIs) and real-world practice that is experienced in school is one of the major issues that ITE in Japan currently faces. This study also clearly highlights the lack of clarity in the goals and standards for EFL student teachers in Japan during ITE as another issue. On the one hand, student teachers are expected to become good subject teachers who are proficient enough and can conduct their classes in English, who can raise their students' overall English language skills to respond to the demands of the international community. On the other hand, they are also expected to become good homeroom teachers with good behaviour management skills because teachers in Japan are considered responsible for the holistic development of their students. These issues are found to be particularly problematic. For example, for some participants, the imbalance between the university-based part of the ITE curriculum and practical teaching experiences resulted in feelings of anxiety, vulnerability and confusion. The latter problem, unclearly defined goals in ITE, also led some student teachers to a dilemma between which goals to reach, whether to be a good subject teacher or a good homeroom teacher. The curriculum content, which lacked consistency and coherence at the HEI and during the school-based practices, also contributed to the variability in the student teachers' experiences in ITE.

A case-study approach was employed in this study to examine student teachers' individual experiences in developing their teacher expertise, while facing these problems in the current Japanese ITE system. A close analysis of the qualitative data resulted in the development of a dialogical process model of filling the gap between theoretical knowledge provided by ITE and practical teaching experiences in the school of the student teachers. As the dialogical model shows, student teachers in ITE in Japan try to employ various mediational activities, such as observation, emulation and peer interaction, in mediating their teacher learning and mitigating the disparity between theoretical knowledge and practical teaching experiences.

What emerged from the qualitative data, therefore, was the student teachers' struggle to adjust and apply their theoretical knowledge bases to their practical teaching experiences on their own. Without systematic and consistent support from the ITE programme and the supervising teachers during school-based practice, the participants struggled to find solutions in mediating their teacher learning, which resulted in the variability of their experiences in school-based teaching practice. Hence, in this final chapter, the four elements in ITE that are found to be influential on the participants' early professional development (observation and emulation, reflective practices, cohort student teachers and supervising teachers) are revisited in order to explore how to provide more practical and systematic support in the ITE programme as well as from supervising teachers so that student teachers' professional development will be more efficiently enhanced.

9.1 Student Teachers' Struggle in Narrowing the Theory/Practice Gap

Developing teacher autonomy is an ultimate goal in teacher education. An autonomous teacher is one who is willing and capable of self-directing their own professional development. Self-regulated professional development is possible and effective for experienced in-service teachers who have theoretical knowledge bases to draw on and places to apply their knowledge and skills. Student teachers often enter an ITE programme without sufficient knowledge bases and practical experiences of English language teaching to draw on, and even less ability and fewer opportunities to apply theory to the practice of teaching. Systematic opportunities thus must be given to student teachers through their teacher education programmes to assist their early professional development.

As was stated earlier, an essential problem of the current ITE system in Japan clearly highlighted in this study is the lack of opportunities for enough practical teaching experiences in school. Student teachers are still at the early phase of the process of laying the foundations for their future professional development, not always equipped with capacities and willingness to self-direct their own learning yet. Therefore, they often find it difficult to apply the theoretical knowledge they acquire in ITE to practical teaching in a classroom, especially because few opportunities are provided for them to experiment with their own teaching and to practise analysing and reflecting on it.

In struggling to find ways to mediate their teacher learning in a short period of time, student teachers find observing and emulating other members of the same learning community beneficial and helpful. This approach has been a much appreciated and accepted element in professional development in Japan. It is beneficial because student teachers can vicariously experience what others are doing and thinking through emulating another teacher's practice. It is also helpful because they can emulate what they think works well in a particular teaching context, and thus, benefit from the teaching practice, rather than through trial and error on their own, or making repeated unsuccessful efforts. The findings of the study also suggest that peer learning, especially with cohort student teachers in the ITE programme, is another mediational tool actively sought by student teachers. Peers can play an important role as co-meaning makers as well as model providers in ITE. As they support and learn from each other, student teachers can collectively develop their expertise as well as their confidence.

However, the results of the study point to the fact that the content and quality of student teachers' struggle is idiosyncratic, which results in varied ITE experiences. Some student teachers are more proactive in finding a good model to emulate, reflecting on their teaching or objectively analysing others' feedback on their teaching; thus, the struggle they experience successfully leads to some improvements, *kaizen*, in their teaching. In contrast, some student teachers struggle because they have not yet cultivated critical reflective skills, or they cannot find a good model to emulate, or they are less able to examine and value others' critical feedback. As the study illustrated, the notion of reflective practices is not so familiar in Japan; thus, some students experience feelings of anxiety, confusion or vulnerability when asked to self-critique and reflect on, or be critiqued during their ITE experiences, which limits their early professional development.

Unsuccessful experiences in student teachers' early professional development are not entirely due to them, however. Failure to find an appropriate solution for mediating teacher learning is not necessarily their fault, since they are still at the early stage of laying a sound base for their future professional development. Their unsuccessful experiences are, rather, due to the shortcomings of the pre-service teacher training programmes, not student teachers' inherent characteristics. Novice teachers who begin the socialisation process of teacher development are peripheral members of the professional learning community. They may not possess sufficient theoretical knowledge to draw on, or possess teaching routines and skills to experiment, or the critical reflective skills to analyse and scrutinise them.

At the same time, it should be noted that interventions that the student teachers in this study participated in, such as writing journal entries by reflecting on microteaching and the ITE coursework, actually encouraged some of them to develop their expertise, as Chie's quote at the start of this chapter suggests. This confirms that more systematic intervention and coherent support must be given to student teachers within the ITE curriculum in Japan. This leads us to suggest that the conditions of the ITE system in Japan ought to be reconsidered. In the following sections, I would like to suggest the kinds of support and mediational activities that should be included – and in a more coherent way – as components of the ITE curriculum.

The meaning of observation and emulation in ITE in Japan

Many researchers and teacher educators have expressed deep-seated scepticism about emulation through observing others. This form of emulation is viewed as a learning strategy that does not necessarily facilitate critical analysis and reflection of teaching, due to beliefs and experiences formed while observing teachers as a learner. However, as the results of this study indicate, the notion of emulation is crucial as a mediational tool in student teachers' early professional development in ITE in Japan. Student teachers actively seek someone who they can observe by focusing on the skills or routines that they wish to emulate and analyse. Observation and emulation are actively used as an essential tool in mediating their learning-to-teach process. The cultural specificity of emulation is also often recognised by ITE tutors as well as supervising teachers.

Rather than directly experimenting with their theoretical knowledge in their teaching, student teachers start their training by observing and emulating the English language teaching strategies of experienced teachers or peers, even when they are not encouraged to do so. Having a model to emulate is beneficial, particularly when student teachers find themselves lacking in confidence and experience. It should also be pointed out that using emulation as a learning strategy does not mean that student teachers are simply uncritical observers, as Chie's successful case of reconstructing the concept of learner-centred pedagogy suggests. This supports Dunn's (2011: 56) 'creative form of imitation' of second language student teachers; novice teachers do not simply imitate experienced teachers' language teaching skills and behaviours, but rather, they try to *transform* what experienced teachers offer them as they experiment and analyse emulated teaching in particular teaching contexts. Emulation can be one possible tool that assists student teachers in promoting their learning, examining their understanding of theoretical concepts in English language teaching and developing their teaching skills.

Emulation is influential in student teachers' early professional development in Japan, since seeking a model in the community to emulate has long been culturally endorsed in the country as part of the professional development process. Emulating the teaching skills and thinking processes of experts is considered a powerful mediational tool for learning, not only in the arts and business industry but also in Japanese in-service teacher training. Thus, student teachers in ITE in Japan are also often implicitly encouraged to identify teaching behaviours and strategies used by others as practices they can try out in their own teaching, which in turn leads to building greater self-confidence.

However, it should be remembered that the mediational activities of observation and emulation are not usually explicitly provided by ITE programmes but are implicitly employed at student teachers' own discretion. Even when some supervising teachers ask student teachers to observe and emulate experienced teachers during the school-based training, they do not specifically instruct which aspects or skills of teaching to focus on, nor do they explicitly provide a model for student teachers to emulate. This is largely due to the cultural connotation of emulation in Japan, by which experienced teachers treat novice teachers as equals and do not offer any explicit advice or guidance; instead, novice teachers are expected to 'steal' ideas and skills from experienced teachers by observing, emulating and interacting with them. Therefore, novice teachers in Japan are not provided with any training on emulation for critical analysis and graduated assistance by the ITE curriculum, which may promote the implicit process of 'apprenticeship of observation' (Lortie, 1975).

Ample opportunities for emulation through microteaching and training of reflective practices on emulated teaching at HEIs prior to school-based practical teaching experiences will greatly benefit student teachers, especially when there is only a limited amount of school-based teaching practice, such as in Japan. Emulated teaching will also be a good starting point for student teachers with lower confidence and fewer prior practical teaching experiences. Furthermore, with explicitly assisted guidance from the ITE programme, student teachers could learn to focus on particular aspects of teaching and to analyse their emulated teaching later by drawing on the theoretical concepts they acquire in ITE. Then, emulation can be a powerful and effective mediational activity and can be increasingly utilised in reconciling the divide between those theoretical principles provided by ITE and teaching practice in school. Having not been given explicit opportunities to critically analyse their emulated teaching, student teachers may intuitively emulate others whose teaching skills they find easy and familiar to emulate, and this may simply lead to the reproduction of current practices of English language teaching in Japan (i.e. focusing on grammatical forms to succeed in an entrance examination). Therefore, the mediational activities of observation and emulation *per se* are limited, if not detrimental to student teachers' early professional development.

The difficulty of developing reflective practices in ITE in Japan

Since the necessity of training in reflective practices in ITE in Japan was mentioned in the previous section, another issue that should be raised is the difficulty of developing reflective practices – a difficulty that some student teachers faced during this study. As discussed earlier, one of the strategies that the participating student teachers in ITE in Japan regularly employed as they struggled to apply their theoretical knowledge base to practical teaching contexts was the use of mediational means, namely observing, emulating and interacting with other teachers (including student teachers). However, as the results have shown, some used these mediational activities without reflecting on the theory and rational underlying their emulated instruction. In other words, they simply emulated others' teaching in order to survive the teaching practice, without reflecting on the deeper theoretical basis of that practice, or critically assessing its value as pedagogical practice. This also means that they are still unaware that the teaching they emulate is not necessarily the best practice, because it might not work well in other teaching contexts and what works for experienced teachers may not work for novice teachers.

Learning to make professional judgements about, and critically analyse, one's teaching is one of the primary goals of teacher professional development, and the development of reflective skills is essential for attaining this ability. With regard to this issue, one challenge that novice teachers face is that, as many prior research studies in ITE have revealed, upon entry into the first phase of professional development, novice teachers are expected to be autonomous to some extent, already equipped with reflective and critical thinking skills. In many ITE programmes outside Japan, they are also provided with extensive opportunities to practise and reflect on their teaching, regardless of the value their programmes attach to theoretical foundations. The implication is that even from the earliest stages of their teacher development programmes, student teachers are introduced to the notion of reflective practice as the medium through which theory and actual practice are effectively mitigated. Consequently, they become aware that developing the cognitive capacities to self-reflect is essential to their early professional development. Reflection is also fairly personal; thus, the responsibility to improve one's teaching is in effect placed on the *individual* student teacher.

However, the findings from the present study provide some conflicting evidence. As Chie's quote at the start of this chapter indicates, being provided with an opportunity to explicitly reflect on teaching practices and the underlying theories and principles (i.e. interviews and journal writing) was greatly appreciated by some participating student teachers in this study. This implies that student teachers in ITE in Japan may find it difficult to narrow the gap between the theoretical knowledge they acquire in ITE courses and their practical teaching experiences in schools, without training or opportunities for reflective practices as a required element of the ITE curriculum at HEIs.

Thus, another essential problem of the ITE system in Japan highlighted in this study is the lack of a systematic and consistent approach to reflective practices, largely due to the limited amount of school-based training in ITE. In Japan, even when student teachers are naturally competent in critical reflection, they do not have many opportunities to implement their thoughts into teaching, and to reflect on their own teaching either through self-reflection or discursive encounters with other practising teachers. Additionally, during informal teaching experiences outside of the ITE curriculum (i.e. teaching at *jyuku* as part-time teachers or working as volunteer teaching assistants) that student teachers voluntarily seek out in order to make up for the imbalance between theory and practice, it is a challenge for them to reflect on their teaching and fill the gap between theoretical principles and practical teaching experiences, without assistance from others.

At the same time, as the findings of this study suggest, the limitations of reflective practices in ITE in Japan should also be realised by teacher educators at HEIs. As discussed earlier, when the term *reflection* is translated into Japanese, it often connotes a negative form of reflection, rather than focusing on the aspect of generating *newer* insights and perspectives due to reflection. Therefore, when the notion of reflective practices is explicitly introduced in the ITE curriculum, a positive form of reflection should be emphasised, through which student teachers are expected to confront, analyse and challenge their pre-existing perspectives and discuss alternatives for making improvements in their teaching. Furthermore, while the benefits of reflection on teacher development are great, as many previous research studies in teacher education have suggested (Atkinson, 2004; Kojima, 2008), this study also suggests that it is effective only after student teachers have acquired a certain degree of capacity to critically reflect on their professional practice. They also need to acquire a certain degree of theoretical knowledge to draw on before they are able to practise structuring, verbalising and restructuring their teaching practices.

Reflection itself is a very individual and subjective activity, and the impact of reflective practices on student teachers in ITE in Japan is an area of research that is as yet underexplored. The practices, *per se*, should not always be assumed an appropriate role in ITE, as other mediational activities are also limited in themselves. How the ITE curriculum can provide more systematic and consistent support in developing student teachers' reflective skills needs to be further investigated.

The impact of others in ITE in Japan

In order to effectively assist student teachers in ITE in Japan in mitigating the gap between theoretical knowledge bases and actual teaching contexts, explicitly providing mediational activities such as observation and emulation – rather than simply asking students to reflect on and critique their own teaching independently – is useful for, and even positively sought by, student teachers at early stages of their professional development. These mediational activities are likely to involve *others* in the same learning community; they provide models to emulate as well as honest and critical feedback on teaching. They can also collectively develop a sense of teacher identity through practising reflection by analysing teaching contexts, as well as going back to their theoretical understandings to underpin their teaching behaviours, develop pedagogical practices and transform their perspectives of English language teaching. This is one way in which student teachers are able to practise and develop their reflective skills.

In one sense, one can draw an interesting parallel between the process of learning to teach and the process through which a foreign language learner progresses to become an autonomous, communicative foreign language speaker, with the help of others in the same learning community. Beginning-level language learners, without confidence or sufficient language skills to articulate their ideas, should first be provided with clear and appropriate instructions as well as a certain degree of topic or subject-matter knowledge so as to feel comfortable in actively participating in communicative language activities. In other words, they cannot engage fully and effectively in language activities without appropriately scaffolded support by teachers or peers and plenty of practice. Similarly, novice teachers, who are not yet ready to be independent teachers, without confidence and significant teaching experience and skills, need not only the theoretical underpinnings provided by HEIs but also some explicit guidance and assistance. In many cases, assistance can be provided by a 'temporary other' (Johnson, 2009: 2), as novice teachers try to articulate their thoughts, reconstruct their personal knowledge and engage in the learning-to-teach process.

A 'temporary other' should be *temporary*, however, since student teachers need to develop the capacity to self-direct their own teaching; thus, assistance and guidance from others should be lessened as student teachers feel more confident. Just as a foreign language learner needs to develop the capacity to self-direct their own learning, as student teachers gain experience, they need to become more independent and responsible for their teaching through the use of reflection. It should also be pointed out that support by others is fluid but can be random at the same time. Since peer support is not usually strategically employed and scaffolded as a required component of the ITE curriculum, student teachers are likely to depend on peers randomly, which can result in variability in their experiences in ITE.

Therefore, the ITE system in Japan needs to recognise, from a sociocultural perspective, that the use of peer learning as a mediational tool for linking theoretical knowledge bases to actual teaching practices should be more strategic and purposeful as an on-going intervention. Student teachers ought to be trained to give constructive feedback, and to be open to and flexible about critical feedback from others that may not match their own expectations or perspectives on teaching. Support by others should be levelled against the goal of cognitive development within the ITE curriculum, so that novice teachers learn to develop their agency and become more confident professionals, on their own.

The impact of supervising teachers in ITE in Japan

The variability of student teachers' experiences partly resulted from the influence of their supervising teachers. This means that student teachers in ITE are greatly influenced by their supervising teachers, along with their perspectives and attitudes towards teaching practice. When a supervising teacher prioritises classroom and behaviour management over subject teaching, a student teacher perhaps comes to focus more on the development of behaviour management skills during his or her practical experiences in school. In addition, when a supervising teacher is able to provide a good role model explicitly as a subject specialist, a student teacher can learn a great deal about subject teaching. However, if a supervising teacher asks a student teacher to observe and emulate experienced teachers, but he or she does not provide any specific teaching points or skills to pay attention to, then a student teacher may emulate their teaching intuitively.

The foregoing examples indicate that what is lacking in ITE in Japan is the view of a supervising teacher during the teaching practice as a mentor, which is a critical aspect of teacher training in many discourses of ITE outside Japan. For example, in the UK, as ITE has come to focus much more on student teachers' school-based experiences, the role of mentors has also been given more importance, whose functions are often described using various metaphors such as a 'reflective coach' (Tomlinson, 1995) and a 'critical friend' (Furlong & Maynard, 1995). In such a discourse, mentor teachers ought to provide models as continuous learners themselves in their professional development. They need to be trained to assist student teachers in analysing existing classroom routines and practices, discussing alternatives and reflecting on the theory underlying their instruction. In this way, the supervising teacher becomes a role model of a reflective practitioner (Schön, 1983). They should also support student teachers to grow professionally and to become a competent and independent teacher, without leaving them to their own capacity and willingness.

As the results of the present study confirm, more systematic training for mentors is needed in ITE in Japan. Mentor teachers should bear a greater professional responsibility to assist in the development of student teachers as autonomous teachers. Well-trained and well-supported mentor teachers can greatly influence and shape student teachers' practice through professional dialogue during school-based teacher training. Student teachers in ITE in Japan seek models to emulate and see peers as co-meaning makers, but the reason why they are placed in such a situation needs to be acknowledged in the first place. Clarification of the role of supervising teachers will certainly raise the quality of their supervision. It will also lessen student teachers' feeling of confusion caused by supervising teachers' attitude towards subject teaching and holistic teaching, as was observed in this study. In addition, it ought to be the responsibility of teacher educators at HEIs to work with schools more closely in order to clarify the roles of supervising teachers in school-based training, to share ideas and principles that are promoted by teacher education programmes and to help them grow as reflective mentors.

9.2 Pedagogical Implications

What does the present study tell us more broadly about secondary school English language teacher education in Japan? Although the main purpose of the study is to depict and interpret the developmental processes and experiences of EFL student teachers, not to critically analyse the current ITE curriculum in Japan, it is worth noting what the results suggest for teacher trainers and educators in Japan and to explore useful insights to better design teacher education programmes.

The implications of the present study are threefold. First of all, the positive effects of emulation on student teachers should not be ignored, but rather be more fully and explicitly incorporated into the Japanese ITE curriculum. As has been discussed in this study, learning to teach is a process of socialisation into the community of learners and seeking a model for emulation in the community has been culturally endorsed in Japan as a step towards professional development. Emulation could be limiting, especially when it is implicitly provided or when student teachers are forced to adhere to the routines and patterns of experienced teachers and/or particular groups. However, if student teachers are provided with opportunities to observe various aspects of experienced teachers with the use of guided observation formats, and if ample opportunities for reflection on observation and emulation are provided, emulation can be useful as an effective and influential mediational activity in ITE, which enables student teachers to narrow the gap between the theoretical knowledge they acquire in ITE and practical teaching experiences at school.

Nevertheless, all the stakeholders in ITE, student teachers, supervising teachers in school and teacher educators at HEIs, need to be made aware that emulation is just one of a number of strategies for novice teachers to use as a springboard to explore and further develop their professional expertise. It is effective since they are still at the early stage of professional development and often lack confidence and extensive teaching experiences; however, they do need to learn to eventually grow out of emulated teaching and be able to make their own professional judgements in teaching and reflect on their own process of developing teacher autonomy.

Second, from a sociocultural theoretical perspective, EFL teacher educators in Japan should attend to the impact of *others* on student teachers' professional development. While it is recognised that people learn from cognitive thinking and problem-solving on their own, this study's data indicate that they also learn from interacting with others and working together to pursue goals and objectives, particularly peers. Even when peer learning is not explicitly incorporated in the ITE curriculum, as in this study, EFL student teachers seek peers who can provide honest criticism and suggestions, as peers are viewed as less intimidating than experienced teachers. Student teachers increase their motivation when they observe the teaching behaviours and skills of peers that they could emulate, which in turn transforms into developing their greater self-confidence. Because peers are more proximal to student teachers' cognitive, social and professional levels, they are easier for the student teachers to identify with. Thus, for student teachers to grow more effectively and professionally, an environment needs to be provided in which they are encouraged to interact with their peers in an informal atmosphere, to practise reflecting on each other's teaching, to learn to provide assistance and guidance and to grow together with an empathic attitude towards others.

Last but not least, the impact of supervising teachers on student teachers' professional development is far-reaching. In view of the very limited amount of practical experiences in school-based work that student teachers gain in their teacher education programmes, a more integrated and consistent approach to ITE is desirable in Japan. In order to make the role of the supervising teachers more central, their roles as mentors first should be clarified. As this particular study shows, student teachers may make arbitrary assumptions of what a good teacher is like, either as a good *homeroom* teacher or as a good *subject* teacher, depending on whether their mentors stress student guidance and classroom management or English language teaching. Supervising teachers also need to continue developing their teacher expertise, become more conscious of their own professional practices and become more aware that they themselves are the central participants of the community of learners in which student teachers are peripheral members who need assistance and guidance from other members, particularly those who are more experienced. As Howe (2006) discusses, 'the power of collaboration' is highly valued among in-service teachers in Japan, which should be extended to ITE and to the relationship between HEIs and schools. Both HEI teacher educators and supervising teachers at school should work more closely together and communicate regularly in order to structure ITE more effectively. For instance, more frequent HEI teacher educator school visits during the teaching practice or more coordination between HEIs and schools in terms of developing a scheme of focused emulated teaching and staged reflective tasks throughout the ITE curriculum are helpful.

9.3 Directions for Future Research

This study provides new insights for teacher educators in Japan to more fully understand a better design for teacher education programmes in future; for example, how *emulation* can improve or inhibit one's teaching and how *others* can effectively benefit novice and experienced teachers in their professional development. Similar studies in the future with more informants at various career stages ought to be conducted to explore the area further.

There are a few issues that should be taken into consideration for future research. First, it is important for future studies to address professional development from a longer-term perspective. As discussed throughout this study, professional development programmes for teachers in Japan lack a perspective of continuity and consistency over career stages. For instance, no agreement has been reached in both pre-service and in-service teacher training with regard to what kind of professional standards and competences should be achieved at each professional stage. A future study employing a longitudinal approach that looks at various sets of teachers' perspectives and experiences can illuminate how the development of teacher expertise proceeds. This may also allow a more fine-grained analysis of teachers' experiences with mediational means such as observation, emulation and reflection. For example, how can student teachers move away from the stage of simply imitating teaching behaviours without a full appreciation of the theoretical principles that underpin them? It may also be worth considering other possible mediational activities so that teacher educators can improve both the ITE system as well as the system of in-service teacher training by offering a more integrated and coherent approach and utilising *others* more effectively in the learning community.

Additionally, although this study stresses the importance of *others* during ITE experiences, student teachers usually cannot choose who they encounter during the process of professional development. For example, as the six cases in this study depicted, the arbitrary arrangement of the teaching practice supervising teachers in each setting resulted in different student teachers having different experiences. Depending on the *others* who the student teachers encounter (e.g. teachers in former schooling, lecturers of methods courses in ITE, supervising teachers during school-based teaching practice, cohort student teachers in ITE, colleagues at *jyuku*) as well as the teaching practice settings, their professional experiences can vary tremendously. The susceptibility of student teachers to the influences of *others* and their effects on how they develop professionally ought to be further investigated. Although this study mainly focused on student teachers' perspective changes and experiences in ITE, in order to develop a fuller picture of the ITE system in Japan, future research should focus on those of *others*, including supervising teachers and teacher educators, in the learning community of teachers. This expanded focus will lead to further understanding of why some student teachers are able to develop more successfully professionally, while others are less so.

As this study was conducted employing a case-study approach, its idiosyncratic nature is a strength of this study. As Strauss and Corbin (1998: 33) argue, the approach to the theory building of qualitative researchers should be 'one of emergence' and concepts and relationships emerge from data that researchers are allowed to interpret, specify the conditions under which actions and behaviours are likely to occur, seek variations and construct their own meanings, as the following quote indicates:

> [I]f one asks a researcher, 'Is this one case representative of all cases?' then the answer probably is 'no' and further study will show why and how. But if one asks, 'Is there something we can learn from this case that will give us insight and understanding about a phenomenon …', then the answer is 'yes'. (Strauss & Corbin, 1998: 285)

In the future, a similar research study ought to be replicated to understand more fully the process of teacher expertise development concerning student teachers in ITE in Japan.

Finally, the effects of participation in this study on some of the participating student teachers and their professional development should be considered. As Chie's quote at the start of this chapter shows, participation in this study resulted in raising her awareness of professional development, since she was instructed to keep a record of and explicitly analyse and articulate her perspectives and practices in her journal entries and interviews. To her surprise, verbalising her thoughts as a participant in this study became an opportunity for her to think about teacher qualities and her own language teaching practices. This implies that participation in this research provided her with an invaluable opportunity to engage in reflective practice and make sense of her professional development as an EFL teacher. Hence, future student teachers in Japan should also be encouraged to more explicitly reflect on their practices during ITE so as to cultivate their willingness and the ability necessary to become more autonomous teachers who can make professional judgements and improvements in their teaching. More research is also needed on how more direct engagement in reflective practices can influence the perceptions and practices of student teachers.

9.4 Final Conclusion

The present study has identified some of the challenges that currently confront the ITE system in Japan: the imbalance between theory and practice due to the short period of school-based training; lack of common goals and objectives between higher education institutions and schools for student teachers; lack of training for supervising teachers to play an active role as mentors; difficulty developing reflective practices in ITE; and the ITE system itself, which lacks consistency and coherence. This qualitative study also explored the perspectives and experiences of the student teachers who were facing these problems and how teacher education programmes influenced their perspectives and experiences. Each struggled in their own way to find solutions, to connect their theoretical understanding developed in ITE with practical teaching experiences and lay the foundations for early professional development. One of the significant findings of this study of student teachers in ITE in Japan is that some mediational activities, such as observation and emulation, and external assistance from others provided them with temporary but crucial support in connecting theoretical understanding and practical teaching experiences. Without the systematic and explicit intervention of the ITE curriculum in mitigating the gap between theoretical principles and practical teaching experiences, student teachers' individual struggles resulted in the variability in their experiences in ITE.

Effective ITE should expose student teachers to a variety of teaching models, approaches, contexts and philosophical ideas that they are allowed to experiment with, critically analyse and practise making professional choices and judgements, informed both by theoretical knowledge and practical experience. As Moore (2000: 127) claims, 'there is no one model of good teaching, any more than there is any one model of the good student or the good school'; pursuing a universal model of competencies will deprive student teachers of their creativity in teaching. Instead, freedom to develop good teaching should be encouraged even in the early phase of professional development, especially when relative autonomy and academic freedom in providing ITE is still allowed in Japan. In collaboration with schools, also with the newly implemented core curriculum, ITE in Japan should play a more significant role as a provider of appropriate intervention that will help student teachers develop the teacher autonomy needed to be confident and effective professionals.

Hence, even if the period of school-based teaching practice cannot be lengthened immediately, the following issues should be considered for assisting future student teachers in ITE in Japan:

(1) more coordination between higher education institutions and schools;
(2) training and providing more substantial roles for mentors;
(3) more professional learning of teacher educators themselves;
(4) more systematic approach for training reflective practices in teacher education courses.

As discussed at the start of this study, the Ministry of Education, Culture, Sports, Science and Technology (MEXT) addresses the urgent task of reforming the English language education system; EFL teachers are expected to improve students' English language abilities so that students will have a better command of English and can live more successfully and be more active in the international community. In order to develop learners' language fluency, not just their accuracy, and motivate them to reach their fullest potential, EFL teachers need to employ more contemporary methods and approaches to language teaching, such as communicative language teaching, learner-centred instruction, cooperative learning and interactive learning, rather than adhering to the current practices that emphasise language accuracy and are often blamed for creating students who are not sufficiently proficient in English. The ITE system needs to be more systematic and coherent as a whole so that student teachers learn to become confident, creative, reflective and autonomous in the process of their early professional development.

With many problems and concerns about ITE in Japan as yet unsolved, in order to raise and ensure the quality of English language education, there is no doubt that the most essential component is to raise and ensure *teacher* quality. Teachers should be at the heart of any educational improvement. Thus, this kind of case study, which delves into individual experiences and perspectives, is relevant and necessary. Furthermore, the challenge for English language teachers and teacher educators in Japan is not only to conduct future research to enhance the understanding of teachers' expertise development, but also to use research of this sort to influence the implementation of educational reforms and to positively affect the ITE curriculum responsible for developing quality language teachers. Future language teachers should be those who can share and develop responsibilities for their professional development, can effectively link theory and practice with the help of mediational activities and reflective practices and can make professional choices and judgements in the classroom. This will, in turn, help prospective Japanese EFL teachers in educating students they will teach in the future and promote the level of English language learning and teaching in Japan.

References

Akbari, R. (2007) Reflections on reflection: A critical appraisal of reflective practices in L2 teacher education. *System* 35, 192–207.

Alexander, E. (2002) Childcare students: Learning or imitating? *Forum* 44 (1), 24–26.

Almarza, G.G. (1996) Student foreign language teacher's knowledge growth. In D. Freeman and J.C. Richards (eds) *Teacher Learning in Language Teaching* (pp. 50–78). Cambridge: Cambridge University Press.

Asaoka, C. (2008) Education reform and its impact on initial teacher education in Japan. *Dokkyo University Studies in English* 65, 19–42.

Asaoka, C. (2012) Initial teacher training in Japan: Trainees' perspectives of language teacher expertise development. *Dokkyo University Studies in English* 70, 159–188.

Asaoka, C. and Ito, M. (2006) English teacher training in South Korea. In JACET SIG on English Education (ed.) *Developing English Teacher Competency: An Empirical Study of Pre-service Teachers, Training and Curriculum* (pp. 79–95). Tokyo: JACET SIG on English Education.

Atkinson, D. (2004) Theorising how student teachers form their identities in initial teacher education. *British Educational Research Journal* 30 (3), 379–394.

Bailey, K.M. (1990) The use of diary studies in teacher education programs. In J.C. Richards and D. Nunan (eds) *Second Language Teacher Education* (pp. 215–226). New York: Cambridge University Press.

Bailey, K.M. and Ochsner, R. (1983) A methodological review of the diary studies: Windmill tilting or social science? In K.M. Bailey, M.H. Long and S. Peck (eds) *Second Language Acquisition Studies* (pp. 188–198). Boston, MA: Newbury House Publishers.

Bandura, A. (1977) *Social Learning Theory*. Englewood Cliffs, NJ: Prentice Hall.

Barnlund, D.C. (1989) *Public and Private Self in Japan and the United States*. Yarmouth, ME: Intercultural Press Inc.

Bassey, M. (1999) *Case Study Research in Educatinoal Settings*. Buckingham/Philadelphia, PA: Open University Press.

Benson, P. (2001) *Autonomy in Language Learning*. Harlow: Pearson Education Ltd.

Borg, M. (2005) A case study of the development in pedagogic thinking of a pre-service teacher. *TESL-EJ* 9 (2), 1–30.

Borg, S. (2003) Teacher cognition in language teaching: A review of research on what language teachers think, know, believe and do. *Language Teaching* 36 (3), 81–109.

Borg, S. (2006) *Teacher Cognition and Language Education: Research and Practice*. London: Continuum.

Bowe, R. and Ball, S.J. (1992) *Reforming Education and Changing Schools: Case Studies in Policy Sociology*. London: Routledge.

Brown, A. and Dowling, P.C. (1998) *Doing Research/ Reading Research: A Mode of Interrogation for Education*. London: Falmer.

Brown, H.D. (2007a) *Principles of Language Learning and Teaching* (5th edn). New York: Pearson Education.
Brown, H.D. (2007b) *Teaching by Principles: An Interactive Approach to Language Pedagogy* (3rd edn). New York: Pearson Education.
Bryman, A. (2004) *Social Research Methods* (2nd edn). New York: Oxford University Press.
Bulte, C., Betts, A., Garner, K. and Durning, S. (2007) Student teaching: Views of student near-peer teachers and learners. *Medical Teacher* 29, 583–590.
Cabaroglu, N. and Roberts, J. (2000) Development in student teachers' pre-existing beliefs during a 1-year PGCE programme. System 28 (3), 387–402.
Carrell, P.L. and Eisterhold, J.C. (1983) Schema theory and ESL reading pegagogy. *TESOL Journal* 17 (4), 553–573.
Central Council for Education. (2006) Kongo no kyoin yosei menkyo seido no arikata ni tsuite (toshin) [The final report on the system of teacher education and teaching certificate programs in the future (final report)]. Tokyo: Ministry of Education, Culture, Sports, Science and Technology.
Chang, V.W. (2004) Training of English Teachers at the Secondary and Primary Levels in Taiwan. Paper presented at the the JAFAE Taiwan Study Tour, National Taiwan Normal University.
Childs, S.S. (2011) 'Seeing' L2 teacher learning: The power of context on conceptualizing teaching. In K.E. Johnson and P.R. Golombek (eds) *Research on Second Language Teacher Education* (pp. 67–85). New York/London: Routledge.
Clarke, A., Triggs, V. and Nielsen, W. (2014) Cooperating teacher participation in teacher education: A review of the literature. *Review of Educational Research* 84 (2), 163–202.
Cohen, L., Manion, L. and Morrison, K. (2000) *Research Methods in Education* (6th edn). London/New York: Routledge/Falmer.
Collins, A., Brown, J.S. and Newman, S.E. (1989) Cognitive apprenticeship: Teaching the crafts of reading, writing, and mathematics. In L.B. Resnick (ed.) *Knowing, Learning, and Instruction: Essays in Honor of Robert Glazer* (pp. 453–494). Hillsdale, NJ: Lawrence Erlbaum Associates.
Collinson, V. and Ono, Y. (2001) The professional development of teachers in the United States and Japan. *European Journal of Teacher Education* 24 (2), 223–248.
Condon, J.C. (1984) *With Respect to the Japanese*. Yarmouth, ME: Intercultural Press Inc.
Connor, U. (1984) Recall of text: Differences between first and second language readers. *TESOL Quarterly* 18 (2), 239–256.
Corbin, J. and Strauss, A. (2008) *Basics of Qualitative Research* (3rd edn). Los Angeles, CA: Sage.
Cousins, S.D. (1989) Culture and self-perception in Japan and the United States. *Journal of Personality and Social Psychology* 56 (1), 124–131.
Croker, R.A. (2009) An introduction to qualitative research. In J. Heigham and R.A. Croker (eds) *Qualitative Research in Applied Linguistics: A Practical Introduction* (pp. 3–24). London: Palgrave Macmillan.
Danzi, J., Reul, K. and Smith, R. (2008) Improving student motivation in mixed ability classrooms using differentiated instruction. Retrieved December 18, 2018 from ERIC database. (ED500838)
Department for Education. (n.d.) Get into Teaching. UK: Department for Education. Retrieved September 12, 2018, from www.education.gov.uk/get-into-teaching.
Dewey, J. (1916) *Democracy and Education*. New York: The Free Press.
Dewey, J. (1938) *Experience and Education*. New York: McMillan.
Dörnyei, Z. (2007) *Research Methods in Applied Linguistics: Quantitative, Qualitative, and Mixed Methodologies*. Oxford: Oxford University Press.
Duff, P.A. (2008) *Case Study Research in Applied Linguistics*. New York: Lawrence Erlbaum Associates.

Duff, P.A. (2012) How to carry out case study research. In A. Mackey and S.M. Gass (eds) *Research Methods in Second Language Acquisition* (pp. 95–116). Chichester: Wiley-Blackwell.

Dunn, W. (2011) Working toward social inclusion through concept development in second language teacher education. In K.E. Johnson and P.R. Golombek (eds) *Research on Second Language Teacher Education: A Sociocultural Perspective on Professional Development* (pp. 50–64). New York/London: Routledge.

Elbaz, F. (1981) The teacher's 'practical knowledge': Report of a case study. *Curriculum Inquiry* 11 (1), 43–71.

Elliott, J. (1993) Professional development in a land of choice and diversity: The future of action research. In D. Bridges and T. Kerry (eds) *Developing Teachers Professionally*. (pp. 23–50) London: Routledge.

Elliott, J. and Labatt, B. (1975) Research and teacher education. *Education for Teaching*, 96 (Spring), 52–68.

Eraut, M. (1989) Initial teacher training and the NVQ model. In J.W. Burke (ed.) *Competency Based Education and Training* (pp. 171–185). London/New York/Philadelphia, PA: The Falmer Press.

Fernandéz, M.L. (2010) Investigating how and what prospective teachers learn through microteaching lesson study. *Teaching and Teacher Education* 26, 351–362.

Friedman, D.A. (2012) How to collect and analyze qualitative data. In A. Mackey and S.M. Gass (eds) *Research Methods in Second Language Acquisition* (pp. 180–200). Chichester: Wiley-Blackwell.

Fujii, A. (2005) Individual differences in task performance: Aptitude profiles, orientation to form, and second language production in the EFL classroom. PhD thesis, Georgetown University.

Funaki, T. (2008) Initial teacher education as an open system. In the Japanese Society for the Study on Teacher Education (ed.) *Reforms of Teacher Education in Japan* (pp. 90–103). Tokyo: Gakuji Shuppan.

Furlong, J. and Maynard, T. (1995) *Mentoring Student Teachers: The Growth of Professional Knowledge*. London: Routledge.

Furlong, J., Barton, L., Miles, S., Whiting, C. and Whitty, G. (2000) *Teacher Education in Transition: Re-forming Professionalism?* Buckingham/Philadelphia, PA: Open University Press.

Grabe, W. (1991) Current developments in second language reading research. *TESOL Quarterly* 25 (3), 375–406.

Grenfell, M. (1998) *Training Teachers in Practice*. Clevedon: Multilingual Matters.

Hare, T. (1996) Try, try again: Training in noh drama. In T. Rohlen and G. LeTendre (eds) *Teaching and Learning in Japan* (pp. 323–344). New York: Cambridge University Press.

Hartley, D. (1993) Confusion in teacher education: A postmodern condition? In P. Gilroy and M. Smith (eds) *International Analyses of Teacher Education* (pp. 83–93). Abingdon: Carfax Publishing Company.

Hatch, J.A. (2002) *Doing Qualitative Research in Education Settings*. New York: State University of New York.

Hedge, T. (2000) *Teaching and Learning in the Language Classroom*. Oxford: Oxford University Press.

Heilbronn, R. (2008) *Teacher Education and the Development of Practical Judgement*. London: Continuum.

Heinrich, P. (2012) *The Making of Monolingual Japan*. Bristol: Multilingual Matters.

Holligan, C. (1997) Theory in initial teacher education: Students' perspectives on its utility: A case study. *British Educational Research Journal* 23 (4), 533–551.

Hooghart, A.M. (2006) Educational reform in Japan and its influence on teachers' work. *International Journal of Educational Research* 45 (4–5), 290–301.

Howe, E.R. (2006) Exemplary teacher induction: An international review. *Educational Philosophy and Theory* 38 (3), 287–297.
Inagaki, M. and Inuzuka, F. (2000) *Wakariyasui Seito Shido Ron [Theory in Student Counseling and Guidance]*. Tokyo: Bunka-Shobo Hakubun-sha.
Ireson, J. and Hallam, S. (1999) Raising standards: Is ability grouping the answer? *Oxford Review of Education* 25 (3), 343–358.
Ito, A. (2011) Enhancing school connectedness in Japan: The role of homeroom teachers in establishing a positive classroom climate. *Asian Journal of Counselling* 18 (1&2), 41–62.
JACET SIG on English Education (2005) *Developing English Teacher Competency: An Empirical Study of Pre-service Teachers, Training, and Curriculum*. Tokyo: JACET.
Jinnai, Y. (2008) Kyoshi to Kyoshikyoiku wo Meguru Konnichiteki Mondaijokyo [Current issues in teacher education]. In N.K. Gakkai (ed.) *Nihon no kyoshikyouiku kaikaku* (pp. 8–18). Tokyo: Gakuji Shuppan.
Johnson, K. (1994) The emerging beliefs and instructional practices of preservice English as a second langauge teachers. *Teaching and Teacher Education* 10 (4), 439–452.
Johnson, K. (2009) *Second Language Teacher Education: A Sociocultural Perspective*. New York: Routledge.
Johnson, K. and Golombek, P.R. (2011) A sociocultural theoretical perspective on teacher professional development. In K.E. Johnson and P.R. Golombek (eds) *Research on Second Language Teacher Education: A Sociocultural Perspective on Professional Development* (pp. 1–12). New York/London: Routledge.
Johnston, S. (1992) Images: A way of understanding the practical knowledge of student teachers. *Teaching and Teacher Education* 18 (2), 128–136.
Kagan, D.M. (1992) Professional growth among preservice and beginning teachers. *Review of Educational Research* 62 (2), 129–169.
Kanno, Y. (2008) *Language and Education in Japan*. New York: Palgrave MacMillan.
Kawaura, Y., Kawakami, Y. and Yamashita, K. (1998) Keeping a diary in cyberspace. *Japanese Psychological Research* 40 (4), 234–245.
Kennedy, J. (1993) Meeting the needs of teacher trainees on teaching practice. *ELT Journal* 47 (2), 157–165.
Kerr, P. (1994) Initial reflections. *The Teacher Trainer* 8 (3), 21.
Kettle, B. and Sellars, N. (1996) The development of student teachers' practical theory of teaching. *Teaching and Teacher Education* 12 (1), 1–24.
Kim, W.J. (2005) *Cultivating and Securing Qualified Teachers*. South Korea: Ministry of Education and Human Resources Development.
Kim, Y.J. (2012) Implementing ability grouping in EFL contexts: Perceptions of teachers and students. *Language Teaching Research* 16 (3), 289–315.
Kojima, H. (2008) A collaborative, autonomous, and reflective teaching approach to student teaching in pre-service EFL teacher education: A case study. *JACET Journal* 46, 1–15.
Kolb, D.A. (1983) *Problem management: Learning from experience. The Executive Mind*. San Francisco: Jossey-Bass.
Korthagen, F.A.J., Kessels, J., Koster, B., Lagerwerf, B. and Wubbels, T. (2001) *Linking Practice with Theory: The Pedagogy of Realistic Teacher Education*. Mahwah, NJ: Lawrence Erlbaum Associates.
Krashen, S. (1985) *The Input Hypothesis: Issues and Applications*. London: Longman.
Krashen, S. (2008) Languag education: Past, present, and future. *RELC Journal* 39, 178–187.
LaBoskey, V.K. (1993) A conceptual framework for reflection in preservice teacher education. In J. Calderhead and P. Gates (eds) *Conceptualizing Reflection in Teacher Development* (pp. 23–38). London: The Falmer Press.

Lantolf, J.P. (2000) Introducing sociocultural theory. *Sociocultural Theory and Second Language Learning* 1, 1–26.

Lantolf, J.P. and Thorne, S.L. (2006) *Sociocultural Theory and the Genesis of Second Language Development*. Oxford: Oxford University Press.

Lave, J. and Wenger, E. (1991) *Situated Learning: Legitimate Peripheral Participation*. Cambridge: Cambridge University Press.

Lawes, S. (2004) The end of theory? A comparative study of the decline of educational theory and professional knowledge in modern foreign language teacher training in England and France. PhD thesis, University of London.

Lee, I. (2007) Preparing pre-service English teachers for reflective practice. *ELT Journal* 61, 321–329.

LeTendre, G.K. (1999) The problem of Japan: Qualitative studies and international educational comparisons. *Educational Researcher* 28 (2), 38–45.

Lewis, C.C. (1992) Creativity and Japanese education. In R. Leetsoma and H. Walberg (eds) *Japanese Educational Productivity* (pp. 225–266). Ann Arbor, MI: University of Michigan Center for Japanese Studies.

Lim, C.P. and Chan, B.C. (2007) MicroLESSONS in teacher education: Examining pre-service teachers' pedagogical beliefs. *Computers and Education* 48 (3), 474–494.

Lortie, D.C. (1975) *Schoolteacher*. Chicago, IL: University of Chicago Press.

Lunenberg, M., Korthagen, F. and Swennen, A. (2007) The teacher educator as a role model. *Teaching and Teacher Education* 23, 586–601.

Lyle, J. (2003) Stimulated recall: A report on its use in naturalistic research. *British Educational Research Journal* 29 (6), 861–878.

MacDonald, M., Badger, R. and White, G. (2001) Changing values: What use are theories of language learning and teaching? *Teaching and Teacher Education* 17, 949–963.

McDonough, J. and McDonough, S. (1997) *Research Methods for English Language Teachers*. London: Arnold.

McIntyre, D. (1993) Theory, theorizing and reflection in initial teacher education. In J. Calderhead and P. Gates (eds) *Conceptualizing Reflection in Teacher Development* (pp. 39–52). London: Falmer Press.

Merriam, S.B. (2001) *Qualitative Research and Case Study Applications in Education*. San Francisco, CA: Jossey-Bass.

MEXT (2001) 21 Seiki Kyoiku Shinsei Plan [Education Reform Plan for the 21st Century]. Retrieved August 10, 2010, from http://www.mext.go.jp/a_menu/shougai/21plan/main_b2.htm.

MEXT (2003a) The Course of Study for Foreign Languages for Primary Education. Retrieved August 10, 2010, from http://www.mext.go.jp/a_menu/shotou/cs/1320008.htm.

MEXT (2003b) 'Eigo ga Tsukaeru Nihonjin' Ikusei no tame no Action Plan [Regarding the Establishment of an Action Plan to Cultivate 'Japanese with English Abilities']. Retrieved August 10, 2010, from http://www.mext.go.jp/b_menu/shingi/chukyo/chukyo3/004/siryo/04031601/005.pdf.

MEXT (2010a) Course of Study: English for Upper-Secondary Schools. Retrieved September 10, 2011, from http://www.mext.go.jp/a_menu/shotou/new-cs/youryou/eiyaku/__icsFiles/afieldfile/2012/10/24/1298353_3.pdf.

MEXT (2010b) Course of Study: Foreign Language Activities for Elementary Schools. Retrieved September 10, 2011, from http://www.mext.go.jp/component/a_menu/education/micro_detail/__icsFiles/afieldfile/2010/10/20/1261037_12.pdf.

MEXT (2010c) Course of Study: Foreign Languages for Lower-secondary Schools. Retrieved September 10, 2011, from http://www.mext.go.jp/component/a_menu/education/micro_detail/__icsFiles/afieldfile/2011/04/11/1298356_10.pdf.

MEXT (2010d) *Heisei 20-nendo koutougakko tou ni okeru kokusai koryu tou nojyoukyou nitsuite* [International Exchange Situations at Upper-Secondary Schools in the School

Year 2008]. Retrieved September 10, 2011, from http://www.mext.go.jp/b_menu/shingi/chousa/shotou/082/shiryo/__icsFiles/afieldfile/2011/04/13/1304154_06.pdf.
MEXT (2017) The Course of Study for Lower-Secondary Schools. Retrieved January 28, 2018, from http://www.mext.go.jp/component/a_menu/education/micro_detail/__icsFiles/afieldfile/2018/05/07/1384661_5_4.pdf.
Ministry of Justice (2017) *Heisei 28 nenmatsu ni okeru zairyu gaikokujin su ni tsuite* [The Number of Foreign Residents as of the End of 2016]. Retrieved January 28, 2018.
Miura, A. and Yamashita, K. (2007) Psychological and social influences on blog writing: An online survey of blog authors in Japan. *Journal of Computer-Meidated Communication* 12, 1452–1471.
Moore, A. (2000) *Teaching and Learning: Pedagogy, Curriculum and Culture*. London/New York: Routledge/Falmer.
Moore, A. (2004) *The Good Teacher: Dominant Discourses in Teacher Education*. Oxford: Routledge.
Murphey, T. and Arao, H. (2001) Changing reported beliefs through near peer role modeling. *TESL-EJ* 5 (3), 1–15.
Nagamine, T. (2008) *Exploring Preservice Teachers' Beliefs*. Saarbrücken: VDM Verlag Dr. Muller.
Nishimuro, M. and Borg, S. (2013) Teacher cognition and grammar teaching in a Japanese high school. *JALT Journal* 35 (1), 29–50.
Nunan, D. (1988) *The Learner-Centred Curriculum: A Study in Second Language Teaching*. Cambridge: Cambridge University Press.
Nunan, D. (1999) *Second Language Teaching and Learning*. Boston, MA: Heinle & Heinle Publishers.
Orland-Barak, L. and Yinon, H. (2007) When theory meets practice: What student teachers learn from guided reflection on their own classroom discourse. *Teaching and Teacher Education* 23 (6), 957–969.
Ota, N. (2000) Teacher education and its reform in contemporary Japan. *International Studies in Sociology of Education* 10 (1), 43–59.
Pachler, N., Evans, M. and Lawes, S. (2007) *Modern Foreign Languages*. London/New York: Routledge.
Pajares, M.F. (1992) Teachers' beliefs and educational research: Cleaning up a messy construct. *Review of Educational Research* 62 (3), 307–332.
Patton, M.Q. (1980) *Qualitative Evaluation Methods*. London: Sage.
Patton, M.Q. (2002) *Qualitative Research and Evaluation Methods* (3rd edn). London: Sage.
Peacock, M. (2001) Pre-service ESL teachers' beliefs about second language learning: A longitudinal study. *System* 29, 177–195.
Poehner, P. (2011) Teacher learning through critical friends groups. In K.E. Johnson and P.R. Golombek (ed.) *Research on Second Language Teacher Education: A Sociocultural Perspective on Professional Development* (pp. 189–203). New York/London: Routledge.
Pring, R. (1995) Standards and quality in education. In T. Kerry and A.S. Mayes (eds) *Issues in Mentoring* (pp. 188–199). London/New York: Routledge.
Richards, J. (1996) Teachers' maxims in language teaching. *TESOL Quarterly* 30 (2), 281–296.
Richards, J. (1998) *Beyond Training: Perspectives on Language Teacher Education*. Cambridge: Cambridge University Press.
Richards, J. and Rodgers, T.S. (2001) *Approaches and Methods in Language Teaching* (2nd edn). Cambridge: Cambridge University Press.
Richards, J., Ho, B. and Giblin, K. (1996) Learning how to teach in the RSA Cert. In D. Freeman and J.C. Richards (eds) *Teacher Learning in Language Teaching* (pp. 242–259). Cambridge: Cambridge University Press.

Richards, J.C. and Lockhart, C. (1994) *Reflective Teaching in Second Language Classrooms*. Cambridge: Cambridge University Press.

Richardson, V. (1996) The role of attitudes and beliefs in learning to teach. In J. Sikula, T.J. Buttery and E. Gyuton (eds) *Handbook of Research on Teacher Education* (2nd edn, pp. 102–119). New York: Macmillan.

Roberts, J. (1998) *Language Teacher Education*. London: Arnold.

Robson, M., Cohen, N. and McGuiness, J. (1999) Counselling, careers education and pastoral care: Beyond the national curriculum. *British Journal of Guidance and Counselling* 27 (1), 5–11.

Rogoff, B. (1990) *Apprenticeship in Thinking*. New York/Oxford: Oxford University Press.

Rogoff, B. (1995) Observing sociocultural activity on three planes: Participatory appropriation, guided participation, and apprenticeship. In J.W. Wertsch, P. del Rio and A. Avarez (eds) *Sociocultural Studies of Mind* (pp. 58–74). Cambridge: Cambridge University Press.

Roth, W.M. and Lee, Y.J. (2007) Vygotsky's neglected legacy: Cultural-historical activity theory. *Review of Educational Research* 77 (2), 186–232.

San, M.M. (1999) Japanese beginning teachers' perceptions of their preparation and professional development *Journal of Education for Teaching: International Research and Pedagogy* 25 (2), 17–29.

Sato, K. (2002) Practical understanding of communicative language teaching and teacher development. In S.J. Sagivnon (ed.) *Interpreting Communicative Language Teaching: Contexts and Concerns in Teacher Education* (pp. 41–81). New Haven, CT: Yale University Press.

Sato, K. and Kleinsasser, R.C. (2004) Beliefs, practices, and interactions of teachers in a Japanese high school English department. *Teaching and Teacher Education* 20 (8), 797–816.

Sato, M. (1992) Japan. In H.B. Leavite (ed.) *Issues and Problems in Teacher Education: An International Handbook* (pp. 155–168). New York: Greenwood Press.

Sato, M. (2004) *Shujukudo-betsu no Nani ga Mondai ka* [What is a Problem of Ability Grouping?]. Tokyo: Iwanami Shoten.

Sato, M. (2008) Kyoshikyoiku no kiki to kaikaku no genritekikento [An analysis of crisis and reforms in teacher education]. In Nihon Kyoshikyouiku Gakkai (ed.) *Nihon no Kyoshikyouiku Kaikaku* [Teacher Education Reforms in Japan] (pp. 20–37). Tokyo: Gakuji Shuppan.

Savignon, S.J. (2005) Communicative language teaching: Strategies and goals. In E. Hinkel (ed.) *Handbook of Research in Second Language Teaching and Learning* (pp. 635–670). Mahwah, NJ: Lawrence Erlbaum Associates.

Schön, D.A. (1983) *The Reflective Practitioner*. London: Basic Books.

Shimahara, N. (1998) The Japanese model of professional development: Teaching as craft. *Teaching and Teacher Education* 14 (5), 451–462.

Shimahara, N. (2002) *Teaching in Japan: A Cultural Perspective*. New York: Taylor & Francis.

Shimahara, N. and Sakai, A. (1992) Teacher internship and the culture of teaching in Japan. *British Journal of Sociology of Education* 13 (2), 147–161.

Shinmura, I. (2008) *Kojien*, 6th Version. Tokyo: Iwanami Shoten.

Shulman, L. (1987) Knowledge and teaching: Foundations of the new reform. *Harvard Educational Review* 57, 1–22.

Shulman, L.S. and Shulman, J.H. (2004) How and what teachers learn: A shifting perspective. *Journal of Curriculum Studies* 36 (2), 257–271.

Silverman, D. (2000) *Doing Qualitative Research*. Los Angeles, CA: Sage.

Silverman, D. (2001) *Interpreting Qualitative Data* (2nd edn). London: Sage.

Silverman, D. (2005) *Doing Qualitative Research* (2nd edn). London: Sage.

Smith, R. and Erdoğan, S. (2008) Teacher–learner autonomy: Programme goals and student–teacher constructs. In T. Lamb and H. Reinders (eds) *Learner and Teacher Autonomy* (pp. 83–102). Amsterdam/Philadelphia, PA: John Benjamins Publishing Co.

Strauss, A.L. and Corbin, J.M. (1998) *Basics of Qualitative Research: Grounded Theory, Procedures and Techniques* (2nd edn). London: Sage.

Stromso, H.I., Braten, I. and Samuelstuen, M.S. (2003) Students' strategic use of multiple sources during expository text reading: A longitudinal think-aloud study. *Cognition and Instruction* 21 (2), 113–147.

Suzuki, A. (2013) Reflective practice as a tool for professional development of in-service high school teachers of English in Japan. PhD thesis, University of London.

Swain, M. (2005) The output hypothesis: Theory and research. In E. Hinkel (ed.) *Handbook of Research in Second Language Teaching and Learning* (pp. 471–483). Mahwah, NJ: Lawrence Erlbaum Associates.

Tann, S. (1993) Eliciting student teachers' personal theories. In J. Calderhead and P. Gates (eds) *Conceptualizing Reflection in Teacher Development* (pp. 53–69). London: Falmer Press.

Tomlinson, P. (1995) *Understanding Mentoring: Reflective Strategies for School-Based Teacher Preparation*. Buckingham: Open University Press.

Triandis, H.C. (1989) The self and social behavior in differing cultural contexts. *Psychological Review* 96 (3), 506–520.

Tsang, W.K. (2003) Journaling from internship to practice teaching. *Reflective Practice* 4 (2), 221–240.

Tsuchiya, S. (2004) *Eigo Communication no Kiso o Tsukuru Ondoku Shido* [*Reading-Aloud Tasks that Develop the Basis of English Communication Abilities*]. Tokyo: Kenkyusha.

Tsui, A.B.M. (2003) *Understanding Expertise in Teaching: Case Studies of ESL Teachers*. Cambridge: Cambridge University Press.

Vygotsky, L.S. (1960/1997) Analysis of higher mental functions. In R.W. Rieber (ed.) *The Collected Works of L.S. Vygotsky* (Vol. 4, pp. 65–82). New York: Plenum Press.

Vygotsky, L.S. (1962) *Thought and Language*. Cambridge, MA: MIT Press.

Vygotsky, L.S. (1978) *Mind in Society: The Development of Higher Psychological Processes*. Cambridge, MA: Harvard University Press.

Wada, M. (2002) Teacher education for curricular innovation in Japan. In S.J. Sagivnon (ed.) *Interpreting Communicative Language Teaching: Contexts and Concerns in Teacher Education* (pp. 31–40). New Haven, CT: Yale University Press.

Wade, S.E., Buxton, W.M. and Kelly, M. (1999) Using think-alouds to examine reader-text interest. *Reading Research Quarterly* 34 (2), 194–216.

Wallace, M. (1991) *Training Foreign Language Teachers: A Reflective Approach*. Cambridge: Cambridge University Press.

Weiten, W., Lloyd, M. and Lashley, R. (1991) *Psychology Applied to Modern Life* (3rd edn). Monterey, CA: Brooks/Cole Publishing Company.

Wenger, E. (2005) *Communities of Practice: Learning, Meaning, and Identity*. Cambridge: Cambridge University Press.

Yando, R., Seitz, V. and Zigler, E. (1978) *Imitation: A Developmental Perspective*. Hillsdale, NJ: Lawrence Erlbaum Associates.

Yoshida, K. (2001) The need for a qualitative change in the teaching of English in Japan in the 21st century. In A. Furness, G. Wong and L. Wu (eds) *Penetrating Discourse: Integrating Theory and Practice in Second Language Teaching* (pp. 159–172). Hong Kong: The Hong Kong University of Science and Technology.

Yoshimoto Asaoka, C. (2015) Mitigating the disparity between theory and practice: EFL student teachers' perspectives and experiences of their professional development. PhD thesis, University College London.

Index

ability grouping (*shujukudo-betsu-shido*) 83, 87, 89–90, 96
academic freedom 13, 19, 154
accreditation 13–15
achievement, learner 30
active learning approaches 9, 112, 116
adaptive process, learning as 23
advanced certificates 13
affective domain 32, 48, 55, 60, 80, 109, 134
affective filters 109
Akbari, R. 24, 25
Alexander, E. 40, 127
Almarza, G.G. 36, 56, 97
apprenticeship 35–41, 81, 126
apprenticeship of observation 36, 40, 56, 81, 102, 103, 108, 119, 145
Arao, H. 129, 133, 134, 138
artistry 23
Asaoka, C. 11, 13, 17
assessment 30, 62
assistant language teachers (ALTs) 8, 9, 19, 71, 94
Atkinson, D. 24, 147
attachment 35
authority, teacher 29, 86
autonomy, learner 73–4, 87, 94, 103, 104, 106, 130, 148
autonomy, teacher 19, 24, 27, 34, 35, 39, 40, 76, 95, 126, 141, 142, 146, 151, 154, 155
Aya
 –ability grouping 90
 –biographical details 53, 69
 –content knowledge 76, 109

–emulation 75–6, 122
–informal teaching experiences 112
–language learner to language teacher shift 108
–learner-centred education 75, 130
–observations of 64
–pedagogical content knowledge (PCK) 15, 76, 109
–peer learning 129, 130, 132, 133
–prior experience of being taught 102
–reflective practice 75
–teacher as subject specialist 75–7, 80, 81, 98

Bailey, K.M. 60
Ball, S.J. 17
Bandura, A. 119
Barnlund, D.C. 50
behaviour management skills 68, 93, 96, 111, 141
behaviourism 34
beliefs 25, 36–7, 43, 47, 55, 103, 106, 144
Benson, P. 116
block practice 16
blogging 63
Borg, M. 56, 102, 103
Borg, S. 30, 98, 99, 102, 125, 128, 136, 137
bounded systems 48
Bowe, R. 17
Brown, A. 62
Brown, H.D. 29, 92, 104, 113, 121, 134
Bryman, A. 49
bullying 14, 85
Bulte, C. 130, 133

business sector, globalisation of 3

Cabaroglu, N. 70, 103, 105
card-sorting exercises 57, 58–9, 72, 113
Carrell, P.L. 15
case-study approach 4, 47–9, 65–6, 142, 153
Central Council for Education 9
certification of teachers 13–15
chain reading 131–2
Chan, B.C. 56
Chang, V.W. 13
character formation (*ningen-keisei*) 89
Chie
 –ability grouping 90
 –biographical details 5, 53
 –content knowledge 70, 71, 109
 –emulation 71, 74, 116–22
 –language learner to language teacher shift 108
 –learner-centred education 72–3, 116–22, 144
 –observations of 64
 –pedagogical content knowledge (PCK) 70, 71, 109
 –peer learning 128, 129, 133
 –prior experience of being taught 102
 –reflective practice 50–1, 74
 –teacher as subject specialist 35, 66, 69–75, 80, 81, 98
 –voluntary teaching practice 112
child development 35–6, 86
Childs, S.S. 128
Chinese, in the Japanese linguistic context 2
chunk reading 104, 131
Clarke, A. 121, 129, 133
class management skills 18, 26, 33, 34, 68, 72, 84, 91
co-construction of meaning 29, 47, 74, 79, 106, 123, 128, 129–32, 138, 150
coding of data 58, 66
cognitive apprenticeship 115
cognitive development 25, 27, 32, 36, 44, 45, 99, 125, 128, 136, 137
cognitive learning theory 35
Cohen, L. 58

collaboration, power of 39, 40, 41, 46, 73, 128, 152
collective identities 47, 128
Collins, A. 115
communicative competence 29, 73, 104
communicative language teaching (CLT) 28–30, 72, 87, 102–8, 155
communities of practice 25, 37, 43, 45, 47, 140 *see also* learning communities
competency-based view of a good teacher 34
Condon, J.C. 50
confidence 13, 17, 22, 97, 109, 134, 144, 151
Confucianism 29
constructivism 137
content knowledge
 –Aya 76, 109
 –Chie 70, 71, 109
 –EFL teachers 27–8
 –intermeshing with other knowledge bases 84
 –Kento 95
 –Mari 81, 82, 109
 –Nana 78, 109
 –teacher expertise 21, 26, 27, 42, 68
 –theory-practice dichotomy 44
 –value of theoretical knowledge 96
 –Yurika 95
content-based instruction 123, 124, 134
continual professional development 11, 19, 149
continuous improvement (*kaizen*) 35, 36, 38, 39, 74–5, 84, 125, 126, 134, 143
Corbin, J. 48, 153
core curriculum for English language teacher training 15, 16, 19, 154
co-researchers, participants as 60
counselling students 33 *see also* homeroom teachers; student guidance (*seito shido*)
Course of Study (MEXT) 3, 7–9, 28, 32, 82, 96–7, 105
coursework 108–11
Cousins, S.D. 49

craft, teaching as 32, 34–41, 74, 75–6, 83, 116, 120, 123, 134
cramming 10, 78 *see also jyuku*
creative form of imitation 38, 39–40, 125, 127, 144
Croker, R.A. 51
cross-curricular thematic projects 11
cultural artefacts 45, 115
cultural knowledge, sometimes lacking in non-native teachers 13, 28
curriculum knowledge 26, 28, 68, 96
cyclic process, learning to teach as 23, 25

Danzi, J. 89
decentralised teacher education system 12, 40, 44, 52
decline in teacher numbers 52
deep learning 9
Democratic Party of Japan 12
demonstration lesson (*kenkyu jugyou*) 18, 40, 63, 89, 94, 125
Dewey, J. 23, 36, 39
dialogical process, learning to teach as 23, 25, 74, 93, 102, 136, 139–40
diary keeping in Japan 63
differentiation 89–90 *see also* ability grouping
dimensions of professional expertise 26–30
discipline 86, 88, 90, 91 *see also* behaviour management skills
Dörnyei, Z. 48, 51, 57, 60
Dowling, P.C. 62
Duff, P.A. 48
Dunn, W. 37, 38, 39, 125, 127, 128, 144

'Education Reform Plan for the 21st Century' (Rainbow Plan) 10–11, 14, 89
educational contexts, knowledge of 26, 28, 68, 71, 73, 80, 96, 118
Educational Personnel Certification Law 13
Educational Personnel Training Council (EPTC) 13–14
educational reform 10–12
Eisterhold, J.C. 15
elders, valuing 37

elementary schools 2, 9, 33, 77–8, 85
eliciting student responses 82, 84, 88
Elliott, J. 34, 109
emic research 49–51
emotional aspects 16, 32, 90, 128–9 *see also* affective domain
emotional distance (*tantan-to-shiteiru*) 90
empathy 50, 130, 151
emulation
 –Aya 75–6, 122
 –Chie 71, 74, 116–22
 –dangers of uncritical 120, 125, 127, 146
 –future research 152
 –greater incorporation into ITE curriculum 150
 –Mari 83–4, 116
 –as mediational tool 37, 38, 41, 71, 74, 75–6, 99, 116–27, 138, 143, 144–8
 –as medium of instruction 139–40
 –Nana 79, 80–1, 116, 121
 –peer learning 128, 133–4
 –role models 70, 91, 99, 116, 121, 122–3, 128, 133–5, 137–8, 143, 149–50, 154
 –social interactionist perspectives 137–8
 –as 'stealing' 39, 83, 126–7, 134, 145
 –teaching as a craft 34–5, 37–41
 –theory-practice dichotomy 5, 22
 –Yurika 94, 95, 116, 125
ends and values, educational 68, 78, 82, 96
English
 –as a foreign language in Japan 2, 7–9
 –in learning logs 61
 –as medium of instruction 3, 9, 21, 27–8, 82–3, 104–5, 132
English for academic purposes (EAP) 87, 106, 138
Eraut, M. 15, 96
Erdoğan, S. 76
European Portfolio for Student Teachers of Languages (EPOSTL) 44

examination-oriented teaching 29
expectations of teaching 102
experiential learning 16, 22, 23, 24, 41, 137
extra-curricular activities 33, 62, 85, 97

facilitator, teacher as 29, 88
Fernandéz, M.L. 112
field notes 64, 92
filial piety 29
Filipino, in the Japanese linguistic context 2
filmed lessons 57, 59, 107, 130
first- and second-class certificates 13
flexibility in the classroom 80
fluency 29, 81–2, 97, 155
form (homeroom) teachers 18, 34, 85, 97, 102, 110, 122, 141–2, 151
form over meaning 29, 130
four skills of language learning 9, 15
Friedman, D.A. 47–9, 51, 59, 60, 61, 62, 64–5
Fujii, A. 49
fun classes 75, 77, 78, 89, 96
Funaki, T. 24, 125
Furlong, J. 22, 34, 35, 95, 102, 111, 113, 116, 124, 125
future research 152–4
'fuzzy' generalisations 47–9

gakkyu-hokai (breakdown in discipline) 88, 96
general pedagogical knowledge (GPK) 14–15, 26, 33, 42, 68, 85–7, 92–4, 96, 110
generalisations 47–9, 153
generic teaching skills 14–15
gesture 134
globalisation 2, 3, 9, 10–11, 29, 32
Golombek, P.R. 44, 45, 46, 74, 126, 128, 138
Grabe, W. 15
grades, for teaching education 18
grammar-translation method 15, 28–9, 75, 104, 122
grammatical knowledge 96, 107
Grenfell, M. 36
group life 34, 39, 40, 41, 50

group work 87–8, 91, 105, 106, 109, 117, 123

Hallam, S. 89
hands-on teacher training 16
hansei (negative reflection) 24, 147
Hare, T. 38, 39
Hartley, D. 16, 23
Hashimoto, Ryutaro 10
Hatch, J.A. 48, 49, 55–6, 59, 60, 61, 62, 63, 64
Hedge, T. 118
hikidashi 88
hikisashi-o-motsu 77, 88
holistic teaching 32, 33–4, 41, 69, 84–96, 97, 141
Holligan, C. 123
homeroom teachers 18, 34, 85, 97, 102, 110, 122, 141–2, 151
Hooghart, A.M. 40
Howe, E.R. 39, 40, 152

idealistic views of student teachers 22
ikiru chikara (zest for living) 11, 32, 33
imitation 35–6, 38–40, 91, 95, 115–16, 124–7, 135, 144 *see also* creative form of imitation; emulation
Immigration Control and Refugee Recognition Act 2
implicit knowledge 37
Inagaki, M. 33
induction training 39
inductive reasoning 48, 121
inferences, making 49
informal teaching experiences 70–2, 78–9, 89–90, 92, 98, 111–14, 117, 126, 138, 147
initial teacher education (ITE)
 –in higher education institutions (HEIs) 12–15
 –history of 12–15
 –professional development in 21–31
 –in secondary schools 16–19
inquiring mind, need for 24
in-service teacher training 23, 39, 40, 44, 142, 145, 152
insider, researcher as 49–51
instrumental purposes, studying for 10

integrated study course (national curriculum) 11
integrative teaching methods 15
interactive learning 9, 104–5, 107, 119, 121, 128, 155
internalisation 45, 126, 138
internationalisation 7, 9
interviews as data collection method 55–8, 66–7
intranational communication, English used for 2, 9
introspection skills 24, 59
intuitive knowing 24, 37, 146, 149
Inuzuka, F. 33
Ireson, J. 89
Ito, A. 18, 33, 85
Ito, M. 13, 17

JACET SIG on English Education 8
Japan Exchange and Teaching Programme 20n(2)
Japanese
 –in the Japanese linguistic context 2
 –in learning logs 61
 –as medium of instruction 3
Jinnai, Y. 12
Johnson, K. 22, 25, 44, 45, 46, 56, 61, 74, 79, 115, 126, 127, 128, 129, 132, 135, 138, 140, 148
Johnston, S. 133
journals 57, 58, 60–3, 66–7, 91, 92–3, 128
judgement, professional 21, 26, 40, 46, 146, 151, 154
jyuku (cram/preparatory schools) 78, 82, 90, 92, 98, 112, 113, 126

Kagan, D.M. 36, 37
kaiho-sei ('open' system of teacher education) 12, 13, 19, 44
kaizen (continuous improvement) 35, 36, 38, 39, 74–5, 84, 125, 126, 134, 143
Kawaura, Y. 63
kenkyu jugyou (demonstration lesson) 18, 40, 63, 89, 94, 125
Kennedy, J. 25
Kento
 –biographical details 5, 52–3

 –communicative language teaching (CLT) 106–8
 –emulation 116, 122–4
 –holistic teaching 1, 66, 84, 85–91
 –journals 62
 –language learner 101, 138
 –learner-centred education 87–8, 110–11, 122–4
 –observations of 64
 –pedagogical content knowledge (PCK) 88, 95
 –peer learning 128, 129, 135
 –practical teaching experience during training 111
 –prior experience of being taught 88, 97, 106, 110, 123, 137
 –reflective practice 87
 –supervising teachers 95, 97, 98
Kettle, B. 58–9
Kim, W.J. 13
Kim, Y.J. 90
Kleinsasser, R. C. 40, 44
knowledge-creation 23
Kojima, H. 24, 147
Kolb, D.A. 22
Korean, in the Japanese linguistic context 2
Korthagen, F.A.J. 74, 93, 98, 128
Krashen, S. 109
kyoshoku-katei 51–2

Labatt, B. 109
language learners, teachers as 75, 81–4, 87, 97–8, 101, 102–8, 116, 138, 148
Lantolf, J.P. 38, 46
Lave, J. 37, 47
learner-centred education
 –Aya 75, 130
 –Chie 72–3, 116–22, 144
 –communicative language teaching (CLT) 108
 –future of ITE 155
 –Kento 87–8, 122–4
 –Mari 110–11, 116
 –in the national curriculum 9
 –teacher expertise 29
 –Yurika 94, 95, 124–7

learning communities 37, 41, 43–4, 48, 128–36, 138–9, 148–9, 151–2, 153
lecturers taking part in study 54, 59–60
Lee, I. 61
lesson flow 119–20, 131
lesson plans 75, 79, 80, 82, 88, 118, 121, 130
LeTendre, G.K. 93
Lewis, C.C. 38, 39
liberal arts education 12
Liberal Democratic Party 11
Licensing Act of Educational Personnel 11
licensing of teachers 13
lifelong career, teaching as 11, 19
Lim, C.P. 56
linear processes of learning to teach 22, 95, 102, 113, 124
lingua franca, English as 2, 9
listening skills 92
logs, learning 18, 61
long-term studies, need for 152
Lortie, D.C. 32, 36, 40, 56, 81, 102, 103, 108, 116, 145
low proficiency students 30, 71, 76, 83, 88, 90, 113, 134
Lunenberg, M. 5
Lyle, J. 59

MacDonald, M. 108
mandatory subject, English as 2–3, 9
maneru 38–41 *see also* apprenticeship; emulation
Mari
 –biographical details 5, 53
 –content knowledge 81, 82, 109
 –emulation 83–4, 116
 –language learner 81–4, 108
 –learner-centred education 110–11, 116
 –observations of 64
 –pedagogical content knowledge (PCK) 81, 82, 84, 109
 –peer learning 128, 129, 130–2, 134
 –reflective practice 83, 131
 –teacher as subject specialist 69, 74, 75, 81–4, 97
Maynard, T. 22, 95, 102, 113, 116, 124, 125

McDonough, J. 60, 65
McDonough, S. 60, 65
meaning over form 29
meaning-making 26, 29, 47, 63, 74, 79, 123, 128, 138 *see also* co-construction of meaning
mediational tools
 –emulation 37, 38, 41, 71, 74, 75–6, 99, 116–27, 138, 144–8
 –informal teaching experiences 111–13
 –internalisation 45
 –microteaching as 112–13
 –peer learning 79, 127–36, 143, 146–8
 –prior experience of being taught 102–8
 –sociocultural theory 25
medium of instruction 3, 9, 21, 27–8, 82–3, 132
mentoring 17, 37, 39, 64, 91, 149–50, 151, 154, 155
merihari (well-modulated) 84
Merriam, S.B. 48
methodology courses in teacher training 14
Methods of Teaching English 52, 53–4, 55, 70, 92, 107, 126
microteaching
 –Aya 75
 –Kento 87–8, 107
 –Mari 83
 –as mediational tool 112–13
 –peer learning 129–30, 132
 –Saori 104
 –study methodology 55, 56, 57, 59, 63
 –Yurika 92, 94
mimicking teacher behaviours 22, 35, 95 *see also* imitation
Ministry of Education, Culture, Sports, Science and Technology (MEXT)
 –ability grouping 89
 –communicative syllabuses 29
 –core curriculum for English 15
 –Course of Study 3, 7–9, 28, 32, 82, 96–7, 105
 –'Education Reform Plan for the 21st Century' (Rainbow Plan) 10–11, 78, 89

–five-year action plan on English education 2, 27, 77–8, 132, 155
–holistic teaching 33
–policies for English Language Education 2, 7–9
–zest for living 11, 32, 33
Miura, A. 63
mixed-ability groupings 90, 92, 112
modelers of practice 133 *see also* role models
models of professional development 21–6
Moore, A. 24, 34, 69, 154
moral education 14, 52, 85
motivation, learner 30, 72, 83, 89–90, 92
multilingual society 2
Murphey, T. 129, 133, 134, 138

Nagamine, T. 44, 46–7, 115, 120, 126, 128, 135
Nana
 –ability grouping 90
 –biographical details 5, 53
 –content knowledge 78, 109
 –emulation 79, 80–1, 116, 121
 –giving clear explanations 80, 112–13
 –language learner to language teacher shift 108
 –observations of 64
 –pedagogical content knowledge (PCK) 78, 109
 –peer learning 128, 129–30, 132, 134
 –reflections on microteaching 113
 –teacher as subject specialist 15, 69, 75, 77–81, 98
'National Commission on Education Reform' 10
national curriculum 7–9, 10–11, 82–3
nationalism 12
native speaker teachers 8
naturalistic settings 48
ningen-keisei (character formation) 89
Nishimuro, M. 30
noh drama 38
non-teaching work of a teacher 33–4 *see also* homeroom teachers; student guidance (*seito shido*)
non-verbal communication 80, 113, 134
noticing 130

Nunan, D. 21, 27, 29, 106, 116
nusumu ('stealing') 39, 83 *see also* emulation

observation (of teaching practice) *see also* emulation
 –and apprenticeship 36
 –apprenticeship of observation 36, 38–41, 56, 81, 102, 103, 108, 119, 145
 –Chie 70, 72, 74–5, 118
 –conclusions on 144–6
 –Mari 83, 84
 –as mediational tool 116–27
 –Nana 79, 112
 –as part of ITE 17, 18
 –peer learning 129–30, 131, 132, 133–4
 –Saori 103
 –teacher socialisation 36
observation (research method) 55, 56, 58, 63–5, 66–7
observer effects 62–3, 64–5
Olympic Games, Tokyo 2020 3
'open' system of teacher education (*kaiho-sei*) 12, 13, 19, 44
Ota, N. 13, 14, 17, 38
output hypothesis 130

Pachler, N. 68, 96, 97, 111, 138
pair-work 88, 89, 105
Pajares, M.F. 36
paraphrasing 82
participant observation 58
participant recruitment 54
participation in study, effects of 51, 54, 84, 153–4
partnership between schools and HEIs 18
Patton, M.Q. 49, 65, 66
Peacock, M. 37
pedagogical content knowledge (PCK)
 –Aya 15, 76, 109
 –Chie 70, 71, 109
 –Japanese teaching culture 42, 44
 –Kento 88, 95
 –and learner-centred approaches 110
 –Mari 81, 82, 84, 109

–models of professional development 21
–Nana 78, 109
–peer learning 133
–teacher expertise 26–8, 30, 68, 69
–value of theoretical knowledge 96
–Yurika 95
pedagogical knowledge, general (GPK) 14–15, 26, 33, 42, 68, 85–7, 92–4, 96, 110
pedagogical wisdom 35
peers
 –co-construction of meaning 29
 –community-based professional development 26–7
 –emulation of others often criticised in professional development 4–5, 119, 125
 –human mediational tools 46–7
 –limitations of peer learning 135–6
 –mediational tools 79, 81
 –peer feedback 71, 113, 116, 128, 129–32, 135–6, 137–8
 –peer learning 38, 75, 79, 127–36, 138, 143, 148–9, 151
 –post-teaching practice course 18
 –social dimension of learning 25
 –whole-person education (*zenjin kyoiku*) 33
personal and social education 32
pilot study 56, 57
planning lessons 75, 79, 80, 82, 88, 118, 121, 130
Poehner, P. 115
post-graduate level teacher education 13
post-teaching practice course 18
practical knowledge bases 68
practical teaching experience during training
 –Chie 70, 71, 75
 –informal teaching experiences 111–13
 –ITE in secondary schools in Japan 16–19
 –Kento 86
 –length of teaching practice 16–17
 –Nana 77, 112–13
 –research process 52, 62
 –sociocultural perspective 46

–theory-practice dichotomy 143
–value of 98–9
–Yurika 92, 93
praise 92
pre-fixed ideas about teaching 36–7, 70
pressure-free education (*yutori kyouiku*) 11
primary schools 2, 9, 33, 77–8, 85
Pring, R. 34
prior experience of being taught
 –apprenticeship of observation 40
 –communicative language teaching (CLT) 30
 –interviews as data collection method 56
 –Japanese teaching culture 41–2
 –Kento 88, 97, 106, 110, 123, 137
 –learner to teacher shift 22, 36
 –as mediational tool 102–8, 137
 –Nana 122
 –Saori 103–6
 –Yurika 91, 92
problem-solving abilities 24, 46, 125, 151
procedural knowledge 45
professional development, models of 21–6
professional expertise, dimensions of 26–7
proficiency, students' 83, 90, 119, 121, 155
proficiency, teachers' 8–9, 27, 31, 52–3, 81, 82–3, 87
proficiency testing 3, 8
pronunciation 81–2, 96, 97

qualifications of teachers 11, 13
qualitative methods 4, 47–9, 54–65, 142, 153

Rainbow Plan ('Education Reform Plan for the 21st Century') 10, 14, 89
rational-autonomous professionals 34
 see also autonomy, teacher
reading, teaching 15, 59, 79, 92, 96, 121, 131–2
reading-aloud tasks 104, 109, 131–2, 134–5
reasoning skills 77

recall protocols 59
recruitment of participants 54
reflection-in-action 23
reflection-on-action 23, 25
reflective journals 60–3, 66–7
reflective practice
 –Aya 75
 –challenges of 91–5
 –Chie 74
 –conclusions on 146–8
 –criticisms of concept 23–5
 –*hansei* (negative reflection) 24, 147
 –Japanese teaching culture 18, 42, 143, 145
 –Kento 87
 –Mari 83, 131
 –peer learning 131, 133
 –recommendations for improvements 155
 –role models 150
 –skills needed for 24–5, 146–7
 –and teaching as a craft 35
 –theory-practice dichotomy 87
 –Yurika 24, 62, 91–5, 116, 124–7
Regulation for the Establishment of University Standards 13
research process 54–5
research site 51–3
rich data 56, 63
Richards, J. 29, 70
Richardson, V. 37
Roberts, J. 37, 68, 70, 94, 98, 103, 105, 136, 137, 138
Robson, M. 32
Rodgers, T.S. 29
Rogoff, B. 35, 125
role models 70, 91, 99, 116, 121, 122–3, 128, 133–5, 137–8, 143, 149–50, 154

Sakai, A. 39, 126
San, M.M. 14, 17
Saori
 –biographical details 5, 53, 54, 69
 –communicative language teaching (CLT) 67, 103–6
 –expectations of teaching 101
 –observations of 64
 –peer learning 135
 –practical teaching experience during training 111
 –prior experience of being taught 102–6
Sato, K. 29–30, 40, 44, 89
Sato, M. 12, 17
Savignon, S.J. 29, 30, 104
scaffolding 148
schema theory 15, 92–3
Schön, D.A. 4, 22, 23, 24, 25, 150
second language acquisition theory 96, 109–10
seito shido (student guidance) 33, 85–91, 93–4, 95
self-directed learning 76, 77, 79, 142, 148
Sellars, N. 58–9
semi-structured interviews 55–8
serial practice 16
Shimahara, N. 29, 32, 33, 34, 35, 39, 76, 85, 126
Shinmura, I. 38
shujukudo-betsu-shido (ability grouping) 83, 87, 89–90, 96
Shulman, J.H. 132, 137
Shulman, L. 5, 14, 21, 26–7, 30, 33, 42, 44, 68, 76, 77, 78, 80, 93, 94, 96, 109, 110, 132, 137
Silverman, D. 47–9, 50, 55, 66
skill level of teachers 8–9
Smith, R. 76
social development 33
social dimension of learning 25
social interactionist perspectives 137
social learning 128
social relationships 29, 45, 46, 115, 127–40, 148–9 *see also* peers
socialisation 35–6, 69–84, 87, 137, 144, 150
sociocultural theory 22, 25–6, 37, 44–7, 74, 127, 137, 138–9, 149, 151
South Korea 17, 90
STEP (Society for Testing English Proficiency) 8, 9
stimulated recall task 57, 59
Strauss, A. 48, 153
student guidance (*seito shido*) 33, 85–91, 93–4, 95

student-centred learning *see* learner-centred education
study abroad 13, 28
'study robots' 10
subject specialist, teacher as a 69–84
subjectivity, interviewees' 58, 60
subjectivity, researcher's 51
subject-specific teaching skills versus generic 14–15, 68–100
supervision of student teachers
 –Chie 120, 121
 –future research 153
 –ITE in secondary schools in Japan 17–18
 –Kento 90–1, 111, 122–3
 –Mari 84
 –teacher expertise 138, 145, 149–50, 151
 –teaching logs 62
 –Yurika 93–4, 95, 125
Suzuki, A. 24, 63
Swain, M. 130

tacit teacher thinking 23, 37
Taiwan 17
tantan-to-shiteiru (emotional distance) 90
teacher education standards 10–12
teacher expertise 26, 68, 74, 76, 95–8, 101–14, 126–7, 136–40, 151–2
teacher talk 113, 119
teacher-centred teaching modes 29, 118
'teaching abilities' 10, 11–12, 19
teaching certificate renewal system 11
teaching culture 32–43
teaching logs 18, 62, 76, 90, 93
teaching standards, in the Rainbow Plan 10–11
team teaching 19, 130
temporary others 46, 129, 132, 148
textbooks 45, 70
theoretical knowledge base 36, 37, 39, 42, 96–7, 108–11, 142–50
theory-building research 48
theory-practice dichotomy
 –Aya 77
 –case studies 44, 70, 74
 –Japanese teaching culture 16, 19, 41–3
 –Kento 86
 –Mari 81
 –mediational tools to narrow the gap 115–40
 –models of professional development 22, 23–5, 26, 30–1
 –prior experience of being taught 103
 –sociocultural perspective 46
 –struggle to narrow 142–50, 154
 –teaching as a craft 36
 –value of practical experience 98–9
 –value of theoretical knowledge 95–7
 –Yurika 92
thick description 48, 49, 50, 56
think-aloud protocols 59
Thorne, S.L. 38
timeline of study 55
TOEFL (Test of English as a Foreign Language) 8, 52
TOEIC (Test of English for International Communication) 3, 8, 9, 52
Tomlinson, P. 37, 91, 149
top-down processing 15
tourism sector, globalisation of 3
transformation of experience 23
Triandis, H.C. 49
triangulation of data 51, 60–1, 62, 64, 65, 66–7
Tsang, W.K. 60
Tsuchiya, S. 131
Tsui, A.B.M. 26, 68, 74, 76, 84, 87, 93, 98, 128, 136
tsutaeru (one-directional communication) 82
tutoring 92

uchi (insiders) 50
UK 12, 13, 16, 17, 44, 71, 89, 126, 137, 149
undergraduate-level teacher training 12–13
United States 33, 39, 89
university entrance examinations 3, 10, 29, 78

values 9, 16, 24, 45, 47, 68, 121, 139
videoing lessons 57, 59, 107, 130
visual aids 80, 89

volunteer teaching experiences 70–2, 78–9, 89–90, 92, 98, 111–14, 117, 126, 138, 147
Vygotsky, L.S. 25, 44, 46, 47, 127, 133, 137

Wada, M. 29
Wallace, M. 37
Weiten, W. 133
Wenger, E. 37, 47, 140
whole-person education (*zenjin kyoiku*) 33–4, 85, 97

Yamashita, K. 63
Yando, R. 35
Yoshida, K. 11
Yurika
 –biographical details 5, 53
 –content knowledge 95
 –emulation 94, 95, 116, 125
 –holistic teaching 91–5, 98
 –learner-centred education 94, 95, 124–7
 –observations of 64
 –pedagogical content knowledge (PCK) 95
 –peer learning 128
 –reflective practice 24, 62, 84, 91–5, 116, 124–7
yutori kyouiku (pressure-free education) 11

zenjin kyoiku (whole-person education) 33–4, 85, 97
zest for living (*ikiru chikara*) 11, 32, 33
zone of proximal development (ZPD) 46, 133, 140, 151

For Product Safety Concerns and Information please contact our EU Authorised Representative:

Easy Access System Europe

Mustamäe tee 50

10621 Tallinn

Estonia

gpsr.requests@easproject.com